St. Benedict was born in the declining years of the fifth century at Nursia and was a student in Rome until he reached his higher studies, when he left the capital to seek God in solitude. He first settled near modern Affile, where he worked his first miracle. This, however, brought him such fame that solitude became impossible in that region, so he left for a new refuge at Subiaco. After three years as a hermit—decisive years in his molding—he became so well known that men began flocking there to place themselves under his guidance. He set up thirteen small monasteries at Subiaco, building them on the bedrock of one of history's great documents, known through the ages as *The Rule of St. Benedict*.

The main elements of the Rule were community life, poverty and obedience, fasting, chastity and stability, manual labor, and regular daily periods of prayer, reading, and study. It was a way of life which could bring out the best in both plain and gifted men, and in the surrounding chaos it shone as a beacon, drawing good men in growing numbers—and arousing the jealousy of the small-minded. A campaign of persecution ensued, reaching its vile climax when a local priest brought a handful of women to dance, naked, in the monastery court! Yet even here the hand of God was manifest: Benedict, deciding to leave Subiaco and spare his followers any future scenes of this sort, began the great foundation that endures to this day, Monte Cassino.

These are the broad outlines of Benedict's life; they give only a partial picture of one of the most appealing saints in the Church. His warm human sympathies, his moderation, his concern for humble people and their everyday problems, all bespeak a man who would make the perfect friend; and these qualities are faithfully mirrored by Abbot Justin McCann in this sensitive, sympathetic study. Yet God also gave Benedict the gift of prophesy and the power to work miracles, and great men and women for over fourteen centuries have numbered themselves among his followers. Benedict was that rare combination: a giant of history and a lovable person.

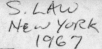

SAINT BENEDICT

Abbot Justin McCann, O.S.B.

REVISED EDITION

Image Books

A DIVISION OF DOUBLEDAY & COMPANY, INC.
GARDEN CITY, NEW YORK

Image Book edition 1958
by special arrangement with Sheed and Ward, Inc.

PRINTING HISTORY

Image Book edition published September, 1958
1st printing . . . . August, 1958

Permissu Superiorum: Ordinis Sancti Benedicti
Nihil Obstat: John A. Goodwine, J.C.D.
                              Censor Librorum
Imprimatur: ✠ Francis Cardinal Spellman
                              Archbishop of New York
                              March 14, 1958

COVER BY MARGOT TOMES

TYPOGRAPHY BY EDWARD GOREY

Library of Congress Catalog Card Number 58–10194

CONTENTS

PREFACE

ST. BENEDICT is separated from us by fourteen centuries, a period which may without exaggeration be called a great gulf of time. It is a space that of itself would make it difficult to reconstruct his life in all its living reality, that is to say, to set the figure of the man before us in the atmosphere and within the social circumstances that surrounded and conditioned his activity. The task would be no easy one even if we had full and accurate historical record of the details of his life; but it is made infinitely more difficult by the serious defect of such historical information. For what is the situation? There are two documents, and two documents only, which may be used by the biographer, namely the famous Rule for Monks and the second book of the Dialogues of St. Gregory the Great. Now the first of these is inevitably defective as a biographical document, for however much it may tell us about the mind and practice of St. Benedict, it tells us nothing about the actual course of his life. And the second document, compiled a half-century after the death of its subject, while it abounds in anecdotes of the saint's spiritual prowess and thus illustrates his career at many points and in a vivid manner, yet gives us no precise and detailed record of that career.

Therefore the biographer of St. Benedict has no easy duty, at least if he feels bound to observe the canons of historical method. And yet his effort is not an impossible one, foredoomed to failure, for there are two factors at hand which tend to alleviate its difficulty. In the first place, St. Benedict is not an isolated and inexplicable figure. He is no Melchisedech 'without father, without mother, without genealogy, having neither beginning of days nor end of life'. He is part

and parcel of the great tradition of monachism, and in that
tradition he has a definite spiritual ancestry just as there can
be no doubt that he has had a spiritual succession. We can
place his life and work in the sequence of a continuous development, and estimate it with reference to a before and an
after.

The second factor which contributes to make it easier for
us to portray the life of St. Benedict is this, that he has left
us in the Rule for Monks a faithful record of his ideals and
his practice. We do not need the assurance of St. Gregory
that 'the holy man cannot have lived otherwise than as he
taught'; the sincerity of the Rule is patent. But St. Gregory's
recommendation that we should go to the pages of the Rule,
if we would know the saint's character and life more perfectly,
is at once a candid admission that he does not regard his own
sketch as complete, and a sound biographical principle. We
may lament that in the case of St. Benedict we have no
genuine autobiographical document other than the Rule,
which of its very nature must be more or less impersonal. The
defect is a real one, and yet we have no right to complain;
it is in complete harmony with the character of the man, with
that self-effacement and that preoccupation with the Divine
which stand out so plainly in the pages of his Rule.

These two factors, then, alleviate the difficulty of the biographer's task, but he could do little with them alone. For the
main substance of his work he has to rely upon the picture
of St. Benedict which is so attractively delineated in the pages
of St. Gregory's Dialogues. What is he to think of this important document, and how is he to use it? Let us now attempt an answer to these questions.

St. Gregory the Great stands in a unique relation to Benedictinism. He was himself a monk and an abbot before he became Pope, and it is practically certain that he used the Rule
which he afterwards approved so highly. It may be said with
justice that he was the greatest and most powerful influence
in the propagation of Benedictinism, and he may even be regarded as its co-founder. He performed his most decisive
service when he devoted the whole second book of his four
books of Dialogues to St. Benedict. Among his various works
St. Gregory wrote none more popular than his Dialogues,

and wherever that book went it proclaimed the sanctity of St. Benedict and the excellence of his Rule for Monks. St. Gregory's testimony is direct and explicit; can we accept it in its entirety with full confidence?

St. Gregory was born at Rome about the year 540, St. Benedict being still alive but not far from his death, which took place about the year 547. We cannot suppose that they ever met. The Dialogues were written at the beginning of St. Gregory's pontificate in the period 593–4, that is to say rather less than fifty years after the death of the saint. Such is the chronological relation of the biographer to his subject. And what of his relations otherwise and opportunities of obtaining exact information about him? Locally St. Gregory was well circumstanced. St. Benedict's life has four landmarks: Nursia, Rome, Subiaco, Monte Cassino. Rome, the place of St. Benedict's education and the refuge of his monks when the Lombards sacked Monte Cassino—a few years before St. Gregory wrote—was the scene of St. Gregory's life and work. The other three lie within easy distance of this centre. There is no direct evidence that he ever visited these places, but it is very probable that he did, and his descriptions have a close relation to actuality. Did he converse with any of those who had known the saint? He gives us the names of many of his informants, and mentions in particular four abbots of St. Benedict's institute. From this it would appear that he was in touch with the men who carried on the saint's work and had the testimony of eye-witnesses, at least at second-hand. Close by him, in Rome, he had the Lateran monastery, where St. Benedict's monks were established when they were driven from Monte Cassino by the Lombards.

It emerges from these considerations that St. Gregory was moderately well equipped for the function of a biographer and that we ought therefore to attach value to his testimony. Nor is there any reason to doubt its accuracy with respect to the general course and chief events of St. Benedict's life. But the design and method of St. Gregory's work tend to reduce its value as history. The Dialogues were written in order to show that Italy, as well as other countries, had produced saints, and that these saints had performed many miracles. Accordingly, when he deals with St. Benedict, St. Gregory is not concerned to give us a connected record of his life, but seeks chiefly to illustrate his sanctity by recounting his miraculous deeds. His biography is professedly selective, and the principle of selection is not history so much as edification. So there is a lack of ordinary detail and a complete absence of chronology, though it is possible to fix one or two events by inference from other sources. These are manifest defects from the point of view of the historian who seeks precise and accurate knowledge concerning St. Benedict. Indeed, it follows inevitably, since St. Gregory is our sole authority for his life, that no complete biography of St. Benedict is possible. We must be content with that series of episodes from his life which is all that St. Gregory's design allowed him to give us.

But there are critics who will not admit that we have even so much substance as this for a life of St. Benedict. Starting from the first principle that all miracles are incredible and finding that St. Gregory's book contains a miracle in its every chapter, they summarily reject the whole and characterize the biography as but pious legend. It is a simple proceeding and drastic, for it leaves us with practically no materials upon which to build a life of St. Benedict. But is it a reasonable procedure? Apart altogether from their unreasoning prejudice against the miraculous—a prejudice no Catholic can share— are such critics acting wisely in thus dismissing St. Gregory's record, a record based on information supplied by St. Benedict's own disciples? We do not think so, but believe that a saner history is bound to accord a substantial value to St. Gregory's materials.

At the same time we are far from insisting that every story in the book must be regarded as history, or from denying that it contains an imaginative and legendary element. The book of the Dialogues belongs in effect to the literature of early monachism, a literature which has its own special atmosphere and character. It would be instructive to compare the narratives of St. Gregory with the lives of the monks of Egypt as written by Palladius, with St. Jerome's lives of SS. Paul, Hilarion and Malchus, with Sulpicius's life of St. Martin, to mention only a part of that extensive literature. But such a comparison would take us beyond the limits of this preface and we must be content to assert, without more ado, that the

Dialogues form part of the Golden Legend of early monachism. We must take them as such and not subject them to
an importunate criticism. And, after all, though St. Gregory
is careful to give us his sources, we are quite unable now to
examine and control them. We are therefore in no position to
discriminate between the narratives of the Dialogues, accepting this and rejecting that. Still less are we justified in attempting any 'rationalization'. Our best course is to reproduce
St. Gregory's materials as they come to us, not claiming for
them any absolute authority, nor yet refusing them the value
which they most certainly have. That is the course which has
been followed in the chapters of this book. The narratives are
by no means lacking in charm, and we hope that the modern
reader will be able, at least, to treat them with sympathy and
understanding.

St. Gregory devotes the most factual of his chapters—the
thirty-sixth—to the Rule for Monks. His testimony is of great
importance and we feel bound to quote it in full. Here is the
information which he gives to his interlocutor:

> I should like, Peter, to tell you much more about this ven-
> erable abbot; but I purposely pass over some of his deeds,
> for I am anxious to get on to the lives of others. Yet I would
> not have you ignorant of this fact, that besides the many
> miracles that made him famous in the world he was emi-
> nent also for his teaching. For he wrote a Rule for Monks
> which is remarkable both for its discretion and for the lu-
> cidity of its style. If anyone wishes to know his character
> and life more precisely, he may find in the ordinances of
> that Rule a complete account of the abbot's practice; for
> the holy man cannot have taught otherwise than as he
> lived.

Age-long tradition has assumed that the Rule for Monks,
here mentioned and highly commended by St. Gregory, is the
Rule that for something like twelve centuries has everywhere
been accepted as the Rule of St. Benedict. This Rule is extant
in many manuscripts and has been printed in innumerable
editions. It has been elaborately commented, and the history
of its text has occupied many scholars. We shall naturally
have much to say about the Rule and its teaching and we had

better make it plain at the outset that we are speaking about the traditional Rule of St. Benedict and nothing else. We shall, however, devote some space to the text-history of the Rule and to the latest theories of the modern scholars.

Having spoken now about the two chief sources which we shall use, we may mention that there are minor sources, of late origin, which have been used by biographers of St. Benedict. Although we shall not make any use of these sources, regarding them as of no historical value, yet we shall give some account of them in an Appendix to this book.

It remains for the author to say that he offers this little book as a Benedictine to Benedictines and to all who admire the venerable figure of St. Benedict. The civilized world owes no small debt to him and to his sons. The ideal for which he lived and the form of life in which he embodied it remain still, in the twentieth century as in the sixth, an ideal and a life that are of value not only for individual souls but for the common welfare of human society.

Turn away from evil and do good:
Seek after peace and pursue it

PS. XXXIII, IN THE
PROLOGUE OF THE RULE

SAINT BENEDICT

CHAPTER I

THE FALL OF THE WESTERN EMPIRE

Venerunt gentes in haereditatem tuam
PS. LXXVII

ST. BENEDICT's life was cast in a period of transition. A few years before the date which is commonly assigned to his birth the line of the Western Emperors ended ignominiously with the deposition of the boy Romulus (Augustulus) by the barbarian chieftain Odoacer (A.D. 476). The saint died (*c.* A.D. 547) during that disastrous war, which, though it destroyed the Gothic Kingdom, laid a devastated and enfeebled Italy open to the attack of the worst of the Teutonic invasions, that of the fierce Lombards. This space of some seventy years does not in its course provide any one moment that we may fix upon as the end of one age and the beginning of another, though the historian may hold that the Gothic War in its calamitous success (A.D. 555) marked the end of the classical period and the beginning of the Middle Ages. 'Amid the frightful storms of the Gothic War classical civilisation perished in Rome and throughout Italy. In cities burnt, desolated and mutilated, ruins remained the sole evidences of former splendour. The prophecy of the Sibyl was fulfilled. The night of barbarism had descended on the Latin world, a darkness in which no light was visible, other than that of the tapers of the Church, and the homely student-lamp of the monk brooding in his cloister' (Gregorovius).

To this we might add that the period contains, in the career of St. Benedict, at least one other original and momentous fact; for the achievement of the Abbot of Monte Cassino, unnoticed then, became in the issue nothing short of epoch-making. And yet, regarded as a whole, this space of years is but a portion of that long process of disintegration which resulted finally in the dissolution of the Western Empire. The process was in full swing during St. Benedict's lifetime and gives its character to the period. It will not then be amiss to consider briefly the causes and circumstances of the prolonged agony which marked the 'death of Rome'.

When St. Jerome, in his cell at Bethlehem, commenting on the prophet Ezechiel, heard the news of Alaric's sack of Rome (A.D. 410) he broke into an impassioned lament. 'The human race', he wrote, 'is included in the ruin.' 'My voice is choked and sobs interrupt the words which I write; the city is captured which took captive the world.' *Capitur urbs quae totum cepit orbem.* St. Augustine, though constructing his *City of God,* built not on war and the lust of power, but on truth and justice and divine love, yet expresses the same dismay. The whole world, Christian no less than pagan, 'groaned at its fall'. It is difficult for us now to appreciate, as did these citizens of the Empire, the majesty and splendour of imperial Rome. The City on the Tiber had then existed for more than a thousand years, and for more than half that time had been the undisputed mistress of the civilized world. *Fecisti urbem quod prius orbis erat.* To its subjects, from Spain to the confines of Parthia and from Britain to the African deserts, the Empire was the very basis and structure of civilization: Rome was the world. They saw its manifest glory and power, they could not imagine its end: Rome must be eternal. Had not the poet given them the sure prophecy: *Imperium sine fine dedi?* The *aeternitas urbis Romae* became a settled conviction in the Roman mind. Tertullian, in the second century, held that Rome would last as long as the world and that her fall would coincide with the Day of Judgment. Yet the ancient city fell and her Empire passed away. At times with a succession of violent shocks, under which the structure seems to reel and totter towards hopeless ruin, the forces of change appear to be racing to a finish; but again the process is retarded and checked by the stability of an order that had rooted itself in the habits of men. The political framework might collapse and fall to pieces; but social traditions and institutions persisted, and the very barbarians did homage to the imperial idea. And yet, however gradual, the process was a real one. The Empire of the West passed away, the nations entered into its heritage.

Technically there was no Western Empire after the year 476, for in that year the line of the Western Emperors ceased. The West was again united to the East and ruled by the Caesar of Byzantium. But it was a poor remnant of the ancient dominions of Rome that now acknowledged the authority of the Emperor in any but a perfunctory fashion. For the fifth century witnessed the occupation of great tracts of the West by Teutonic tribes. Britain, Gaul, Spain and Africa passed under their domination and it was soon to be the turn of Italy itself. Thus was the whole aspect of the West changed, almost beyond recognition.

In briefest summary the Western Empire may be said to have fallen through the operation of two forces, the one internal decay, the other external assault. The great Augustus, carrying forward the work of his greater predecessor, the dictator Julius Caesar, founded a polity which rested practically on the personal authority of one man. This centralization was intensified under his successors. Under good emperors the all-embracing, absolute bureaucracy worked well, and gave its subjects good government and genuine prosperity. But it enervated them. Too much was left to the central authority, and the citizens of the Empire lost that independent strength and self-reliance which had built up the Roman state and were soon to be so sorely needed for its defence. Moreover, the central authority being vested in one man and the method of his choice being uncertain and accidental, there was in the heart of the organism a deadly weakness which was not slow to manifest itself. The benevolent despot might be, and often was, succeeded by a tyrant who worked the imperial machine as an engine of oppression. One of the most obvious evils under which the Empire suffered in its decline was a financial one, and this is largely to be set down to misgovernment. Taxation became intolerable, and an exhausted middle class had to be forced to undertake the duties of local government. Agriculture and commerce languished, and the Empire took on the semblance of a once prosperous family that is endeavouring in decay to support its ancient pretensions.

Not all, however, was due to misgovernment, or rather misgovernment was not wholly due to the imperial machine and the accident of evil emperors. For another and a potent cause began early to operate and increased in strength as the Empire declined. It was frontier war very often that drained the imperial treasury and led to excessive taxation, and frontier war soon became a constant and menacing fact. For the barbarian peoples on the frontiers were beginning to move and to cross the boundaries of the Empire. At first a sporadic and infrequent thing, this movement soon becomes general, and in the fifth century we are in the full tide of the Wandering of the Peoples.

The emperors of the third and fourth centuries had relieved the pressure on their frontiers by allowing large masses of the barbarians to settle within the Empire. It was a solution that gave immediate relief, but it lacked stability and finality. The frontiers were assailed again and the peoples admitted to the Empire were constrained or tempted to further invasion of its territories. Alaric and his Visigoths were denizens of the Empire; but Alaric in A.D. 400 led his people into Italy and in A.D. 410 he sacked Rome. His successor, Ataulf, is found in Gaul fighting for the Empire, and the next Visigothic leader was the founder (with the approval of the emperor Honorius) of a Visigothic monarchy in south-western Gaul. In the same way and at about the same period another rich province, Spain, became divided among three Teutonic tribes, the Vandals, Suevi and Alans. In theory both Gaul and Spain remained parts of the Empire and recognized the emperor's authority; in fact they had become independent principalities.

The barbarian progress was now in full swing. The Vandals invaded Roman Africa in A.D. 429 and their kingdom was soon firmly established. In A.D. 451 came the scourge of Attila and his Huns, devastating and terrifying, but resulting in no permanent settlement. In the year A.D. 455 Rome was again sacked, this time by Genseric and his Vandals from Africa. From that time until the year A.D. 476, though a succession of puppet emperors of the West was preserved, the real power passed into the hands successively of the barbarian officers, Ricimer, Orestes and Odoacer. The last-named deposed the boy Romulus and caused an embassy to be sent to Zeno at Constantinople, representing to him that the West desired no emperor of its own but was content to be ruled by his imperial majesty of the East. Only let Odoacer be his vicegerent. Zeno accepted the situation, for he had no alternative, and Odoacer was invested with the title of Patrician. The date of this important event, A.D. 476, marked the beginning of a new epoch. Italy, as also Spain and Gaul, did not cease to be Roman in language, administrative system and social tradition; but they were now emancipated from direct imperial control. The age of distinct and separate nationalities has now come into view. It is the end of the Western Empire.

Odoacer, his authority recognized by senate and by emperor, assumed the title of King and proceeded to rule Italy with a strong yet just hand. A third part of the soil, the *sors barbarica*, was given to his followers; for the rest he allowed the whole machinery of Roman government to function as usual, himself and his military power being held in the background, as the real but unobtruded sanction of the political and social order. The years of his undisputed rule were to Italy welcome years of peace and prosperity. It was during this happy space that St. Benedict was born, about the year A.D. 480.

But Odoacer was not to be left in secure possession of his kingdom. The Emperor Zeno had never regarded him as anything but a usurper. He now enlisted the services of another great barbarian king against him, and, while punishing the usurper, at the same time relieved himself of a dangerous neighbour. Making a formal alliance with Theodoric, king of the Ostrogoths, he gave him the titles of Consul and Patrician and invested him with authority over Italy. Forthwith Theodoric and his people marched into that country to claim possession of their inheritance. This was in the thirteenth year of the rule of Odoacer (A.D. 489). There followed three years of war in which Odoacer made a gallant but hopeless resistance. He surrendered in the spring of the year A.D. 493, only to be murdered treacherously by his conqueror.

Thus had Italy—still nominally a Roman province—acquired another Teutonic ruler. And again the experience was a happy one. Theodoric was a strong and just king. He ruled his Roman subjects according to the forms to which they were accustomed and paid due deference to tradition. Himself an unlettered barbarian he employed a minister, Cassiodorus, who stands out as the chief representative in the Italy of his day of the old classical tradition of humane letters, a man of a noble and admirable character. For the thirty-three years during which Theodoric was the master of Italy (A.D. 493–526) the country enjoyed a just and stable government. He was an alien and his Roman subjects could not be expected to be wholly satisfied with his rule. He was an Arian heretic and the people he ruled were Catholics; but he did not persecute nor interfere other than wisely with the Church. Except for the stain which attaches to his last years, when, embittered by real or supposed Byzantine intrigue, he executed Boethius and Symmachus, he would stand before us as the model of a great king. His death was certainly a disaster for Italy.

Meanwhile the Eastern Empire remained strongly entrenched in Constantinople. Though, like the West, it had its barbarian invaders, the barbarians never succeeded in penetrating to its vital centre. There were times when internal and dynastic troubles seemed to threaten ruin here also, but the East was not wholly unfortunate in its emperors, and the strong official system which they created brought it safe through many crises and enabled it to survive the West by nearly a thousand years. The great city of Constantine upheld the name and something of the majesty of imperial Rome until it fell in A.D. 1453 before the onslaught of the Ottoman Turks.

But our concern is with the Western Empire and in particular with its heart and centre, the peninsula of Italy. The poet Virgil sang the praises of Italy as the homeland of Roman virtue and Roman might. It was, moreover, a land singularly blessed with the gifts of nature: a productive soil, a genial sky, a charming beauty. And these things also, and especially, are celebrated by the poet. But when the rampart of native valour broke down, Italy's natural gifts were its undoing. The wild northern tribes were tempted by its wealth and beauty, and poured down into its fertile plains. Of their invasions and the ruin which they caused something has already been said. The progress of civilization in Italy was seriously interrupted. Great spaces of once productive land went out of cultivation. The population was sadly thinned by war and famine. Prosperous towns languished in decay, and the arts of civilized life suffered partial eclipse.

At the time of St. Benedict's birth, which took place towards the end of the fifth century, Italy was no longer the prosperous and vigorous society of the Republic and early Empire. A Roman of the Augustan age would have been puzzled and saddened by what he saw in his fair Ausonian land, as indeed he would have been at a loss to understand its political status. He would have been puzzled at the outset to find the successors of the Caesars ruling, not from the imperial City on the Tiber, but from distant Byzantium. He would have marvelled still more at the actual composition of the Western Empire. Franks and Burgundians, Suevi, Visigoths and Vandals dominated its fairest provinces. And Italy, once the mistress of the world, was under the strong control of a Gothic king.

These facts represent a real and enormous change. The Wandering of the Peoples is no mere poetic phrase, but the name of a genuine historical fact by which the face of Europe was transformed. And yet it must not be supposed that this transformation entailed the utter uprooting and destruction of all that went before. Nothing gives us so just a measure of the immense power of Rome as the evidence of the influence which it exercised, even in its decline, upon the barbarian peoples who supplanted it. Teutonic kingdoms were established throughout the West, but the rulers of these kingdoms continued to regard themselves, however perfunctorily, as vassals of the Caesars. The law and custom of Rome in large measure survived. In Italy, for instance, the forms of government suffered little or no change. Rome kept its senate; the provincial towns continued to administer their local affairs; though the whole administrative machine was in the hands and subject to the will of a barbarian chieftain. And it would appear that throughout the West there remained, along with much of the structure of the Roman civilization, a consciousness, born of long custom and association, of a real and fundamental unity.

But the West was seriously disorganized. The disruptive effects of war were manifest on all hands. Never was reconstruction more needed. Yet it was to be long before the new Europe emerged from the social chaos that had now come upon it. And the process was to be retarded at first, not merely by the difficulty of assimilating the barbarian elements with their conflicting social customs and traditions, but by a profound religious problem. In fact a most serious obstacle to the reconstruction of the West, which made its disruption more violent and its progress towards a new unity more difficult and slow, was religious difference. Vandals, Visigoths and Goths were either pagans or Arians. The Vandals and Visigoths persecuted their Catholic subjects; the Goths were tolerant but alien. Indeed the picture which is presented to us of the religious state of the Western Empire at the end of the fifth century is a gloomy one. It seemed as though Arianism would everywhere triumph and oust the orthodox faith. Away in the far West, where the legions of Rome had never reached, St. Patrick was preaching the Catholic faith to the heathen Irish and founding the centre of a great future apostolate. At Christmas of the year 496, Clovis, king of the Franks, was baptized by St. Remy. But these things were of promise for the future; the present saw heresy or paganism dominant over large tracts of western Europe.

In Italy, however, Catholic Christianity was not in such grievous plight as elsewhere. Italian Catholics had the City of the Apostles, a long and glorious tradition of loyalty to the faith, and near at hand the central authority of the Papacy. Already, fifty years before, St. Leo the Great could claim that the spiritual empire of Christian Rome was greater than the secular sway of the Caesars. 'These men', he says, speaking of the apostles Peter and Paul, 'brought thee the light of the Gospel. And thou, Rome, that wert mistress of error, hast become disciple of truth . . . These are they that have brought thee to this glory that thou art a holy nation, a chosen people, a priestly and royal city. By the See of Peter thou art made the head of the world, and rulest more widely by divine religion than by earthly dominance.' And again: 'The toil of war brought thee no such empire as the Christian peace.' With this centre of orthodoxy in its midst Italy became the rallying-point for the forces of Catholic Christianity.

The poet hailed Italy as the great mother of crops and men:

> Salve, magna parens frugum, Saturnia tellus,
> magna virum . . .

If at the end of the fifth century the first member of his phrase was belied by the devastation wrought by invasion and war, the second was to prove true even in those disastrous times. The last years of that century saw the birth of St. Benedict who was to found an institute and write a Rule which were to be among the most powerful forces working for the civil and religious regeneration of the West.

But that regeneration was still in the future and the sixth century brought to Italy an experience of war and desolation worse than any that she had hitherto endured. At the beginning of that century, as we have seen, the Western Empire in general was under the government of barbarian rulers who gave a nominal allegiance to the Emperor of the East. But there came to the throne of the East, in the year 527, an emperor who was not content with this unreal subjection, but determined to assert his imperial authority to the full. This was the great Justinian (527–65). Taking advantage of Vandal dissensions he first reconquered a great part of Roman Africa for the Empire (533–48). A like opportunity presenting itself in Italy, where Theodoric had had no worthy successor, Justinian embarked on the reconquest of this province also. Thus began the Gothic War which raged through the unfortunate peninsula for twenty years (535–55) and caused more ruin and devastation than any of the barbarian occupations. Rome was three times besieged, and at one time was in the possession of Belisarius, the imperial general, at another in that of Totila, the Gothic king. At one moment, in the year 547, the ancient capital of the Empire was emptied of its inhabitants, and history has to record the strange and moving fact that imperial Rome became for forty days an empty solitude. But the persistence of Justinian achieved its end. Italy was recovered for the Empire, though at a price of impoverishment and devastation that robbed the reconquest of the promise of permanence and stability. Not long after—in A.D. 568—came Alboin and his Lombards; and, as a result of the wars which followed, though the authority of the emperor was maintained at Ravenna and Rome, the greater part of the soil of Italy passed under the control of the Lombard dukes.

It is unnecessary to continue this summary further, for we have now passed beyond the limits of St. Benedict's life. But it will be abundantly plain, even in such a brief survey, what was the character of the inheritance into which Benedict entered as a Roman born at the end of the fifth century. And it will be clear also that his life was cast in no peaceful and untroubled epoch. It was in fact rounded with a war. He was born under Odoacer. His boyhood witnessed the campaigns in which Theodoric defeated and supplanted the Herule. In youth and early manhood he enjoyed the security and peace of the Ostrogothic kingdom. His declining years saw the devastating campaigns of Totila and Belisarius. There is an air of melancholy about the records of those times. Italy had now suffered so much and so grievously that its people began to give up hope; Romans at last despaired of the Republic. And this melancholy and brooding pessimism seem to have affected even the Abbot of Monte Cassino. St. Gregory depicts him as foretelling the utter decay of Rome and as mourning prophetically over the future fate of his own monastery, one day to be sacked by the Lombards.

And yet, in the main, St. Benedict's life would seem to have been singularly unaffected by the secular circumstances of his period. Whether at Nursia, Rome, Subiaco, or Monte Cassino, it would seem to have passed securely and peacefully, vexed not at all by the excursions and alarms of war, concerned only with the inner moral struggle of his spiritual enterprise. The story of his life recounts a famous interview with the heroic Totila, and implies that the saint followed as from a watchtower the fortunes of the war that raged over his devoted country. But, for the most part, the history of his monastic career, so far as it has reached us, and above all the calm and untroubled pages of his Rule, reveal a security and stability that justified the confident creation of an enduring edifice. Let us grant that his life was lived in places remote from the scenes of contemporary conflict, and that his monasteries, while they required only a minimum subsistence, offered no attraction to the spoiler; although Monte Cassino at least was in no lonely retreat but planted by the side of the Latin Way, on the high road from Rome to Naples. It was something that such quiet oases were possible, and the fact of their existence should prevent us from conceiving the Italy of that period as a scene of unmixed desolation and social ruin.

In the centuries which followed the disciples of St. Benedict were to become acquainted often with similar social conditions. Their monasteries were often to be as islands of peace in a sea of turmoil and unrest. Their strength lay in a life which was conceived in similar circumstances and in a Rule which was written amid the echoes of war.

CHAPTER II

EARLY YEARS

Fuit vir vitae venerabilis, gratia Benedictus et nomine
DIAL. II. INIT.

THE Flaminian Way, striking due north from Rome, passes by Etruria and Umbria to the Adriatic. Narni, Spoleto, Foligno, Assisi lie in its course and it brings the traveller to Rimini and Ravenna. The Salarian Way takes another and a shorter course to the eastern sea, traversing the Sabine country and Picenum, in a direction north-east of Rome. Midway between these two great highways, at a distance of about seventy miles from Rome, in the northernmost part of the Sabine country and encircled by the ranges of the Apennines, lies the little town of Norcia, the Roman Nursia. An ancient Sabine township, it was subjugated with the rest of the Sabine territory after the third Samnite War (290 B.C.) and at first was granted only the subject status of citizenship without franchise. But, when the power of Rome grew to include the whole of the Italian peninsula and her position was secure, the Sabine towns were admitted to the full franchise and became self-governing communities. Nursia then became a prosperous Roman borough (*municipium*).

Its citizens were Sabines, that is to say of a stock noted for its toughness of fibre and rough virtue. They were built morally to the stature of the rugged hill-country in which they lived. They were eminently a people of character. The inhabitants of the plains to the south, of Latium and Campania, had a great respect for the Sabines. To Cicero they were *severissimi homines,* that is to say, men of a certain austerity of character and gravity of demeanour, the very incarnation of the old Roman ideal. And to this they held, in their hardy upland country, when Rome itself had fallen from its high estate and lost by internal corruption and foreign admixture the qualities which had made it great.

Nursia was not a large town nor an influential one, yet it has left some record of itself in the pages of history. It was remote enough in its broad Apennine valley, and yet it lay within sixteen miles of the Flaminian Way and must have been cognizant of the busy life both in war and in peace that passed by that great highway. Virgil enumerates, among the array of Turnus, the Sabine warriors of 'cold Nursia': *quos frigida misit Nursia* (*Aeneid*, iii, 175). It was no upstart town, but one of a venerable antiquity; St. Gregory is right in calling it 'ancient Nursia', *vetusta Nursia*. Other writers tell us of a *Nursina durities*, that strength of character as well as of muscle which is characteristic of the highlander. In the last civil war of the expiring republic, the men of Nursia took the side of Antony and erected a memorial to their citizens who fell at Mutina (Modena) in 43 B.C. with the inscription: 'They fell for freedom.' For this bold act Augustus punished them with a fine that they could not pay and then drove them from their town. From this brave folk sprang the gallant Quintus Sertorius and the bluff soldier-emperor, Vespasian. It was in Nursia, or in the district of which it was the centre—St. Gregory says the 'province' of Nursia—that St. Benedict was born, in the declining years of the fifth century.

Of his parents we know next to nothing. St. Gregory tells us that they were of good or at least of more than ordinary social status: *liberiori genere*. The words have been variously interpreted, but they lend little countenance to the view that Benedict was of patrician birth. The Roman system of provincial administration employed the towns as its units and for this purpose organized them according to certain well-known types. Nursia was a borough (*municipium*) and as such enjoyed the special municipal constitution. There was a town council—with more power and less responsibility than town councils as we know them—consisting of a hundred members. This council was chosen from among the richer citizens who could face the not inconsiderable obligations of office. And there was the mass of ordinary, less well-to-do citizens. The official class was distinguished from the other, not merely by the possession of greater wealth, but often also by long tradition of public service. It formed at its best a sort of provincial gentry and was not without its own pride of birth and position. On either side of these classes may be distinguished two others. At the lower end of the social scale were the entirely unprivileged slaves, a numerous element in an ancient community. At the upper end were the Roman nobility, the patrician owners of great landed estates, who figure often in the titular capacity of patrons of the municipalities. It is possible that St. Benedict's father was a well-to-do burgher of Nursia, and he may in his time have been a councillor and even a magistrate of his town. We are disposed, in fact, to make him a member of the small provincial gentry, as described above. Not only St. Gregory's phrase, which might be rendered 'of goodish birth', but also the journey to Rome, with its purpose and circumstances, lends colour to such a theory of his social status.

But this solution, itself obviously conjectural, has seemed to imaginative biographers to make all too modest a claim for the Patriarch of Western Monachism, with the consequence that the saint has been endowed with important relatives and a remarkable genealogy. The structure, indeed, lacks historical foundation, but it may be of interest to record briefly some of the additions which it makes to St. Gregory's meagre narrative. They are as follows: St. Benedict's parents are named Eupropius and Abundantia, his nurse Cyrilla; they are of the noble and famous Anician family and lived in a splendid palace, adorned with marble and mosaic, statues and paintings, in beautiful grounds just beyond the walls of Nursia; as a scion of the Anician family the saint has among his relatives the Emperor Justinian and Pope St. Gregory the Great; finally—and this is the most remarkable discovery of all—the saint is connected through the same Anician family with the Counts of Habsburg, and when we think of him we may let our imagination range to the glories of the Kings of Spain and Emperors of the Holy Roman Empire, to the 'royal palace of the Escorial and the imperial eagle of the House of Austria'.[1]

[1] The family names come from Peter the Deacon, for whom see Appendix, Note 6. The remarkable genealogy is the achievement of

St. Gregory, however, tells us none of these things; he has little to say about St. Benedict's parents and nothing about their genealogy; he is content to introduce to our notice two members of his family circle and two only: his sister Scholastica and his nurse. Both help to illustrate the life of the saint as a saint, and that is all that St. Gregory is interested in. St. Scholastica, whom we shall meet again later in the course of this narrative, was consecrated to God in her earliest years. It has been surmised that she received this consecration at the hands of the local bishop, and that her consecration did not involve any separation from the paternal home. It was common then for Christian women to live the religious life, not only in communities, but also in the bosom of their family. However, it would appear from St. Gregory's narrative that in later life at least St. Scholastica left Nursia and lived in a *cella*, whether that imply a hermitage or a convent, at no great distance from her brother at Monte Cassino.[2] Tradition has it that Benedict and Scholastica were twins and had a special mutual affection. The narrative of St. Gregory testifies that there existed between them the love of brother and sister, a love which was not destroyed but rather intensified by their consecration to the service of God.

The nurse is an interesting, if somewhat puzzling, adjunct to the story of Benedict's early years. She enters the story abruptly and abruptly leaves it, having tended her charge devotedly and having before her exit given occasion for his first miracle, the immediate cause of his final flight from the world. She has been christened Cyrilla, and some of the saint's biographers are able to tell us a good deal about her thoughts as she tended him and about the intimate relations which existed between them, so that Benedict found in Cyrilla the sympathetic confidante of his soul's aspirations and a guide on his way to God.

Of Benedict's home life we know nothing. Imagination has painted an attractive picture of the tender friendship of the boy and his 'twin-sister' Scholastica, of their ordered family life in

Dom Arnold Wion, a monk of the Cassinese Congregation, in his *Lignum Vitae* (Venice, 1595).

[2] This convent is usually located at Plumbariola, about three miles from the foot of Monte Cassino.

a model Christian household, of their youthful aspirations and intimate spiritual converse. It is very possible, though our sources are silent and no record survives to enable us to draw a parallel with another famous history of saintly childhood. 'One of my brothers', writes St. Teresa, 'was nearly of my own age (seven years); and he it was whom I most loved . . . He and I used to read the lives of the saints together. When I read of martyrdom undergone by the saints for the love of God, it struck me that the vision of God was very cheaply purchased; and I had a great desire to die a martyr's death . . . and I used to discuss with my brother how we could become martyrs. We settled to go together to the country of the Moors, begging our way for the love of God, that we might be there beheaded; and our Lord, I believe, had given us courage enough, even at so tender an age, if we could have found the means to proceed; but our greatest difficulty seemed to be our father and mother. . . . As soon as I saw it was impossible to go to any place where people would put me to death for the sake of God, my brother and I set about becoming hermits; and in an orchard belonging to the house we contrived, as well as we could, to build hermitages, by piling up small stones one on the other, which fell down immediately; and so it came to pass that we found no means of accomplishing our wish.' Perhaps the early years of Benedict and Scholastica were indeed such as this. When the hardy Sabine folk abandoned their ancient paganism—after the preaching of St. Felician of Foligno—they became a community of earnest and practical Christians. Nursia in St. Benedict's time was the seat of a bishopric. Let us suppose then that he was brought up in an atmosphere of genuine Christian piety and faithful observance. That profound sense of the presence of God and of the importance of duty, which is so marked a feature of his manhood, must have been implanted in his soul from his earliest years. St. Gregory tells us that from his boyhood he had the wisdom of age and surrendered his mind to no pleasure. It would seem that he received a thorough grounding in his Christian faith and understood already the meaning of asceticism.

As to secular instruction we may presume that he was given the elements of a good education as it was understood in those times. This education was doubtless begun at home in the bosom of his family and continued afterwards in the public schools. A Roman boy was generally sent to school at the age of seven years and began his career with instruction in reading, writing and arithmetic, under a *litterator* or *magister litterarius*, the elementary schoolmaster. There was doubtless such a school in his native town and to this Benedict probably went, unless we suppose that he was instructed at home by a private tutor. For the next stage the boy was transferred to the 'grammar school' and placed under the care of a more advanced teacher, the *grammaticus*, to begin an education of a predominantly literary character. This *eruditio liberalis*, or liberal education, consisted mainly in the study of the classical writers, both Greek and Latin. Juvenal testifies to the assiduous use of such authors as Virgil and Horace, and in the best times a large amount of Greek literature also was read. A Roman boy was trained especially in the power of expression and his education paid more attention to form and style than to substance. The satirists frequently criticize the unreality and triviality that tended to characterize this literary education.

For the generality this double course was considered sufficient; but for those who intended to take up a public career there was a third stage, the school of rhetoric. In this school, under a skilled *rhetor*, the youth made a careful study of oratory, with all its principles and methods, and practised declamation. He was exercised in the composition of speeches upon a variety of topics and trained in the use of every rhetorical artifice. Here again form tended to triumph over substance and reality.

St. Gregory gives us very little information as to the character and scope of Benedict's education, but he tells us that his parents sent him to Rome for his 'liberal education': *Romae liberalibus litterarum studiis traditus fuerat*. These words seem to compel us to conclude that, after his elementary education was completed, Benedict was sent to a Roman grammar school for the second stage. The Roman boy was generally accompanied from his home to school by a *paedagogus*, frequently a Greek slave, who acted also as a private tutor. Benedict, however, is accompanied to Rome by a 'nurse'. Perhaps we may see in this an indication that his parents were not able to afford the more expensive male tutor, or perhaps 'Cyrilla' was intended to act also as housekeeper and mother to the young scholar, for it does not appear that Benedict had any relations in Rome. But the presence of such a companion combines with St. Gregory's words, quoted above, to urge the conclusion that it was for his grammatical education that St. Benedict was sent to Rome.

What then was his age when he made this momentous journey? Let us suppose that he was of the age at which the elementary schoolboy now finishes his education and set him down provisionally as of fourteen years. It is a conclusion that is by no means generally accepted. Many writers object to so low an estimate and would have it that Benedict was at least seventeen when he went to Rome. They suppose that he was going to Rome, not for his grammatical training, but for what may be called a university course. He was to be an undergraduate and not a schoolboy. They argue that it is unlikely that he should have left home at a tender age to be plunged into the dangers of a great city. They infer from the temptation to which he was subject at Subiaco that he must have been of an age appropriate for a romantic experience. To this last point it may be replied that this is to make too much of the implications of the story; it requires no such background. Or, granting the probability of this interpretation, it is to be remembered that we know nothing as to the length of Benedict's stay in Rome; it may have extended to several years. On the whole it seems better to accept St. Gregory's words at their face value, and to set Benedict on the way to Rome in his early teens.

Here then, in early youth, Benedict leaves his native Nursia. There is no reason to suppose that he did not return to it at intervals during his schooldays—it was no great distance from Rome—but of this St. Gregory gives no hint. Accompanied by his nurse he journeys southward from the Sabine country towards the plains of Latium and the imperial City. His emotions, as he said farewell to his parents and the home of his childhood, must have been much the same as those of any other schoolboy setting forth to the great adventure of his first school. We may picture his astonishment and admiration when he gained his first view of the majestic buildings of Rome. His heart would beat quicker with excitement and expectation as he drew nearer to the city, and he would enter it with high hopes and serious resolves, wondering what experience would be his in the ancient capital of the Caesars.

CHAPTER III

ROME

Romae liberalibus litterarum studiis traditus fuerat
DIAL. II. INIT.

AT THE time of which we are writing the City on the Tiber no
longer enjoyed its proud eminence among the cities of the
world. The magic of its great past still clung to it, Rome was
still an impressive memory in the minds of men, but its ancient
secular power had gone from it, never to return again. The
Caesars themselves began the work of its degradation. The
Eastern trend of the Empire caused the foundation of New
Rome, on the Bosphorus, and Constantinople began its long
rivalry with the ancient seat of Empire. Moreover, the gover-
nors of the West found Milan or Ravenna a more convenient
and less embarrassing capital than the southern and turbulent
City. Political convenience and the circumstances of administration began this process by which Rome was deprived of its
high estate; barbarian inroads and devastation hastened the
course of policy. *Facta est quasi vidua domina gentium.*

The period of 168 years from Alaric to Alboin, a space of
five generations, has been specifically denominated the period
of the 'death of Rome'. The first campaign of Alaric and his
Visigoths took place in the years 400–2, but it was in the second invasion (408–10) that Rome itself suffered. Each of those
three years saw the city besieged and the last witnessed its
sack. After the Visigoths came the Huns under their terrible
leader, Attila (452); but the majesty of Pope Leo the Great
availed to save the city from a repetition of the excesses of the
Visigoths. Genseric followed with his Vandals (455) and Rome
endured three terrible days of pillage and destruction. There

followed under the Ostrogoths a period of comparative quiet; but the Gothic War in which their domination ended was even more disastrous for the City than the sack of Visigoth or Vandal. In the fifth generation came the Lombards under Alboin (568) and with them the decay and mortal sickness of the imperial City.

St. Benedict came to Rome in the calm between two storms. The fifth century was just ending as he entered upon his school life. He found the Rome of the Emperors, resplendent in marble and bronze, still decked out in most of its ancient magnificence. There were scars here and there: Alaric and Genseric had left their mark upon it; but the real destruction was yet to come. The aqueducts were not yet cut; the Campagna was no desolate and unwholesome waste; Rome still enjoyed her *Thermae*. Coliseum, temples, palaces: there was much in all this to justify Cassiodorus, St. Benedict's contemporary, in setting down Rome as one of the wonders of the world. We can easily imagine the feelings of the young provincial when confronted with all this splendour.

And in the streets of the ancient city there was busy and continual life. Rome had become a cosmopolitan centre. All that was good and all that was bad had flowed into it, until the city was a veritable medley of diverse peoples and diverse faiths. The Orient and its subtle vices were well represented there. It was a place full of manifold attraction and allurement.

Then, alongside the pagan city, and gradually encroaching upon it, was Christian Rome with its catacombs and its shrines of apostles and martyrs. There was much to remind the fervent Christian of the great crises in the history of the Church and to take his mind back in devout recollection to the times of persecution. St. Jerome had come to Rome from the province of Dalmatia, more than a century before, to devote himself to the same 'liberal studies'. He speaks thus of his schooldays:

When I was at Rome as a boy and was being instructed in liberal studies, I was wont on Sundays, in company with others of the same age and vocation, to go the round of the tombs of the apostles and martyrs. Frequently would we enter those vaults which are dug in the depths of the earth. In their walls on either side as you enter are the bodies of the

dead. So dark is everything there that the words of the
prophet are almost fulfilled: 'Let them go down alive into
hell.' The horror of the darkness is tempered very occasionally by light from above, yet so that it seems to come not
from a window but through a slit or hole. And again
we grope our way forward, surrounded with impenetrable
night. It recalls the line of Virgil:

'Horror ubique animos simul ipsa silentia terrent.'

So too may we suppose that Benedict acted. We may surmise
that the serious young stranger from the Sabine hills would be
attracted especially by this aspect of Rome and would seek
refuge from pagan allurements in the Christian memories of
the dark and silent catacombs.

St. Gregory has very little to say about Benedict's residence
in Rome and gives us no clue as to the part of the city in which
he lived, nor any information as to the routine of his daily life.
In the biographer's eyes nothing in his connection with Rome
became him so much as his leaving it. But a tradition exists, of
very late and dubious origin, which is more explicit. It centres
round the little church of San Benedetto *in Piscinula* which is
situated in the region beyond the Tiber, Trastevere, and it employs generally the assumption that the saint belonged to the
Anician *gens*. The chronicler Leo of Ostia (twelfth century)
tells us that there was a church of St. Benedict in Rome in
the tenth century and that it was given by the abbot of Monte
Cassino to one Adelarius under certain conditions. He says that
the church belonged 'anciently' to the Cassinese monks. But
even if we assume that this church is identical with San
Benedetto *in Piscinula*—which cannot be proved—we have yet
to establish the saint's connection with it. That connection is
inferred in some such way as this. The *Via Anicia* of Trastevere
shows that the Anicii held considerable possessions in that
quarter. It is highly probable that either the family palace—
the *Domus Aniciana*—or else a hospice founded by them—
Xenodochium Anicianorum—was situated in this region. It may
have occupied the exact site, or have stood next to the site of
the church of San Benedetto. There were considerable ruins of
a large building visible as late as the seventeenth century. Now
if Benedict belonged to the family of the Anicii, what more

natural than that he should lodge in the (probable) palace of his *gens?* But, even if he did not belong to this family, an institution such as the *Xenodochium Anicianorum* (of uncertain existence in his time, and unknown position) was a highly suitable place for his lodging. After the saint's death this palace (or hospice) was converted into a monastery, first of monks and then of nuns, and to it was joined a church dedicated to Our Lady and subsequently re-dedicated to him. Or perhaps he himself in his lifetime, following the example of other Christian patricians in the early centuries, erected a church in or near his paternal mansion, which the piety of the faithful afterwards dedicated to him. Tradition is even able to point to a little oratory on the left of the entrance as the favourite resort of the saint, and to indicate the picture of Our Lady before which he said his prayers. But in all this there are only two certain points: the tenth-century church of St. Benedict and the present church of San Benedetto *in Piscinula;* the rest is conjecture. We must be content therefore to remain ignorant as to the place where Benedict resided during his stay in the city.

Nor do we know any more about the routine of his daily life. The horarium of a Roman school was severe and the discipline strict. We are told that school began early, even before dawn, and that the boys brought lamps with them. The Roman parent seems to have believed in corporal punishment, which was administered generously by the schoolmaster. And holidays were infrequent and brief. All this would suggest what appears to our minds a rigorous regime. But the life of a schoolboy in Rome could not have been a dull one. Public festivals and games, the splendid surroundings amid which he lived, and perhaps more than all the infinite variety of characters, occupations, customs: all this would stimulate and interest the growing boy. Nor did it lack an element of danger. Rome was a cosmopolitan city. The satirists tell us that all that was evil and corrupt found a home within its walls. There East met West, and the sensuous Syrian vied with the brutal Goth. The Orontes had flowed into the Tiber. There were many temptations on every side, and a receptive boy would be peculiarly sensitive to their influence. We learn from St. Gregory that many of Benedict's companions became involved in vicious courses. Benedict saw them rushing headlong to moral ruin. Fearing a like fate for himself—for he felt as much as any the seductive power of the temptations which surrounded him—he determined on a drastic remedy. He had held aloof from evil; perhaps his companions had teased him for his 'simplicity' and boasted of their own experience and knowledge of the world; Benedict would have no such knowledge 'lest by tasting it he should himself fall headlong down the dreadful precipice' to eternal disaster. He withdrew 'knowingly ignorant and wisely unlearned' and abandoning his studies set out to seek the monastic life.

How old was he when he formed this resolution? We do not know; but it is reasonable to suppose that he was then approaching manhood. St. Gregory tells us that he 'drew back the foot which he had set on the threshold of life', from which we might even infer that he had finished his secondary studies and taken up some vocational training. It is supposed by some that he attended the schools of rhetoric and law and made no small progress in these studies before his abrupt departure from Rome. It is suggested that he was influenced by the Roman law—that specifically Roman creation which amid the unrealities of literature and rhetoric preserved close contact with life and a direct simplicity of language—and that its influence is manifest in his Rule. But, however this may be, Benedict did not complete his course. 'He abandoned the schools and left his father's house and possessions, and desiring to serve God alone sought the habit of a monk.'

The information which St. Gregory gives us about the life of the saint—and especially about this early phase—is so small that it leaves considerable latitude for speculation. A recent writer, Abbot Herwegen, dissatisfied with St. Gregory's account, has ventured to correct the biographer on a material point. To understand his argument it is necessary to consider the state of the Roman Church about the year A.D. 500.

The year 484 saw the commencement of the Acacian schism, the first schism between East and West, which lasted until 519 in the reign of the Emperor Justin, that is thirty-five years. Acacius became Patriarch of Constantinople in the year 471 and at first was strictly orthodox. But in the year 482 he composed his *Henoticon*, a formulary which endeavoured by means of reticence and compromise to reconcile the churches of the East, still distracted by the Eutychian controversy. The Council of Chalcedon was ignored. Acacius has been described as the 'forerunner of Photius', and his purpose, strongly supported by the Emperor Zeno, was to establish the independence of the See of Constantinople and its ascendancy over the eastern Patriarchates. The action of Acacius was vigorously opposed by Pope Simplicius and by his successors Felix III and Gelasius I. In the year 484 Pope Felix excommunicated Peter Mongus, the intruding Patriarch of Alexandria, and this act marked the beginning of the schism. The successor of Gelasius, Anastasius II (496–8), attempted a policy of conciliation with unfortunate results. At once there arose among the Catholics of Rome two rival parties, the one in favour of making concessions to the Emperor and the Patriarchate of Constantinople, the other insisting on the pure orthodox faith and the supreme authority of the Holy See. When Anastasius died (498) the two parties each chose a Pope, the orthodox Catholics electing the deacon Symmachus, the partisans of the Emperor the anti-Pope Laurentius. Thus began the Laurentian schism, which lasted until the death of Symmachus and election of Pope Hormisdas (514) and was marked by considerable disorder and even some bloodshed in Rome.

St. Benedict's residence in Rome probably coincided with the early part of the Acacian schism and he may even have seen the beginnings of the trouble caused by the faction of the anti-Pope Laurentius. The experience would not edify him. No doubt he knew where truth and right lay and did not hesitate in his allegiance; but the spectacle of dissension in the principal See of Christendom and the behaviour of the rival parties would distress his soul. At such a time and in such circumstances it is supposed (by Abbot Herwegen) that he abandoned his preparation for a secular career and resolved to devote his life to the service of the Church. With this end in view—without as yet any monastic purpose—he left Rome and took up his residence with the priest of Enfide, in order to prepare himself for the sacred ministry. It was only after his experience at Enfide that he determined to be a monk.

But, however attractive this account may be, it is only a theory, and it traverses the evidence of our sole authority. It

would therefore seem better to adhere to the account given by
St. Gregory. According to him it was at Rome that Benedict
determined to become a monk. Perhaps he had already begun
his acquaintance with the literature of monachism and read
with admiration the lives and sayings of the fathers of the
Egyptian deserts. Certainly he could not be ignorant of the institute itself, for there were monks of every conceivable kind—
solitary, cenobitic and nondescript—throughout his own province of Valeria. And, as for Rome, there had been monasteries
of sorts in the city since the days of St. Athanasius and St.
Jerome. For the provincial monks, St. Gregory in his Dialogues
has some vivid pictures of the exploits of such a missionary
monk as St. Equitius, or of such a 'character' as Isaac the Syrian. For the Roman monasteries, he has no such sanctity to report. Were they feeble and half-hearted communities, without
any genuine monastic vitality? We do not know; we know only
that the young Benedict did not choose to join himself to one
of them, nor indeed to any existing institute, but struck out for
himself. That very fact is perhaps an indication of his opinion
of contemporary Italian monachism; and, if we desire a more
express indication, we have the incisive judgments of the first
chapter of his Rule. After speaking with approval of true hermits and cenobites, he goes on thus to characterize and con-
demn the debased monks who were all too much in evidence
in the Italy of his day:

The third kind of monks is that detestable one of the
Sarabaites, who not having been tested, as gold in the fur-
nace, by any rule or by the lessons of experience, are as soft
and yielding as lead. In their actions they still conform to
the standards of the world, so that their tonsure marks them
as liars before God. They live in twos and threes, or even
singly, without a shepherd, in their own sheepfolds and not
in the Lord's. Their law is their own good pleasure: whatever
they think of or choose to do, that they call holy; what they
like not, that they regard as unlawful.

The fourth kind of monks are those called Gyrovagues.
These spend their whole lives wandering from province to
province, staying three days in one monastery and four in
another, ever roaming and never stable, given up to their

own wills and the allurements of gluttony, and worse in all respects than the Sarabaites. Of the wretched life of all these folk it is better to be silent than to speak.

These are severe words and express a determined judgment. The young saint did not intend to become a monk after such patterns. That resolve having been made, he turned his back upon Rome and his secular studies and directed his course towards the east. There amid the coolness and purity of the hills, he would find peace and security for his soul, unvexed by the corruptions and dissensions of the city. He was now a young man, perhaps seventeen years of age, with all the brave idealism of youth. With a sense of great relief, and yet perhaps not without some apprehension for the future, he passed out of the city gate and began his life anew.

His faithful nurse accompanied him. Leaving Rome either by the Via Praenestina, or by the road that leads to Tivoli, they made their way to the little hill town of Enfide (now Affile), once a Roman colony, about thirty-five miles distant from Rome. There, St. Gregory tells us, 'they were detained by the charity of many good people, and abode awhile in the church of the Apostle St. Peter', by which we may suppose that he means that they stayed in some annex or dependency of the church and were charitably entertained by the good Christians of the place. Or, if we adopt the alternative suggestion that was given above, we are to surmise that Benedict entered into association with the local clergy and commenced his pastoral studies.

However, St. Gregory says nothing of this; his account is quite different. According to him Benedict's resolution to become a monk was formed in Rome, and when he left Rome it was in pursuit of the monastic life and of solitude. To him also Benedict's stay at Enfide is no more than a temporary detention, due to the charity of the good people of that place, so that Enfide was by no means his goal, but only a stage in his journey. He tells us nothing regarding the length of his stay at Enfide, though his narrative would imply that it was a brief one. It may very well be that that stay was of some considerable duration and that Benedict had time and opportunity for further study in the literature of monachism, a study which confirmed him in his purpose and determined him to the great decision which he presently took. St. Gregory's design, which was to report especially the miraculous episodes of the saint's life, would lead him to pass over such an interval of quiet and unobtrusive preparation; or it may simply be that he knew nothing about it, for he tells us explicitly that his information about Benedict's career was incomplete. But, for whatever reason, he makes it appear that his stay at Enfide was a short one, devoting no more than a phrase to it and hastening at once to the account of that miracle which heralded his departure for the hermitage of Subiaco. So we, for our part, must not argue further for a longer stay, however likely such a stay may appear, but imitate the reticence of St. Gregory.

The biographer, as we have said, has nothing to report of Benedict's life at Enfide but the miracle which ended it. Let us give the story in his own words:

Meantime the nurse borrowed an (earthenware) sieve from some women of the place in order to sift some grain, but left it imprudently on a table; an accident befel it and the sieve was broken into two pieces. When the nurse returned and saw what had happened, she began to weep most violently because the vessel she had borrowed was broken. But Benedict, pious and loving youth that he was, when he saw his nurse weeping, had pity on her sorrow, and taking with him the two pieces of the sieve set himself to earnest prayer. When he rose from his knees the sieve beside him was whole and entire, nor was there any mark to show that it had been broken. Going then he comforted his nurse with kindly words, and restored the sieve whole which he had taken away broken. The fact became known to all who dwelt in that place, and caused so much admiration, that they hung the sieve in the porch of the church, so that all, both then and afterwards, might know in what perfection Benedict began his holy life. The sieve was there for many years, obvious to all, and hung over the door of the church down to these times of the Lombards (ch. 1).

Benedict was embarrassed by the consequences of his action. The whole trend of his life was towards self-effacement and the quiet service of God. He had fled from Rome to seek a life wherein his spirit might be free to commune with its Creator without interruption. And now he found himself the centre of praise and admiration. It was a severe trial for his modesty, but it was more than that. He had hoped perhaps to find the monastic peace in the retirement of Enfide, without wholly severing himself from the society of his fellow-men. He now saw that this hope was vain. He found himself deprived of that peace and security of the spirit for which he sought, and the deprivation revealed to him with complete and startling clearness his real vocation. In the shock of this experience he realized fully to what he was called, and his resolution was soon taken. He would flee again, but this time it would be into complete solitude away from the haunts of men. He had already renounced much, he would now cut the last ties that bound him to his fellow-men and go forth into the wilderness alone. Secretly then, as it seems, and without any leave-taking, he left Enfide and sought a remote spot where none might discover him and interrupt his solitary prayer. After some time spent in search by mountain tracks, he found the retreat that he sought to the north of Enfide, in the valley of the Anio, at the place called Sublaqueum.

Such is St. Gregory's account of the miracle of Enfide and such the interpretation of that episode which his narrative would suggest. We have already surmised that St. Gregory has perhaps foreshortened and simplified the actual history, and that St. Benedict's resolution may have resulted rather from a gradual spiritual evolution than from such an abrupt crisis. The miracle of Enfide would then provide the occasion, rather than the cause, of his departure for Subiaco. But, whatever the truth of the matter may be, the saint now abandoned the society of the clergy of Enfide, cut himself adrift from his fellowmen and embarked upon the monastic life in its sternest form, the solitary struggle of the hermit.

Here then, in all earnest, begins the monastic career of the patriarch of the Western monks. The time is the end of the fifth century, about the year of Our Lord 500. Benedict is perhaps twenty years old.

CHAPTER IV

SUBIACO

Elongavi fugiens et mansi in solitudine
PS. LIV

THE founder of Christian monasticism in its eremitical form, St. Antony of Egypt, regarded his vocation as a call to the perfect fulfilment of the counsels of the Gospel. He had a great desire to imitate the life of the apostles and early Christians, and hearing one day in church when he was twenty years old the words of the Gospel: 'If thou wouldst be perfect, go, sell what thou hast and give to the poor, and come, follow me', he took them as addressed personally to himself and fulfilled them literally. And indeed, if we would understand monachism we must conceive it thus, as an attempt to fulfil the evangelical counsels. There was at first no specific 'rule' apart from the words of Christ. Nor was it till long afterwards that monachism was organized into the ordered state of life and compact structure that is familiar to the student of the Middle Ages.

Long before St. Antony, from the earliest days of Christianity, the ascetic impulse was present and vigorous in the Church. Ascetics, both men and women, lived the life of the counsels within the Christian communities or in close juxtaposition to them. The many efforts which have been made, in the interests of a nonascetic Christianity, to find for monachism an alien, non-Christian origin have failed; the latest research is compelled to admit that it is a native Christian growth. But if St. Antony was far from being the first Christian ascetic, he has a good title to the claim of being the first Christian monk; for the anchoretical movement which he started turned the ascetic into the solitary, set him apart in a striking manner from his fellow-Christians, and led directly to the recognition of monachism as a distinct state of life.

But it was to be long yet before monachism became an organized thing, and meanwhile the first and fundamental monastic rule was the Gospel. The words of Our Lord counselled voluntary celibacy for the sake of the kingdom of heaven, self-denial and the bearing of the Cross, the abandonment of father and mother, wife and possessions for His sake, the selling of property and giving of it to the poor, in order to follow Him in complete poverty. Particular monastic rules were to be nothing more than applications or declarations of this first and general rule, adapted to places and persons.

In the time of St. Benedict this specification and determination of monachism had not gone beyond its earliest stages. The Church had not taken any particular monastic rule and given it a definite sanction and authority. Therefore we find—and this is true for some centuries after St. Benedict—that monachism is not at all centralized. It is a loose and general thing. There are many monasteries, but no uniform observance. It is sufficient that all are aiming, each in its own way, at the fulfilment of the Gospel counsels.

Moreover, the entrance into religious life was a much simpler thing than it has since become. No Canon Law had as yet laid down conditions and forms. It was enough that a man should adopt a monk's way of life, separate himself from the ordinary life of the world, and manifest his resolution in some simple form of dress and the tonsure. In this ready fashion was it that St. Benedict became a monk.

When he fled from Enfide he was seeking some place where he might satisfy his desire for solitude, where his life might be 'hid with Christ in God'. There were many lonely and desolate spots in the Italy of his day, and St. Benedict had not far to go before he found just such a retreat as he sought. About three miles north of Enfide he came to a narrow and deep valley, the gorge of the Anio. The river flowed through it with a continual murmur of rushing water, but at its lower end, where the valley broadened, it was held up by substantial barriers of masonry, so that two lakes were formed, the one above the other. From the second of these the waters fell some twenty feet into the ancient bed of the stream and continued this course until they joined the Tiber close to Rome. The barrage was the work of the Emperor Claudius, and Nero had constructed by the side of the lake a villa and baths. In St. Benedict's day these buildings were no longer standing, though extensive ruins testified to their former splendour. But the dams still held and the lakes of Subiaco survived until the year 1305 when a sudden flood burst the masonry and the waters escaped, causing no small devastation in their wild course down the lower valley. Below the lakes was a marble bridge crossing the stream, and by this bridge, it would seem, the young Benedict now passed. He was attracted by the desolation around him. There was no sign of human habitation. So he put the stream between him and Enfide and began to climb the opposite side of the valley.

As he was climbing arduously up the rocky slope he encountered a monk—to his surprise perhaps—and yet he was familiar with other solitaries in the Sabine hills, and may at first have recognized in him one who was pursuing the same purpose as himself. However, this was no solitary, but a monk of a monastery which lay on the rocky heights above the valley. Romanus—such was the monk's name—interrogated the youth. Benedict answered truthfully and explained all his desire: he wished for a solitude where he could serve God undisturbed. Did Romanus know of one? Would he help him to effect his purpose? He spoke eagerly and confidently, with an ardour that must have moved the experienced monk deeply. Perhaps Romanus at first tried to dissuade him from his purpose, and represented to him that it would be more prudent to come to his monastery and there pursue his holy purpose. But Benedict was not to be dissuaded. He had already suffered from association with men and feared a repetition of the distractions of Enfide. He wanted to be utterly alone, alone with God. Romanus yielded to his fervent appeal and promised to help him in his purpose. He showed him a cave where he might dwell, he supplied him with a *melota*, the plain sheep-skin garment that was the robe of the Eastern monks, and promised to keep his secret safe from all. He himself would bring him at stated times his meagre pittance of bread.

Thus began St. Benedict's three years of hermit life in the narrow cave on the rocky mountain-side. Below him were the stream and the lakes, and the ruins of pagan splendour and voluptuous living. Around him and above him was the cold rock, his own habitation giving little shelter indeed from winter's rain and frost, or from the heats of summer. But he was alone in the pure and calm solitude. He was free to give himself wholly to the desire of his soul, to commune in long hours of unfettered prayer with God. We can imagine, but we can hardly realize, the story of those three years of silent prayer, of struggle and victory. The life of the fathers of the desert, of a Paul the Simple, of a St. Antony, of many another heroic solitary, was repeated in the solitude of Subiaco. Day followed day and night succeeded to night, and the months sped by, and still the hermit pursued his life of constant patient prayer. The sun rising above the silent walls of the valley would shine on this peaceful existence; rain and storm would beat on him in his inhospitable cave; the cold mists of night and the stars, with their silent doctrine of infinitude and eternity, would find him still studying in the school of prayer and contemplation, learning therein self-knowledge and the knowledge of God. It was in this long apprenticeship of prayer that he acquired that profound attitude of soul, that concentration of all upon the thought of God and His all-seeing eye, which was to be the pervading and transforming motive of his later teaching.

This silent life, wholly absorbed in prayer and contemplation, was no easy, effortless existence. It was not full of external activity, and yet it was a life of keen and vigorous action. There is no energy that can compare with the energy of the contemplative. There were consolations in it, the unspeakable joys that are known only to the consecrated soul; but there was trial also and desolation. Not every soul is called to such a life. High courage is needed, sane judgment and equipoise of mind, faith and hope and love. St. Benedict had these in full measure. His soul did not wither in the hermit life, but grew to its full stature of wisdom and sanctity. But he learnt much from his experience, and we may read in his Rule the fruits of that experience, for he has given us there a brief criticism of the solitary life. We read in the first chapter that there are four kinds of monks: Cenobites, Anchorites, Sarabaites and Gyrovagues. Of the anchorites, or hermits, he speaks as follows: 'These are they who, not in the first fervour of their religious life, but after long probation in the monastery, having learnt in association with many brethren how to fight against the devil, go out well-armed from the ranks of the community to the solitary combat of the desert. They are able now to live without the help of others, and by their own strength and God's assistance to fight against the temptations of mind and body.' Plainly he does not regard his own example as one to be indiscriminately followed. His vocation had been a special and individual one, and his success was due to the gift and grace of God. But others must not plunge thus into solitude, without any preliminary training. Their first fervour must be schooled in the society of religious brethren, and thereby only will they gain strength and mastery for the hermit life.

St. Gregory the Great gives us little detail about the three years of solitude, and indeed the record of those years would scarcely provide the substance of history. *Solus in superni spectatoris oculis habitavit secum:* there is little more for us to do than to appreciate the implications of those simple words. Yet he does recount two incidents which belong to this period: the story of the devil and the bell, and the great temptation. They shall be given as nearly as possible in his own words:

Romanus, the monk who befriended Benedict on his arrival at Subiaco, undertook, as we have said, to supply him with bread for his sustenance. But between the monastery of Romanus and the cave of Benedict lay the precipitous cliff, and the monk was compelled, if he was not to go a long way round, to adopt the following device. He used to let down the bread over the cliff by means of a very long rope, and fastened to this rope a small bell, so that the man of God, Benedict, might know when he was sending him bread and come out to receive it. But the old enemy, envying the one his charity and the other his meal, one day when he saw the bread going down, threw a stone and broke the bell. Romanus, however, did not cease to minister to Benedict in fitting manner (*ch.* 1).

On attaque les places fortes par l'assaut ou par la famine; a fortress may be taken either by slow famine or by sudden assault. There came a more serious trial for the saint:

One day when he was alone the tempter came. A small black bird—and so it is commonly called—began to flutter round his face and persistently to beset it, so that the man of God might have grasped it in his hand, had he so wished; but he made the sign of the Cross and the bird departed. However, when the bird had gone, there followed such a temptation of the flesh as the holy man had never before experienced. The evil spirit brought before his mind the image of a woman he had once seen and by this picture inflamed the servant of God with such a heat of passion that his breast could hardly contain it. Almost overcome by desire, he was on the point of abandoning his solitude. Then suddenly, being moved by heavenly grace, he returned to himself, and seeing hard by a dense thicket of nettles and briars, threw off his garment and cast himself naked amid the sharp thorns and stinging nettles, and rolling in them for a space came out with his body torn and wounded . . . From this time forth—as he used afterwards to tell his disciples—the temptation of lust was so conquered in him that never again did he feel any such thing (*ch. 2*).

Towards the end of the three years Benedict's solitude began to be invaded. And first it was in a way that helps us to realize the completeness of the isolation which he had achieved:

The time was now come [says St. Gregory] when God Almighty willed that Romanus should rest from his toil and the life of Benedict be displayed to men for their instruction, so that his light being placed on a candlestick might shine brightly and give light to all in the house of God. The Lord, therefore, appeared in a vision to a certain priest at a distance who had prepared himself an Easter meal and said to him: 'Thou preparest a feast for thyself but My servant in yonder place is tormented with hunger.' The priest forthwith arose and set out on Easter Day itself, taking with him the food he had prepared. Over the rugged hills and through the valleys and in the holes of the ground he sought the man of God, and at last found him hidden in his cave. They prayed, and blessing Almighty God sat down together. After sweet talk of heavenly things the priest said: 'Arise, let us eat, for to-day is Easter Day.' The man of God replied: 'I know it is Easter Day, because I have been granted the sight of thee.' For he was so remote from men that he knew not that the feast of Easter fell on that day. Then the reverend priest insisted again: 'Verily, to-day is the feast of the Lord's Resurrection, and it by no means befits thee to abstain. Yea, and for this was I sent, that we might partake together of the gifts of God.' So with blessing they took the food. And when the meal and talk were finished the priest returned to his church (*ch.* 1).

His retreat was discovered also by some of the rude and scattered inhabitants of that wild country-side. Some shepherds descried him amid the thickets round his cave, and, clad as he was in his rough sheepskin, they mistook him for some wild animal. But approaching nearer they discovered their mistake, and entered into converse with the saint. That intercourse grew frequent, with great benefit to the rough and ignorant peasants. They had lived before in a manner which was scarcely human; they now came to the knowledge of the Christian faith and practice.

St. Gregory tells us that the name of Benedict became known to all throughout the neighbourhood and that he now had to receive many visitors who 'brought him food for his body, while they carried away in their hearts the food of life that fell from his lips'. Some of those who thus came to him desired him to take them under his direction and to become their spiritual master. Benedict found himself invited to change his hermitage into a monastery. It would appear, as we should expect, that he shrank at first from this reversal of his previous way of life, that he resisted all such requests, and clung steadfastly to his hermit existence. But an experience befell him which altered his view of his duty.

The monks of a neighbouring monastery had recently lost their abbot. They had heard much of the sanctity of St. Benedict, and one day they sent a party of their brethren to wait upon him and invite him to be their abbot. Their action shows them capable at least of high aspiration; but the event proved them sadly lacking in the practical performance of their duty. We do not know what rule or rules they followed. It would

appear that their life was a highly individualistic one, in which
the principle of obedience had little play. The very structure
of their monastery suggests a congregation of solitaries rather
than a community of cenobites.

Vicovaro—for that is the name of the monastery which
tradition connects with this incident—was situated in a steep
cliff overlooking the Anio, some eighteen miles below Subiaco
on the way to Tivoli. The monastery was literally *in* the rock,
consisting as it did of a series of caves, and for this reason survives to this day, while many more pretentious monasteries
have perished utterly. Steps led down from the surface to these
cells which were cut in the rock, each having a small window
which looked out over the river. Each cell measured about
six feet by four and was eight feet in height. For furniture
there were two ledges cut in the rock. At the end of the series
of cells was a larger one for the common refectory. Its arrangements were curious. It was twenty-eight feet square, and in
the centre the monks had shaped the natural rock into the
form of a table. From this level steps led down to another
grotto below, which served them for their church, a sufficiently
rude one. Its length was twenty-four feet; at the eastern end
the width was nineteen feet, at the western twelve. In the
centre the original rock had been left as a pillar to support the
roof.

The monks of this singular monastery had now come to beg
St. Benedict to undertake their governance. The saint was by
no means ready to assent to their request. He was not yet
prepared to abandon his solitary life, and it would appear also
that there was something in their appearance or in their reputation which led him to the conviction that the undertaking
would be abortive. He told them plainly that 'their way of life
and his would by no means agree', but the monks would take
no refusal. So in the end he gave a reluctant consent and went
with them to their monastery. Benedict took his new duties
seriously, and set himself to mend many laxities which he observed in the community. He was no complaisant ruler, who
would suffer those under his charge to live as they liked, but
rebuked severely such as he found indulging in practices which
were inconsistent with their vocation. It was not long before
the monks of Vicovaro began to repent of their impulsive

choice. There was murmuring first and then fierce anger. And presently they formed the desperate resolve of removing their obnoxious abbot by poison. The monks were at dinner in their subterranean refectory with the abbot at their head. The server came in with the jug that contained the wine for the meal, which had first to be blessed and tasted by the abbot. Into this vessel poison had been put. The monk set the glass vessel down before the abbot, while the conspirators silently and anxiously awaited the event. Benedict

stretched out his hand and made the sign of the Cross, and at that sign the vessel, though at some distance from him, was broken, and broken exactly as though he had cast a stone at it and not a blessing. The man of God at once understood that it had held a deadly potion which could not endure the sign of life, and rising immediately from the table, called the brethren together and thus addressed them: 'My brethren, may Almighty God have mercy on you. Why would ye treat me thus? Did I not tell you before that my ways and yours would never agree? Go then and seek an abbot according to your way of life, for me ye can have no longer.' With these words he returned to his beloved solitude, and alone under the eye of God dwelt with himself (*ch.* 3).

Thus failed the experiment of Vicovaro. We might have thought that this experience would have strengthened Benedict in his resolve to abide far from men, to mingle as little as possible in human association. And certainly his solitude was doubly sweet to him after this startling episode. But we find, after this event, that Benedict listened more readily to the prayers of those who besought him to take them under his guidance. The soul of the solitary was already alive to the spiritual needs of the poor countryfolk around; he had already learnt to sympathize with them in their joys and sorrows, and to give them generously of the fund of faith and love that abounded in his own soul. His solitary life had not hardened or soured him; rather it had widened his sympathies and enlarged his understanding of human need. And now he realizes that a larger work is calling him, a work of greater moment and wider result than the instruction of the poor rustics of

Subiaco. He can no longer refuse the requests of the many souls that come to him seeking guidance on the way to God. He can no longer send them away to the care of other masters in neighbouring monasteries. For he had learnt by sad experience that such a course might not be the salvation but the destruction of their souls. And so he renounces his solitary life and begins to gather disciples around him, there in the valley near his cave. He takes the second decisive step in his life. The hermit becomes the cenobite, and presently the great father of monks.

CHAPTER V

MONASTIC BEGINNINGS

---

*Laetabitur deserta et invia et exsultabit solitudo et florebit
quasi lilium*

IS. XXXV

ST. BENEDICT in his own life summarized the development of
monachism. Monachism, as its very name implies, began in
individualism; the first monks were solitaries; the cenobitic life
was a development of the solitary life. As in most of the things
of the spirit, so here also the East was the pioneer. Egypt,
Syria, Asia Minor: all had their monks and great monastic
teachers; from them monachism spread to the West. But
above all others Egypt is the source and origin of monachism.
There lived Antony and Paul and Pachomius and many another great name in the history of its development. There first,
under Pachomius, did monachism find organization and a
written rule, and there in effect did it become cenobitic.

There is no direct evidence that St. Benedict was familiar
at this time with monastic literature; but it is very probable
that he knew something about it. And when he wrote his Rule
he certainly had a considerable acquaintance with the chief
monastic legislators and their work. For the present we may
regard him as one who had read most in the book of his own
experience, and had made practical acquaintance with the
fundamental conditions of the monastic life. As has been said
already, the law of monachism was simple and ready at hand
for every Christian instructed in his faith: it was the book of
the Gospels itself. But the counsels of the Gospel needed application and adaptation to circumstances of persons and
places. This was the work that Benedict now had to under-

take, guided in it by his own experience and such knowledge of monastic enterprise as had come his way.

The disciples who flocked to him increased rapidly in number. At first he erected a monastery near the lake and dwelt there with his infant community. But he was soon under the necessity of building others in the valley and on the hills above, until, as St. Gregory tells us, there were twelve such monasteries gathered round the saint at Subiaco. They were not elaborate structures, these first Benedictine monasteries. They were probably simple, quickly erected buildings of wood. Each contained twelve monks and an abbot.

St. Benedict kept near himself those disciples who seemed to him to require his personal care. Such is the information given to us by St. Gregory. Perhaps we may see in this the beginnings of the novitiate, and suppose that St. Benedict himself undertook the early training of all who came to him. But it is apparent that he kept also a considerable influence over the other monasteries of his disciples in the Anio valley. Each had its own abbot, and would so far be self-contained, but it seems that St. Benedict reserved to himself a general supervision over all. Indeed it would appear that we should regard these foundations as forming a single monastic colony, closely bound together in their life and under the rule of their common founder.

St. Gregory tells us that the fame of Benedict's sanctity had now spread to Rome:

At that time the nobles and pious folk of the city of Rome began to flock to him and to give him their sons to be brought up for the service of Almighty God. It was then that Equitius brought his son Maurus, and the patrician Tertullus his son Placid, two youths of great promise. Maurus was a young man of many virtues and presently became his master's assistant; Placid was still but a boy of tender years (*ch.* 3).

Tradition has lingered lovingly on the names of these two early disciples of St. Benedict, and a marvellous structure of legend has been built up around them. Controversy has raged, and is not yet entirely silent, about the part assigned to them in later chronicles. But that does not concern us here. St.

Gregory mentions but few of the disciples of St. Benedict; to Maurus and Placid he has devoted several pages, which will serve to illustrate the atmosphere of that first Benedictine colony, and to display the qualities of its founder:

Three of the monasteries which he had built in that place [writes St. Gregory] were placed aloft among the rocks of the mountains, and the monks had much labour in descending to the lake for their water, especially as the mountain was so steep that they used to go down fearfully and in much danger. So the brethren of those three monasteries met together and coming to the servant of God, Benedict, spoke as follows: 'We have great toil in descending daily to the lake for water, so that the monasteries must needs be changed from that place.' Benedict consoled them with kindly words and that same night took with him the boy Placid, whom I mentioned before, and climbing the rock of the mountain prayed there for a considerable time. When his prayer was ended he put three stones there to mark the place and returned to his monastery (the brethren knowing nothing of what he had done). Now when the aforesaid monks returned to him next day, because of their need of water, he said to them: 'Go to the rock and in the place where you find three stones placed, one over another, dig a hole; for Almighty God can produce water even on that mountain top, and in His goodness relieve you of the toil of so great a journey.' They went and found the spot which Benedict had indicated already wet with moisture. As soon as they had made a hollow in it, it filled at once with water which flowed abundantly; and even to this day there is a plentiful stream running from that mountain top to the valley below (*ch.* 5).

In this narrative we have depicted for us the careful solicitude of the father, anxious to succour his children in their need. In the night, when all are asleep, he is thinking of them, and praying that God would help them and relieve their necessity. And by his side, serving his apprenticeship in prayer, is the boy Placid. We can imagine him following with wondering eyes the actions of his abbot, and again inspired to purest fervour of devotion by the sight of the saint's long and complete absorption in prayer. Already we can see the strength and tenderness of that character which made Benedict admirably fitted to be the father of many monks.

The next story associates all three, Benedict and his favourite disciples, Maurus and Placid. St. Benedict is in his monastery near the lake, Maurus is close at hand, Placid has gone to the lake to fetch water. The boy is impetuous, leans over the water, and, his bucket filling quickly, is pulled in. The current seizes him and carries him an arrow's flight from the bank. Benedict, though in his cell, knows the peril of the boy and sends Maurus quickly to his rescue. Maurus obeys promptly, rushes straight to where Placid is struggling in the water and pulls him safely to land. It is not till they are both safe again on the bank that he realizes that he has walked on the water. Both return to Benedict and there ensues a friendly controversy, Benedict ascribing the miracle to the obedience of Maurus, Maurus to the prayers of his abbot. But Placid interrupts and settles the debate: 'When I was being drawn out of the water', he said, 'I saw the abbot's cowl over my head and I judged that it was he who was taking me out of the water' (ch. 7).

In this story again we have a picture of the relations between the abbot and his disciples. The chapter of the Rule which speaks of the reception of the postulant makes certain stipulations as to the character of the novice master who is to be set over him. 'Let there be assigned to him a senior who is skilled in winning souls, who may watch over him with the utmost care and consider anxiously whether he truly seeks God, and is zealous for the Work of God, for obedience, and for humiliation.' Benedict himself was just such a wise and anxious father, *aptus ad lucrandas animas*.

The monastic colony of Subiaco was, as we have seen, a congeries of small monasteries. It was not a new type, but had already existed in the East. Nor again would the life and occupation of its members offer anything novel, except where local circumstances or the peculiarities of the Western temperament counselled some modification. The main purpose of the monk is the pursuit of perfection by the practice of the evangelical counsels. It follows naturally from this, and we find the consequence everywhere, that his life expresses itself in two main activities, in prayer and in work. St. Benedict makes this plain enough in his Rule, but already in the years at Subiaco these essential aspects of the monastic life must have received their necessary emphasis. In each monastery there would be a chapel, the *Oratorium*, where the monks assembled at stated hours of the day and night for the public service of God. This service had already been fixed in its general outlines; the psalms were its main substance; we shall find St. Benedict systematizing the 'Work of God' with the greatest nicety in the pages of his Rule. This primary duty would entail upon the monks a certain preparation, in reading and study. Not a few, perhaps, would have to begin with the very elements of education; but all were to think no toil too great, so that they might take their part worthily in the chief duty of their day.

St. Gregory does not deal explicitly with this side of the life at Subiaco, but he alludes to it in the quaint story of 'the monk who would not stay at his prayers', a story which shows us also another aspect of Benedict's governance:

In one of those monasteries [says the biographer] there was a monk who could not stay at silent prayer. As soon as the brethren set themselves to this work he would go out and with distracted mind occupy himself with vain and transitory things. When he had been admonished frequently by his abbot he was brought to the man of God, who also rebuked him severely for his folly. He returned to his monastery, but observed the admonition of the man of God scarcely two days. For on the third day he reverted to his own ways and went wandering during the time of prayer. The abbot of that monastery sent word of this to the servant of God and Benedict replied that he would come and himself reform him. So when the man of God had come to that monastery, and, at the appointed hour, the psalmody being finished, the brethren had set themselves to silent prayer, he observed a little black boy dragging the monk who could not stay at prayer by the fringe of his cowl. Then secretly he asked the abbot, whose name was Pompeianus, and the servant of God, Maurus, did they not see who was dragging the monk away. 'No,' they replied. 'Let us pray then,' said

Benedict, 'so that you too may see whom this monk is following.' When they had prayed for two days the monk Maurus saw, but Pompeianus, the abbot of the monastery, could not see. So on another day, when prayer was finished, the man of God went out of the Oratory, and finding the monk standing outside, struck him with a rod because of the blindness of his heart. And from that day he yielded no more to the persuasions of the tempter, but stayed fast at the practice of prayer; the old enemy, as though he himself had received that blow, dared no longer lord it over his mind (*ch. 4*).

The second main activity of the monk's life was manual work. The very construction and furnishing of their monasteries would devolve upon the monks themselves, and often they would have to labour in the cultivation of the soil, so as to win their frugal sustenance. Here again St. Gregory gives us no explicit information, but tells us a story which has reference to this manual labour. One of the many postulants that came to Benedict at this time was a simple Goth, one of the nation that then dominated Italy, who had been converted from his Arianism and felt drawn to the service of God in the monastic life. Benedict saw the goodness of his heart and admitted him willingly to his novitiate. One day he set him to clear the briers from some ground so that it might be tilled, and provided him with a bill-hook for that purpose. The piece of ground was situated on the very bank of the lake. The worthy Goth set to work with a will—he was probably strong of muscle—and wielded his tool with great zeal and vigour. Suddenly the head came off the handle, flew over the lake and was soon lost in its depths. The Goth was overcome with distress at this unhappy accident, and went tremblingly to tell his misfortune to Maurus, doing penance for his fault. Maurus reported the matter to Benedict. The abbot, doubtless pitying the distress of his well-meaning disciple, went to the edge of the lake and threw the handle after its head. Immediately the iron head rose from the bottom of the lake and attached itself again to its handle. Then Benedict returned the tool to the astonished Goth, with the encouraging words: 'There now, work on, and be sad no longer.' *Ecce labora et noli contristari* (*ch. 6*).

From these stories of St. Gregory, and from legitimate inferences as to the course of the monk's life, we may piece together a picture of the quiet and happy existence of the now populous solitude of Subiaco. But the day came when their peace was to be sadly interrupted. The priest of a neighbouring church, by name Florentius, had conceived a dislike for the saint. We do not know the cause of his dislike beyond what St. Gregory tells us. According to him it was the hatred of a vicious man for one whose life was a standing condemnation of his own. Doubtless his position had been easier but for the uncomfortable proximity of the zealous monastic colony. Against the background of their virtues, his own lax and vicious courses showed up in their true colours. So he disparaged the saint's life and endeavoured to prevent all he could from visiting him. Finally, finding that his efforts were of no avail, he determined to rid himself of the presence of him who was the source and cause of his discomfiture.[1]

It was the custom in those times for Christians to send one another little presents of blessed bread, as a symbol of their oneness in faith and love. Florentius decided to use this token of communion as the instrument of his malicious purpose. He sent the saint a poisoned *eulogium*—apparently a token of friendship, really a minister of death. Benedict accepted the present, but had some presentiment of the purpose that lay behind it. He cannot have been ignorant of the hostility of Florentius, and while not returning hatred for hatred must have been forced into an attitude of caution and reserve. St. Gregory gives the sequel in the following words:

At the hour of dinner a raven used to come from a neighbouring wood and take bread from Benedict's hand. That day it came as usual, and the man of God threw it the loaf which Florentius had sent, bidding it take it in the name of the Lord Jesus Christ and cast it in such a place that no one might find it. Then the raven opened its mouth and spreading its wings began to hop this way and that around

[1] St. Gregory was in a position to know all about this curious story (apart from his Benedictine sources) for one of his own subdeacons was a grandson of this Florentius. The subdeacon gave St. Gregory some trouble in 592 by refusing to become bishop of Naples, and figures in the Pope's correspondence (III, 15).

the loaf, and to croak the while, as who should say that it wished to obey yet could not fulfil the command. The man of God repeated his order again and again, bidding the raven take it without fear and cast it where none might find it. The raven then, after long delay, took the bread in its mouth, picked it up and departed. After three hours' space, having cast the bread away, it returned and received from the hand of the man of God its usual portion (*ch.* 8).

Florentius was not daunted by the failure of this attempt to remove Benedict. He returned to the attack and this time aimed a blow at the saint through his disciples. He attempted by means of some depraved women to seduce their virtue. We can scarcely believe that his hatred could have reached such a point, but if he wished to dislodge the saint he could have chosen no better way. Benedict realized that he must act and at once. It was against him that the efforts of this unscrupulous man were directed, he was the rock of offence. He would leave Subiaco and give place to his hatred. This resolution once taken St. Benedict lost no time in putting it into effect. He was now nearly fifty years old. His colony of monks was firmly established and could persevere successfully in the course which he had laid down for them. He made his final dispositions, constituted his monasteries as independent families, and fared forth from the valley which had been his home for thirty years and had witnessed the peaceful triumphs of his saintly life.

On his way (St. Gregory tells us) he heard of the sudden death of Florentius, by the manifest judgment of God; but Benedict would not listen to the suggestion that he should return to Subiaco. His mind was made up and he pursued his way to the south. Perhaps he had conceived the plan of another type of monastery, an ideal which had been growing clearer and clearer in the long experiment of Subiaco. Some have supposed that he was yielding to the persuasions of powerful friends who desired to extend the influence of the saintly abbot. Perhaps one of those Roman patricians, who had come to know his work at Subiaco and had entrusted their sons to his care, now provided him with the refuge of Monte Cassino, thus setting his light upon a magnificent candlestick where it could not be hid. But this is no more than speculation. The monk-poet, Mark of Monte Cassino, makes no mention of Florentius or of any other human agency as determining Benedict's decision. It was his own choice, or rather his choice as guided by a divine call. Mark would surround the whole event with an atmosphere of the supernatural:

When thou wert called from other mount one day,
Christ was thy Guide, and through the waste thy Way;
For ever where the roads apart did lead,
Two youths appeared to guide thee in thy need.
And to the saint that once had lived hereby
Was said, 'Give place, another friend is nigh'.

He tells us also that all Subiaco mourned the saint's departure: hills, woods and lakes joining with his disciples in grief for the loss of his saintly presence.

More than this our authorities do not tell us. Benedict left the valley of the Anio, taking some of his disciples with him, and then pursued his way steadfastly to the south, until he arrived at the towering mass of Monte Cassino.

CHAPTER VI

MONTE CASSINO

Levavi oculos meos in montes unde veniet auxilium mihi
PS. CXX

THE ancient Latin Way, which ran from Rome to Capua and Naples, passed midway in its course, at about eighty miles from Rome, the important town of Casinum. It was an ancient *municipium,* and in the days of Rome's greatness had enjoyed considerable prosperity. In Benedict's time, after the evil century which had just ended, Casinum was ruined and impoverished, and like many another Italian town of that day was little better than a struggling village. In our own day there is nothing remaining of the ancient town except the ruins of its amphitheatre; the modern railway passes over the spot where once stood Casinum.

The town was established at the foot—St. Gregory says in the lap—of the mountain now known as Monte Cassino, an imposing mass which is projected like an outpost from the central system of the Apennines, and watches sentinel-wise over the fertile plain of the Liris. Its summit shows, in the remains of Cyclopean masonry, the evidences of a pre-historic fortress, and in Roman times also there were fortifications there, the mountain top thus serving as the acropolis or citadel of the town which lay at its foot. Moreover, it was a sanctuary where sacrifice was offered to the gods of paganism. The sides of the mountain were then clothed with dense woods, where in sacred groves and on marble altars the worship of Jupiter, Apollo and Venus was celebrated. This worship outlasted the prosperity of Casinum and survived the introduction of Christianity, for we learn from St. Gregory that the countryfolk,

arts, still resorted to the ancient sanctuary
ore an idol of the god Apollo. It was thus
red on in many remote parts of Italy, re-
ven in Christian districts amid the demoral-
arian invasions.

have it that St. Benedict had a predilection
for

> Bernardus valles, montes Benedictus amabat,
> oppida Franciscus, celebres Dominicus urbes.

The monk-poet, Mark of Monte Cassino, whose verses cannot
be dated exactly but belong at the latest to the eighth century, gives us to understand that the saint was directly called
to Casinum, in order that he might evangelize the pagan rustics and turn them from their idolatry. They were wholly
devoted to the worship of Jupiter, but Benedict came, 'called
from his distant monastery', broke the idols, cleared the ground
of all traces of the false rites, and built instead a temple to the
true God. The mountain was currently known as the 'citadel
of Campania' (*arx Campaniae*). When given over to pagan
worship it was, says Mark, a citadel of impiety and death; but
now, under St. Benedict, crowned no longer with a pagan
fortress but with the cloister's tower, it had become a citadel
of godliness and life.

Apart from this testimony of Mark our sources do not explain why St. Benedict directed his steps to Monte Cassino.
Later writers have surmised that the place had been given into
his possession by the patrician Tertullus, the father of St.
Placid. In default of such a donation we are at a loss, humanly
speaking, to explain the choice of St. Benedict or his conduct
on taking possession. For he soon began to act as absolute lord
of the mountain. He destroyed the idols and every other trace
of pagan worship; he built Christian shrines in the place of
the temples and he set to work to establish himself and the
disciples who came to him in a substantial and comprehensive
monastery. Our knowledge of the circumstances of the time,
and the terms of St. Gregory's record, would suggest that there
was none to dispute the saint's occupation of the mountain.
Mark, however, speaks of a hermit who was bidden make way
for him. The same writer depicts the mountain at St. Bene-

dict's coming as a barren wilderness of rock and thicket, and is enthusiastic over the transformation which the saint wrought. The ground was cleared of its wild overgrowth; fields were laid out and cultivated; a water supply was provided; and a gently-winding road from the plain to the mountain top allowed visitors to approach the monastery without excessive fatigue.

> Ah! justly does the mountain honour thee,
> For thou hast made it rich and fair to see.
> Its barren sides by thee are gardens made,
> Its naked rocks with fruitful vineyards laid;
> The crags admire a crop and fruit not theirs,
> The wild wood now a bounteous harvest bears.

Perhaps the saint obtained such authority as he needed from the people of Casinum; and, in the matter of the destruction of pagan sanctuaries, he had imperial edicts on his side. But the most natural explanation is something of this sort: St. Gregory's narrative is so rapid in regard to historical detail that it tends to foreshorten the saint's career. It is extremely unlikely that he began at once as soon as he had arrived at Monte Cassino to erect a monastery and establish a monastic community. It is more natural to suppose that his arrival at Monte Cassino was similar to his arrival at Subiaco and that his life there developed in much the same way. He began as a hermit; then he felt compelled to wean the ignorant inhabitants of the mountain from their idolatry. In so doing, just as at Subiaco, he won their hearts. The lordship that he came to exercise over the mountain was a lordship of love rather than of territorial right. It was a personal success. Some such account as this would appear to agree with the information given us by Mark. He tells us of Benedict withdrawing for a while from the people into complete solitude, and of their pressing eagerly round his retreat and bewailing the loss of his presence. Later writers report that the saint made it his regular habit to go into such complete retreat for the season of Lent. The tradition surely depicts the conduct of a hermit and not of an abbot, and may be assigned with probability to the first period of his residence at Monte Cassino. Doubtless the process by which he became again the ruler of many monks and the founder of his greatest monastery did not take so long as at Subiaco. He was now in the prime of life; he had won a certain reputation; his new home was more accessible; disciples soon flocked to him. And so his foundation grew and his beneficent influence was widely felt and none questioned his dominion over the mountain.

However, St. Benedict, with whatever purpose or mission, climbed the mountain-side and came upon the ruined fortifications and the pagan survivals. The saint dealt drastically with the heathen worship: 'When the man of God arrived there [says St. Gregory] he broke to pieces the idol of Apollo, overturned the altar and cut down the sacred groves. In the temple of Apollo he put an oratory dedicated to St. Martin, on the site of the altar of Apollo he erected an oratory in honour of St. John; and preaching continually to the people round about he summoned them to the faith.' At this point the record of St. Gregory reflects manifestly the vigorous building activity which presently occupied the new-comer. Benedict took up his habitation in an ancient tower of the citadel wall; for a hermit such a dwelling was more than sufficient. But he soon found himself compelled to provide for the needs of those disciples who flocked to him in increasing numbers at this new centre. St. Gregory speaks explicitly only of the oratories which were built; but we may infer from incidental allusions and from the provisions of the Rule that the saint set to work to construct a complete series of monastic buildings.[1]

[1] Monte Cassino has been several times more or less destroyed (by Lombards, Saracens, Spaniards, earthquakes) and several times restored and rebuilt. The present great Church of St. Benedict dates from the beginning of the eighteenth century. It occupies the site of that oratory of St. John which St. Benedict erected apart from his monastery on the highest point of the mountain, where the pagan altar had stood. It was in this oratory that he provided the grave for himself and his sister. The church of his monastery, where his monks sang their office and where the saint died, was at a lower point, within the enclosure of the citadel, and took the place of the pagan temple, probably using much of its structure. This was the oratory of St. Martin. It was of solid construction and would seem to have survived the Lombard sack, at least substantially, for Petronax at the beginning of the eighth century made it his church and lengthened it by adding an apse. It was a small basilican structure and when enlarged had no greater length than

The mountain top had been the scene of pagan worship, and the ancient gods did not—it would seem—abandon it to the monks without a struggle. St. Gregory has much to tell us of diabolical machination:

The ancient enemy did not bear all this in silence, nor was he content to act secretly or by vision of the night. He showed himself plainly to the Abbot's eyes and clamorously complained that he was suffering violent treatment; even the brethren heard his cries, though they did not see his form. Benedict used to tell his disciples that the old enemy would appear before him in most foul and furious fashion, and rage against him, whilst flames issued from his mouth and flashed from his eyes. But his words could be heard by all. First would he call Benedict by his name, and then, re   no reply, would break into abuse. He would be   Benedict, Benedict', and then, getting no   Maledict, what do   me?' (*ch.* 8).

                                              ted to interfere

                                              the cells of that
                                              ch they intended
                                              or three failing to
                                              e stone remained
                                              nd, so that it was

_____

he time of Petronax
son than the Anglo-
f Bavaria and bishop
in the restoration of
At a later date, the
other ch   . Martin's took second
place. But, whereas no trace   y of St. John can be
discerned in the magnificent edifice which has superseded it, the primitive oratory of St. Martin may still be identified. It is embodied in the buildings of the so-called 'Torretta' and disguised by later constructions, yet not so that its exact position and original form may not be determined with reasonable certainty. I owe the substance of this note to the essay of Dom Germain Morin: 'Pour la topographie ancienne du Mont-Cassin' (*Revue Bénédictine*, xxv, 1908, pp. 277–303).

plain, since so many men could not move it, that the old enemy himself was sitting upon it. In this difficulty the monks sent for the man of God that he should come and by his prayers repel the enemy, in order that the stone might be moved. Benedict came and praying gave his blessing, and then the stone was raised so speedily that it seemed to have no weight at all (*ch.* 9).

At the suggestion of the saint the brethren dug the ground where the stone had stood and found buried there a bronze idol. The same idol was thrown on one side in the kitchen, where again it was the cause of a diabolical manifestation.

But Satan went further still in his efforts to baulk the plans of Benedict. His disciples were busy one day erecting a wall. Perhaps they were only amateur masons, and the wall a somewhat imperfect structure. At any rate it fell suddenly in the midst of their toil, and falling crushed one of the brethren under its ruins. He was a boy monk, the son of a curial, that is to say a person of standing in provincial circles. The distress of his brethren was extreme. They extricated the poor shattered body from the debris and carried him on a blanket to the abbot, with much lamentation. Benedict bade them leave him with him in his cell and return to their work. Then he gave himself to more than usually fervent prayer and within the same hour the boy was back at his work, entirely restored and taking his part once more in the building of the wall.

Such are the traces which the construction of the monastery of Monte Cassino has left in the pages of St. Gregory's biography. As to the actual form and quality of the monastic buildings he gives us no further information than has been already quoted. But from the narrative of the foundation of the monastery of Terracina, and from the ordinances of his Rule, we may glean further detail.

He had been asked by a devout man—doubtless when Monte Cassino was firmly established and already well known —to send monks and build a monastery on his estate near the town of Terracina. 'Benedict consented, and, having appointed the brethren who were to go, gave them an abbot and a prior. When they were leaving he made them the following promise: "Go," said he, "and I will come on such a day and will show you where you should build the oratory, the refectory, the guest-house, and all that is necessary."' The promise was fulfilled, St. Gregory tells us, in a dream, when Benedict appeared both to the abbot and to the prior, and 'indicated with great nicety the several sites and what they should build upon them' (ch. 22).

In the sixty-sixth chapter of his Rule, where he speaks of the porter, or gate-keeper, of the monastery, the saint makes clear the general lines upon which he would have a monastery constructed. And we may fairly assume that his requirements were fulfilled at Monte Cassino. In the first place he would have the monastery securely enclosed, with one gate giving access from the outside world. At this gate there was to be placed a wise old man who would know how to deal with all who came and whose maturity of age could ensure stability as well as prudence. 'This porter should have a room near the gate, so that those who come may always find him there to answer them.' And further in the same chapter we read: 'The monastery should, if possible, be so arranged that all necessary things, such as water, mill, garden, and various workshops may be within the enclosure; so that the monks will not be compelled to wander outside it, for this is altogether inexpedient for their souls.' From other chapters of the Rule we infer these chief items of the monastic establishment: oratory, guest-house, refectories (several), kitchens for each refectory, novitiate, dormitories, library, infirmary, and offices where the crafts were exercised and the tools of the monastery kept. At Monte Cassino there was no well within the enclosure nor could there have been any considerable garden. The monks would have to go out of the enclosure for their work in the fields, a state of things which is definitely contemplated in the Rule.

For the rest we can easily construct for ourselves from the data of the Rule a picture of the daily life that Benedict organized in his new home. It was a life compounded as at Subiaco of two elements: prayer and work. Very early in the morning, at an hour which varied with the season, but corresponds roughly with our 2 a.m., the monks rose for the night office. They would assemble in the church of St. Martin, and, if we remember that there was no heating and that windows

were plain unglazed apertures in the wall, we can imagine
that vigils on a winter morning was an exacting exercise. The
office lasted from one to two hours, after which, in winter,
there was a considerable interval which was devoted to study.
Then the monks reassembled in the church for Matins, the
Office which is now known as Lauds. And so, throughout the
day, there are Offices to be recited at stated hours, until Com-
pline terminates the monk's day and he retires, soon after sun-
set, to a well-earned rest. But the Divine Office is not the
whole of his duty. There was Mass and Holy Communion on
Sundays and great Feasts, and there was labour, both intellectual and manual. St. Benedict frequently speaks of *sacred
reading*, by which we are to understand the study of the Scriptures and of the Fathers of the Church. The time allotted to
this study varied according to the season of the year, being
more in winter than in summer. It was not an inconsiderable
amount. Though it cannot fairly be argued that St. Benedict
legislated for study as for a substantive pursuit, yet he secured
his monks about four hours daily of intellectual work. His aim
was practical and spiritual: he wished his monks to learn the
psalms which they used so constantly in the 'Work of God',
and to assimilate the spiritual teaching of Holy Scripture, of
the orthodox Catholic Fathers and of the great writers of
monachism. Their study was designed to assist them directly
in their monastic life and to bring them to the summit of monastic perfection in the exercise of contemplative love. St.
Benedict's great contemporary, Cassiodorus, conceived monastic study after a different fashion.[2] Though at one with St.
Benedict in regard to the main purpose of that study, he
wished it also to serve the needs of the Church and for that
end gave it a wider scope. Consequently he envisaged intellectual labour as a chief activity of the monks of his monastery
of Vivarium, and provided elaborately for it. But the institute
of Cassiodorus did not survive, while St. Benedict's took firm
root and flourished exceedingly. His disciples went forth admirably adapted for that material and moral effort which the
reconstruction of Europe demanded. They set themselves to
prayer and to arduous manual toil; and all the time they kept

[2] More is said about Cassiodorus in Chapter XII.

alive in their monasteries that sacred reading which preserved
the literary tradition. When the foundations of faith and
civilization had been laid, then their labour turned more and
more to the things of the mind, and they began to carry out
the ideals of Cassiodorus.

The forty-eighth chapter of the Rule, 'Of the daily manual
labour', begins with the famous words: 'Idleness is the enemy
of the soul', and continues: 'The brethren, therefore, must be
occupied at certain hours in manual labour, and again at other
hours in sacred reading.' We have said that about four hours
daily were allotted to sacred reading: the time given to manual
labour also varied according to the season of the year, but
would perhaps be about six hours daily. However, St. Benedict
contemplates occasions when the monks might have to devote
practically their whole day to it, sacrificing, it would seem,
the hours of sacred reading. Perhaps they had, from very need,
to labour themselves in gathering in the harvest. But 'let them
not be discontented, for then are they truly monks if they live
by the labour of their hands, like our Fathers and the Apostles'.
St. Benedict enjoined manual labour because it was the traditional occupation, sanctioned by the practice of the great
monks who had preceded him. It was recognized to be an excellent instrument in the training of the soul, and essential, as
by some law of nature, to the health and well-being of the
monastic life. It was good for the body, and, by keeping the
body healthy, it preserved the monk from many spiritual dangers. But St. Benedict does not regard manual labour as a
wholesome exercise only; he gives it a special function in the
economy of the monastery. He would have a monastery self-
supporting: the monks should live by the labour of their hands.
He did not conceive a monastery so rich in worldly possessions
that its monks would be under no necessity of working for
their living, though he does imagine degrees in their poverty.
History has justified his conception. Monasticism has flourished when there has existed a real relation between work and
livelihood. Few monasteries have died of poverty, many have
been corrupted by wealth.

The main toil of St. Benedict's monks would consist in
agriculture, the fundamental human labour. His monks were
to distinguish themselves in the centuries that followed as

great agriculturists, carrying to the barbarians the ordered system of the ancient civilization. Their monasteries were to be missionary centres, not only of the faith, but of the fundamental arts of civilization. They were a great economic factor in the new Europe that emerged from the disturbed period of the wandering of the nations. But agriculture was not the only craft exercised by the monks. St. Benedict devotes the fifty-seventh chapter of his Rule to the 'craftsmen' of the monastery. In his eyes manual labour, that had once been considered suitable only to slaves, bore with it no stigma of degradation. All manual toil was honest toil, and the monk was to regard no honest labour as beneath him. That principle of itself was a valuable contribution to human progress, and Benedict carried it out practically by legislating for the exercise of any species of craft in the workshops of the monastery. We should remember further that no hard distinction was then made between crafts in general and the fine arts in particular. Doubtless St. Benedict did not promote the merely decorative; but his monks would be free to develop their capacity and skill to the full in those crafts which had a vital connection with the occupations of their daily life. 'If there be craftsmen in the monastery', he writes, 'let them practise their crafts with all humility, provided the abbot give permission.' He is anxious that his monks should not become mere craftsmen; he would have them always remember the main purpose of their lives. And later in the same chapter he deals with the dangers that might bring harm to the community. He would not have his monastery become a money-making concern, a sort of unscrupulous monastic factory. 'If any of the work of the craftsmen is to be sold, let those through whose hands the business passes, take care that they be not guilty of any dishonesty. Let them always remember Ananias and Saphira, and take care lest they, or any others who deal dishonestly with the property of the monastery, suffer in their souls the death which they incurred in their bodies. And as regards price let not the sin of avarice creep in; but let the goods always be sold a little cheaper than they are sold by people in the world, that in all things God may be glorified.'

That last phrase is the keynote of all St. Benedict's legislation: he would have the occupations of his monks serve the main purpose of human life, the glory of God. Nor should we, in considering the part played in the lives of his monks by manual work and intellectual work, forget to give its proper emphasis to that labour which the saint himself denominates the 'Work of God'. We have already alluded to the Divine Office, the liturgical service of God, to the regulation of which St. Benedict devotes so large a part of his Rule. Obviously it is in his eyes the main occupation of his monks. He regulates it with great care and minuteness of detail. He is most anxious for its exact performance. He assigns to the abbot, as a sacred duty, the function of summoning the brethren to it. 'Let nothing', he says, 'be put before the work of God.' Plainly we are here in the presence of that which he regarded as the principal duty of his monks. Doubtless he would not say that this liturgical worship is essential to the very idea of a monk; for three years at least he had no other fellow-choristers but the birds that nested in the rocks by his solitary cave, or soared singing in the blue sky above. But when he came to regulate the life of his cenobites, this work is primary. They were to pay daily a stated 'measure of service' in the public worship, by psalmody, of their Lord and Creator.

The effect of St. Benedict's regulations in this matter of the Divine Office deserves a passing notice. The Rule lays down a programme of daily psalmody, specifies its amount and character, and defines its importance in the monk's life. The psalter thus arranged has been used by Benedictine monks now for fourteen centuries. Augustine brought it to England, Boniface propagated it in Germany: wherever the Benedictine missionaries went they took with them this systematic scheme of daily worship. The Benedictine Office was soon to be heard throughout the entire West. At first it was in the primitive wooden churches of pioneer settlements, and then in the noble choirs of splendid abbeys, which still remain, if only in ruin, to testify to the purpose for which they were built. We read of the Venerable Bede in his Northumbrian monastery that he was exact and unremitting in the performance of this daily task. 'If the angels find me not among my brethren in the choir, will they not say: "Where is Bede? *Ubi est Baeda?*"' And so, too, of Anselm, and of every one of the great names of Benedictine history. It is a striking record, these centuries of a regulated measure of reverent worship. Monasteries have lived and died, many choirs have been silenced, but still the work goes on; and now in countries also and in continents, of which St. Benedict never knew, the same 'Work of God' for which he legislated is being performed according to his Rule.

There are two chapters of the Rule, the nineteenth and twentieth, which are of paramount importance if we would understand St. Benedict's conception of prayer in general and of the Divine Office in particular. They speak for themselves. In the first he writes:

> We believe that God is present everywhere, and that *the eyes of the Lord in every place behold the good and the wicked;* but let us especially believe this, without any doubt, when we are assisting at the Divine Office. Therefore let us ever remember the words of the prophet: *Serve ye the Lord in fear:* and again, *Sing ye wisely;* and, *I will sing to thee in the sight of the angels.* Let us then consider how we ought to behave ourselves in the presence of God and his angels, and so sing the psalms that mind and voice may be in harmony.

The second passage (*ch.* 20) is of a similar strong and genuine piety. In comparison with what he has to say in regulation of the Divine Office, St. Benedict's instructions for private prayer are very brief; but we cannot mistake their wisdom and sincerity:

> If we wish to prefer a petition to men of high station, we do not presume to do so without humility and reverence; how much more ought we to supplicate the Lord God of all things with all humility and pure devotion? And let us be sure that we shall not be heard for our much speaking, but for purity of heart and tears of compunction. Our prayer, therefore, ought to be short and pure, unless it chance to be prolonged by the inspiration of divine grace.

CHAPTER VII

ABBOT BENEDICT

Dirum magistri, pium patris ostendat affectum
REG. C. II

IN THE course of his Rule St. Benedict has occasion to say
many things about him whom he calls the 'father of the monastery', about the character and governance of the abbot. We
have St. Gregory's word for it that 'the saint cannot have lived
otherwise than as he taught', and indeed the sincerity of the
Rule is obvious. We may take it, therefore, that St. Benedict
makes no demand of the abbot which he has not first required
of himself. But the saint is so copious upon this subject of the
abbot that to deal fully with the points which he makes would
require not a chapter but a book. It will be sufficient here to
mention the chief qualities that he seeks in an abbot, illustrat-
ing them as far as possible with the narratives of St. Gregory.

Like the practical, direct Roman that he was, St. Benedict's
first stipulation is that the abbot should be sincere. 'An abbot
who is worthy to rule over a monastery ought always to remember what he is called (*Abba,* father) and correspond to
his name by his deeds.' St. Benedict continually reminds him
of the account which he will have to render at the judgment
seat of God. He has to be continually alive to the responsibili-
ties of his position and to live up to his high vocation. He is
not abbot for his own pleasure, or for any other purpose but
the service of God's chosen flock, in order that he may bring
them all safely to Him. He is *servus servorum Dei.* Therefore
he must never allow himself any other conception of his life,
and must strive with complete self-forgetfulness to secure perfect concord between his acts and his duty. In every act of his

governance, when dealing with proud and difficult souls, as well as when instructing the humble and obedient, he must seek God and God's glory, not the satisfaction of his own personal feelings.

St. Gregory tells us a story that illustrates St. Benedict's government in this very quality of religious sincerity and directness:

One day, when it was evening and the venerable man was at his supper, one of the monks—he was the son of a great person[1]—was holding a light for him at the table. While the man of God ate his meal and the monk stood there with the lamp, the spirit of pride entered into him and he began secretly to ponder and indulge such thoughts as these: 'Who is this man that I am waiting on as he eats, whom I serve and give light to? Who am I to be doing such service?' At once the man of God turned to him and began to rebuke him severely: 'Sign thy heart, brother! What is this thou art saying? Sign thy heart!' And then, summoning the brethren, he bade them take the lamp from his hand, and dismissed the monk from his waiting, bidding him retire by himself for a while. The brethren afterwards asked him what he had had in his heart, and he told them in order how he had been puffed up with pride and of the words that he had spoken against the man of God in the secrecy of his thoughts (ch. 20).

The abbot's rebuke was stern and uncompromising, but its purpose was plain: it was directed not to the punishment of a personal affront, but to the amendment of his disciple's soul. That was the mark that Benedict ever had in view, and to that mark he directs the whole vigour of his straightforward character.

Benedict was a practical Christian. In the first sentence of the prologue to his Rule he invites the disciple to 'fight for the Lord, our true King'. He describes the monastery as a 'school of the Lord's service'. He tells the abbot that he is 'Christ's

---

[1] The son of a Defensor, says St. Gregory. This official was intended to be the champion of the people, whether of city or country-side, against the possible injustice of other imperial officials. He had necessarily to be a man of rank and importance.

vicegerent' in the monastery. His monks are to see Christ in everything and everywhere, but especially in the sick, in guests and in the poor. 'Before all things and above all things care must be taken of the sick, so that they may be served in very deed as Christ Himself; for He said: "I was sick and ye visited me", and, "As long as ye did it to one of these, my least brethren, ye did it to me".' 'Let all guests that come be received like Christ, for He will say: "I was a stranger and ye took me in".' 'In the greeting of all guests, whether they be arriving or departing, let the greatest humility be shown. Let the head be bowed or the whole body prostrated on the ground, and so let Christ be worshipped in them, for indeed He is received in their persons.' 'In the reception of poor men and pilgrims special attention should be shown, because in them is Christ more truly welcomed.' His monks are to follow Christ in obedience, in patience, in self-denial, and must cast down their temptations at His feet. The perfect monk lives by His love, and must prefer nothing whatever before Him. 'Let them prefer nothing whatever to Christ, and may He bring us all alike to life everlasting.'

St. Benedict's manner of conceiving the service of Christ as a service of love, as a deep inner attachment of soul, and not a service of legalism and constraint, is illustrated aptly by St. Gregory's beautiful story of Martin the hermit. This hermit lived in a cave on a mountain-side at no great distance from Monte Cassino. In order to keep himself faithful to his vocation he had fastened himself to the rocky walls of his cave by an iron chain. The circumstance was reported to St. Benedict and forthwith the abbot sent him the following message: 'If thou art a servant of God, let no chain of iron hold thee, but the chain of Christ.' St. Gregory tells us that the hermit at once dispensed with the chain, and remained faithful to his service by the constraint of love alone (*Bk.* III, *ch.* 16).

Sincerity and the love of Christ, these two characteristics of the saint are subsumed in and so to say dominated by his realization of the fact of God, of his duty as a creature towards his omnipotent Creator. 'The fear of the Lord is the beginning of wisdom.' That profound attitude of reverence, which is to the Psalmist another name for religion, is manifested by Benedict in his Rule and in his life. He was a Roman, and a Roman of a stock that was noted for its *severitas*, for gravity and rectitude. His view of duty is precise and strong, to the point of sternness. When in his prologue he lays before the disciple his view of the meaning of life, he insists on God and on judgment. He would have the abbot always remember the judgment and the account which God will require of him. The first degree of humility is 'that a man keep the fear of God before his eyes, altogether shunning forgetfulness. Let him ever remember all the commandments of God, and how hell will burn for their sins those that despise Him; and let him constantly turn over in his heart the eternal life which is prepared for those that fear Him.' Obviously St. Benedict was not shy of the 'Four Last Things', of death, judgment, hell and heaven. They are at the very basis of his thought.

St. Benedict conceived life as a journey to God, the last end of the rational creature. The monastic life was a special grace to chosen souls to whom God deigned to reveal with startling clearness the perils of the world and the privileges of His chosen servants. But they were never to idle on the way. They must be up and doing, they must run while they have the light of life, they must ever be seeking God. When a man comes to his monastery to ask admittance into the community he is to be severely tested to see whether he 'truly seeks God'. That is the point; the novice must have that basic purpose. He does not come to the monastery for a quiet life, or because he is a disappointed man, or that he may practise his craft, or devote himself to study; he does not come even for the ordered liturgical life, for the pure joys of choir and of cloister, but to *seek God*. That is the fundamental and essential purpose.

Benedict saw all things *sub specie aeternitatis*, in the light of God. His biographer illustrates this character of his mind and soul in the story of the Great Vision. This is his narrative:

Another time Servandus, a deacon and abbot of that monastery which was founded formerly in Campania by Liberius the noble, came to visit him as was his wont. He used to come often to the monastery because he too was a man of heavenly wisdom, and that they might hold sweet converse of sacred things and at least taste in words of yearning desire the delights of heaven which they could not yet perfectly enjoy. Now when the time came for them to take their rest, they retired to their rooms which were in the same tower, Benedict being above and Servandus below and the rooms connected by a stairway. Facing the tower was a large building in which the disciples of both were sleeping. Then the man of God, Benedict, keeping vigil while others slept, and anticipating the Night Office, was standing in prayer at his window, when suddenly in the depth of night he beheld a light pouring from the sky. The darkness of the night was utterly dispelled, and so great brightness succeeded that the light which illumined the darkness outshone the light of day. And as he gazed upon it, there followed a wondrous marvel; for, as he afterwards declared, the whole world seemed to be gathered into one sunbeam and brought thus before his eyes . . . Desiring to have a witness of so great a miracle he called loudly to Servandus, the deacon, repeating his name two or three times. Surprised by this unusual clamour on the part of the man of God, Servandus went up to his room, looked out and saw a portion of the light still left. He was amazed at the miracle and the man of God told him in order what had happened.

St. Gregory stops in his narrative to comment upon this vision and his comment is to the point:

Animae videnti Creatorem angusta est omnis creatura: to a soul that sees the Creator all creation becomes small. Though it see but a glimpse of the light of the Creator, all that is created becomes little in its eyes. By the light of that inward vision the grasp of the mind is so extended and enlarged in God that it transcends the world (*ch.* 35).

The Great Vision is true biography. It was indeed thus that Benedict lived with his gaze fixed on God, so that all else took its value in the light of that chief preoccupation. In his Rule he urges the disciple to remember always the eye of God and he would have him do everything as in God's presence. The twelfth degree of humility carries this endeavour even to matters of external deportment, and tradition holds that in this twelfth degree Benedict has given us a description of his own absorbed and saintly presence as it moved about the cloister and in the precincts of Monte Cassino:

The twelfth degree of humility is that a monk should not only be humble of heart, but should also in his behaviour always manifest his humility to those who look upon him. That is to say, that whether he is at the work of God, in the oratory, in the monastery, in the garden, on the road, in the fields, or anywhere else, and whether sitting, walking, or standing, he should always have his head bowed and his eyes downcast, pondering always the guilt of his sins, and considering that he is about to be brought before the dread judgment seat of God. Let him constantly say in his heart what was said with downcast eyes by the publican in the Gospel: 'Lord, I a sinner am not worthy to raise mine eyes to heaven.' And again, with the prophet: 'I am bowed down and humbled on every side.' Then when all these degrees of humility have been climbed, the monk will presently come to that perfect love of God which casts out all fear: whereby he will begin to observe without labour, as though naturally and by habit, all those precepts which formerly he did not observe without fear; no longer for fear of hell, but for love of Christ, and through good habit and delight in virtue. And this will the Lord deign to show forth by the power of His spirit in His workman, now cleansed from vice and from sin.

Fear of God, love of Christ, deep sincerity: these three are the great characteristics of St. Benedict. There are others which follow from these. The Rule uses various figures in speaking of the governance of the abbot: he is father, master, shepherd, physician, steward. The two first comprehend the others and cover the whole field of the abbot's activity. To St. Benedict the abbot is a loving father, in the fullest sense of paternal care and authority; and he is a master, one who is able and instant to instruct the souls committed to his charge.[2]

[2] The first sentence of the Rule is an appeal to the monk to give attention and obedience to the abbot as to his 'master' and 'loving father'. Commentators have missed this curiously, supposing that St. Benedict meant himself personally, or—as more compatible with his modesty—the Holy Spirit.

Certainly he must himself have been a wise and earnest teacher, speaking with the authority of conviction and out of a fund of spiritual experience. Nor did he lack severity, when occasion required it. His Rule is evidence that he had himself laboured to acquire that wise learning which he would have the abbot possess, by assiduous study of the Holy Scriptures and the Fathers of the Church; but in particular he displays an intimate acquaintance with monastic literature. He does not seek the quality of originality—he is eminently a man of tradition—but he has assimilated the best elements in the teaching of his monastic predecessors and reproduced them all transfused with his own fatherly wisdom and his eminent moderation. A wise discretion is one of his most characteristic qualities and the direct consequence of his paternal spirit. St. Gregory's chief purpose being to illustrate the supernatural quality of his subject, he has little to say about Benedict's ordinary government, about the normal course of his activity as abbot. But he gives us several narratives which illustrate a certain faculty of supernatural insight. One of these, the story of Valentinian's brother, gives us an interesting picture of a devout layman of the time:

This layman used to visit the monastery every year, both to get the prayers of the servant of God and to see his brother, and it was his practice to make the journey fasting. Now one day, when he was journeying to the monastery, he was joined by another traveller who carried food to eat on the way. When the day wore on this stranger said: 'Come brother, let us take food, so that we be not fatigued by the journey.' 'God forbid,' replied the other, 'I must not do so, for 'tis my custom ever to go fasting to the venerable Benedict.' No more was said for a while, but when they had accomplished another stage of the journey, his fellow-traveller again urged that they should eat. The other refused again, being determined to go through his journey fasting. So his friend held his peace, and agreed to go fasting with him for a short distance further. Now when they had been journeying a long time, and the hour was late and they were weary with walking, they came to a pleasant lawn and a spring of water, and all else that could seem delightful for the refreshment of the body. Then his companion said: 'Lo, here is water, and a lawn, and a very pleasant spot in which we can refresh ourselves and rest awhile, so that we may be able presently to finish our journey.' His ears were cajoled by these words, his eyes by the beauty of the place, so that he yielded to the third persuasion and took food. Arriving at the monastery in the evening, he was taken to the venerable abbot, Benedict, and begged his blessing; but the man of God presently reproached him with what he had done on the way. 'How is it, brother,' he said, 'that the evil one, who spoke by the mouth of your fellow-traveller, could not persuade you the first or second time, but succeeded on the third, and won you over to do his will?' Then the other, acknowledging his guilt and weakness, prostrated himself at his feet and began to lament his fault and to be ashamed of it, and this the more vehemently because he knew that he had done it in the sight of the Abbot Benedict although he was far away (*ch.* 13).

But while he was obviously the master, the wise instructor of his disciples, Benedict was still more plainly their father. In the first sentence of the Rule he gives the abbot the title of 'loving father'; he is several times referred to as the 'father of the monastery'; and Benedict requires from him all the love, tenderness and solicitude of a true father. And this he must display in more abounding measure when he has to deal with refractory brethren. Benedict's regulations about the treatment of offenders, of the sick, of old men and children, all breathe the spirit of the loving father. Nor did he confine his solicitude within the walls of his monastery. His love was large enough to embrace the countryfolk around, whom he sought to aid in their necessities, both of body and soul:

Nor should I omit [says St. Gregory] the story told by his disciple Peregrinus, which is as follows. A certain good man had fallen into debt, and in his need saw only one remedy, that he should go straight to the man of God and tell him of the debt which oppressed him. So he came to the monastery, found the man of God, and told him that he was being sorely afflicted by his creditor for a debt of twelve shillings. The venerable abbot replied that he did not possess twelve shillings, but consoled him in his need with kindly words: 'Go,' said he, 'and return in two days, for to-day I have nought to give thee.' Now during those two days Benedict, as was his custom, busied himself in prayer. On the third day, when the debtor returned, thirteen shillings were suddenly found on the top of the bin that held the corn. The man of God bade them be brought and gave them to his poor client, telling him to pay the twelve and to keep the extra shilling for his own expenses (*ch. 27*).

Another of St. Gregory's narratives deserves to be given for the reference which it makes to the social conditions of Italy under the Gothic rule:

In the times of King Totila [he writes] there was a Goth by name Zalla, an Arian heretic, who raged with exceeding cruelty against religious men of the Catholic Church, so much so that no cleric or monk could meet him and escape from his hands alive. One day, impelled by avarice, he was cruelly afflicting a poor countryman and subjecting him to various tortures in order to rob him. The peasant, overcome by his sufferings, declared that he had entrusted all his prop-erty to Benedict, the servant of God, hoping that his torturer might believe him and suspending his cruelty give him some hours of life. Then Zalla ceased his torturing and binding his victim's arms with strong cords began to drive him be-fore his horse, bidding him show him who was this Benedict that had taken charge of his property. So the peasant, his arms bound, marched thus before him and led him to the holy man's monastery where they found Benedict at the gate, sitting there alone and reading. The peasant turned to the angry Zalla and pointing to the saint said: 'Look, there is the man I told you of, there is Abbot Benedict.' Zalla re-garded Benedict with hot anger and evil rage, and thinking to carry matters through by terror as he was wont, began to shout noisily: 'Get up, get up, and give back this fellow's property which thou hast taken.' At these words the man of God lifted his eyes from his book and looked at him, and then turned his gaze to the peasant. When Benedict's eyes fell on his arms, the cords that bound them began marvel-lously to unwind, and that with such speed that no human hand could have done it so rapidly. In a moment the prisoner stood free. At the sight of such power Zalla fell terrified to the ground and bowing his cruel head to Benedict's feet, begged him to pray for him. The saint, however, did not leave his reading, but summoning some brethren bade them take him into the monastery and give him hospitality. This done they brought him back to Benedict, who admonished him to cease from his cruelty. So Zalla departed crestfallen, nor dared again to persecute the peasant (*ch.* 31).

The history of Benedict's life from the time when men began to visit him in his solitude, through the first settlement at Subiaco and the foundation on the mountain of Casinum until his death, is a consistent testimony to the fact that he was endowed with those qualities which attracted the admiration and won the confidence of all who sought him. He fulfilled his own ideal of the perfect abbot, teacher and father of his monks. And tradition, although it has mingled legend with fact so that it is now beyond our power to disentangle the two, has yet seized the essential quality of his personality. His was a large and generous spirit, a mind practised in the contemplation of eternal issues, a heart warm with broadest love and sympathy, a soul united in closest supernatural union with the Source of all life. St. Gregory compares the abbot of Monte Cassino with the great figures of the Old Testament and declares that he was full of the spirit of all the just.

NOTE.—Some writers have propounded the view that St. Benedict was perhaps a priest, if not a bishop. I do not propose to discuss this view, except so far as to say that I regard it as a speculation which, however attractive, rests on no serious evidence and is really in conflict with the Dialogues. It is not merely that St. Gregory in his very full account of St. Benedict makes no mention of any such clerical status, whereas he is careful in the brief notices of many others of his saints to give them their precise clerical title and diocese. It seems to me clear that his whole account is designed to portray St. Benedict as endowed with that non-hierarchical, 'charismatic' authority which he ascribes also to the great Abbot Equitius (I. 4) and to others of his monastic, non-clerical saints. Abbot Equitius, as he tells us, was taken to task for exercising such authority and triumphantly vindicated. It was definitely a period when conspicuous personal sanctity was considered to give spiritual authority, and the devout laity of the time accorded it in no uncertain a manner. Nor did the bishops object. St. Gregory himself discusses and allows such spiritual authority in the opening pages of his Dialogues, a natural preface to a book which contains so many instances of its exercise.

CHAPTER VIII

THE TEXT-HISTORY OF THE RULE

*Scripsit monachorum regulam discretione praecipuam,
sermone luculentam*

DIAL. II, 36

THERE are two standard modern editions of the Latin text of
the Rule, those of Abbot Butler (2nd ed., 1927) and Dom
Benno Linderbauer (1928). Dom Linderbauer's is a critical
text with apparatus; it gives St. Benedict's text as nearly as it
can be determined and with none but orthographical changes.
For the scholar who desires an exact text and to be informed
regarding the manuscript evidence, this is the best edition of
the Rule. Dom Linderbauer published earlier (1922) a philo-
logical commentary. The Rule is an important monument of
Late Latin, and this commentary explains it carefully throughout with reference to the vocabulary, grammar and syntax of
that form of the language. Dom Linderbauer's two books are
essential for a student of the Rule.

Abbot Butler's edition of the text is a 'critico-practical' one.
It also is based on a full study of the manuscripts; it contains
a valuable introduction, very full indication of sources, select
variant readings and important appendices; but the text is a
revised one. The more serious irregularities of St. Benedict's
Latin, as judged by the standards of normal Latin, are corrected, so that the text may be more serviceable for liturgical
use. Since there is no full apparatus, it becomes necessary at
times to turn to Linderbauer's text in order to determine what
St. Benedict actually wrote. For the general reader who wishes
to understand the Rule and to appreciate St. Benedict's use of
his sources, this is the best edition.

These two editions are for readers who have Latin. There

are, however, some modern editions, with substantially the same Latin text as Linderbauer or Butler, which are designed for readers who like to have the assistance of a translation. One such edition, in Latin and English, was prepared by the present writer in 1952 and is published by Messrs. Burns & Oates, London, and by The Newman Press, Westminster, Maryland. For French readers Dom Philibert Schmitz of Maredsous published a similar bi-lingual edition in 1950. (Dom Schmitz had previously published a Latin text, with a useful concordance. Prefixed to the latest issue of this Latin text, 1955, is a valuable essay on St. Benedict's latinity by Dr. Christine Mohrmann, entitled 'La langue de saint Benoît.')

Both Butler and Linderbauer in their introductions give an account of the history of the text—down to their own day—and both underline the importance of the work done by the great palaeographer, Ludwig Traube, in his Text History of the Rule.[1] It is not too much to say that Traube effected a revolution in the study of the text comparable to the revolution effected by Copernicus in astronomy. Let us be allowed at this point to sketch the situation as Traube found it, and as he left it.

To begin with, it is a curious fact but a true one, that the Rule though issued in innumerable editions, of greater or less value, was not subjected to an exact critical study until the late nineteenth century. No thorough examination of all the manuscript evidence was made and no scientific interpretation of the conflicting tradition attempted before the year 1880, when Dom Edmund Schmidt of Metten published his *Regula S. Benedicti juxta antiquissimos codices cognita*. Dom Schmidt was in a true sense a pioneer. After him came a series of scholars: Traube, Plenkers, Morin, Butler, Linderbauer, carrying forward the work which he had begun. As a result of their work it is possible now to speak with some certainty of the

---

[1] *Textgeschichte der Regula S. Benedicti*, 1898. Traube was preparing a second edition of his work when he died in 1907. The second edition was published in 1910. The editor of that edition (Plenkers) says in his foreword that he has no doubt that Traube would have brought his work to even greater perfection had he lived to complete it; but 'of this inexorable death has robbed us'.

true text of the Rule and of its history. Let us set forth succinctly the results which have been attained.

St. Benedict did not write his Rule, so to say, at one sitting; the Rule itself falls into independent sections and it bears evident traces of revision and addition. We should regard it, not as a code of law that was first devised as a whole by the legislator and then imposed on his disciples, but as the redaction of rules that had been in practice long before they were codified.[2] It is most probable, for instance, that the long section regarding the Divine Office existed separately as the liturgical regime of St. Benedict's monasteries from the earliest date. So also the section on faults and their punishment, which the Germans call the *Strafkodex*, forms a self-contained unity and probably had had an independent existence. The last seven chapters of the Rule would seem to be an addition, and the prologue was probably written last of all. At what date did St. Benedict put together the whole Rule, with its prologue and seventy-three chapters, as we have it now? We cannot say, but can only surmise that he did the work at Monte Cassino and towards the end of his life. Abbot Chapman, in his *St. Benedict and the Sixth Century*, argued from the traces of the Rule which he considered that he had found in contemporary documents, that the Rule was composed about the year 525; but the argument is of uncertain quality and will not bear close

[2] It is Abbot Chapman's striking thesis that St. Benedict wrote his Rule at the instance of Pope Hormisdas (514–23) to provide a single, clear code for Western monachism. It is an attractive thesis. He is able to point out very justly that codification was then the order of the day; he shows reason to believe that St. Benedict's phraseology copies the style of the canons; he is right in maintaining that the Rule is a well-ordered code of monastic law and was designed for use in other monasteries. On the other hand, any positive evidence for the thesis is lacking, and the actual history of the slow diffusion of the Rule would seem to conflict with it. It may be, too, that it is something of an anachronism to suppose that the conception of a unitary monachism was then present to the minds of monks or Pope. Certainly Rome attempted no general regulation of the institute until long afterwards. However, the age of Hormisdas is separated as by a gulf from the period which follows. The disastrous Gothic War baulked many projects and interrupted the continuity of ecclesiastical life and culture in Italy in the most decisive fashion. I hesitate, therefore, to dismiss the thesis as no more than a brilliant fancy.

examination. To take but one point: he found plain echoes of the Rule of St. Benedict in the Rule of St. Caesarius of Arles, of which the probable date is 534, and argued that St. Caesarius had St. Benedict's Rule before him when writing his own. But the texts of Caesarius which were available to him were bad ones, containing much interpolation of late date *from the Benedictine Rule.* And as to the genuine resemblances between the two Rules, not due to such interpolation, Dom Morin agrees decisively with Abbot Butler that St. Benedict used St. Caesarius and not vice versa.[3] Which conclusion, if we could rely on the date given for the Rule of St. Caesarius, would manifestly place St. Benedict's work after 534. However, the evidence which we possess does not, in fact, allow us to give a precise date for the composition of the Rule and we must be content to suppose that it was written, in the form in which we have it, well on in the first half of the sixth century, without attempting greater exactitude.

St. Gregory describes St. Benedict when he fled from the world as *scienter nescius et sapienter indoctus* (consciously ignorant and wisely unlearned). He had in fact abruptly broken off his schooling, and these words may fairly be interpreted as a graceful apology for the saint's lack of a full literary training. It is quite clear from the pages of the Rule itself that St. Benedict subsequently acquired a considerable measure of monastic learning, for the Rule contains abundant evidence of wide and fruitful study; but it is clear also from the same Rule that he did not take pains to write a classically correct Latin. For the Rule is largely written in that Late Latin of his period which departs considerably in grammar and syntax from the standards of classical Latin. A man who can write: *Post quibus lectionibus sequantur ex ordine alii sex psalmi cum antiphonas* and similar sentences, is not concerned to write correct Latin, but is adapting himself to the usage of his time. In doing so St. Benedict doubtless consulted the convenience of his immediate disciples, but he left behind him a text which inevitably attracted the hand of the corrector. In fact the subsequent

---

[3] See Morin: S. *Caesarii Arelatensis Episcopi Regula Sanctarum Virginum* (Bonn, 1933), p. 2. Abbot Chapman required an early date for his chief thesis.

history of the Rule was largely determined by its original character.

For it would appear that at once, in the next generation after his death, the disciples of St. Benedict began to edit the text of their founder. There survives in some manuscripts a verse prologue to the Rule which is of doubtful import but would seem to attach the name of Simplicius, the third abbot of Monte Cassino (about 560), to such an edition, and Traube accepts this as fact. However that may be, a revised edition of the Rule *did* appear in the sixth century and had a wide vogue, practically supplanting the original text. This revised edition is represented, for instance by Oxoniensis, the oldest of all extant manuscripts, which was probably written at Canterbury about the year 700. So by that year there were in existence two distinct forms of text, the original of St. Benedict and the early revised version (also called the 'interpolated text'). In the course of the eighth century there came into existence a third form of text, a mixture of the other two with 'improvements' of its own. This is known as the Textus Receptus, the received text or vulgate of the Rule. It was a text from which all difficulties of grammar and syntax had been removed and the whole redressed in a fair Latin. It is sufficiently true to say that some such vulgate text of the Rule has been the current text among Benedictines until the present century.

But, meanwhile, what were the fortunes of St. Benedict's original text? Monte Cassino was sacked by the Lombards about the year 580 and the monks fled to Rome, taking with them, says Paul the Deacon, 'the book of the holy rule which the aforesaid father had written, some other books, the weight for bread and the measure for wine, and what furniture they could get away'.[4] It is the conviction of most scholars that Paul in this passage intends not just a copy of the Rule, but the autograph itself. This autograph was taken to the Lateran monastery and from that probably passed into the papal library. For, when Paul comes to narrate the history of the restoration of Monte Cassino under Abbot Petronax (717–47) he records that Pope Zachary 'gave him many helps, namely books of Holy Scripture and other things useful for a monas-

[4] *Historia Langobardorum*, IV, 17.

tery, and moreover, of his fatherly love granted him the rule which the blessed father Benedict wrote with his own holy hands' (vi. 40). The precious autograph thus returned to Monte Cassino and stayed there until the year 883 when the monastery was attacked by the Saracens and the community fled to Teano near Capua, taking the autograph with them. The monastery of Teano was destroyed by fire in the year 896 and the autograph with it. But the Cassinese monks evidently, and naturally, possessed copies, for there are extant still at Monte Cassino manuscripts of the tenth and later centuries which though by no means free from other influences are judged to derive their descent from this source. Yet, strangely enough, it is not to these Cassinese manuscripts, but to a German manuscript, that we must go for a faithful copy of the autograph.

It happened in this way. The Emperor Charlemagne, as a promoter of learning, set a high value on correct texts. He was anxious also to regulate the monasteries of his empire. In the course of his Italian campaign in the winter of 786–7 he visited Monte Cassino and doubtless there saw the autograph of the Rule with his own eyes. Shortly after his return to Aachen, in the summer of 787, he wrote to Abbot Theodemar of Monte Cassino and asked him for a faithful copy of the autograph. Abbot Theodemar sent him the copy with a covering letter written by Paul the Deacon. That letter contains this sentence: 'Behold, according to your order we have transcribed the rule of our blessed father from the very codex which he wrote with his own holy hands and have sent it to you.' That is the first stage: Charlemagne has obtained a copy of the autograph to serve as the standard for the text of the Rule in the monasteries of his empire. The next stage was the dissemination of this text among these monasteries. Many copies were made from this standard text and began to supersede that revised text which had hitherto reigned supreme. The royal copy has perished but some of the copies of it remain, and of these copies—grandchildren so to say of the original—one stands out above the rest for its completeness and accuracy and for its precisely-known history. This is Sangallensis 914, transcribed at the beginning of the ninth century for the abbey of Reichenau. Its history is as follows:

Charlemagne's successor, Louis the Pious, held a synod at Aachen in the year 817 which ordained that the Rule of St. Benedict should be observed in all the monasteries of the Empire, and made regulations for its exact observance. As part of this monastic policy Louis established the great reforming abbot, St. Benedict of Aniane, in a special monastery near Aachen which should set the standard of observance for all other monasteries. It was provided also that inspectors should visit these monasteries to see that the emperor's wishes were being carried out. In order to comply with these regulations, Haito, abbot of Reichenau and bishop of Basle, sent two young monks of his abbey, by name Grimalt and Tatto, to Aachen to be instructed in the standard observance. The librarian of Reichenau, by name Reginbert, took advantage of their visit to ask the two emissaries to make him an exact transcript of the imperial copy of St. Benedict's Rule. Grimalt and Tatto fulfilled his commission with great fidelity. They made a very careful transcript and dispatched the copy to Reichenau with a letter to their 'most excellent and most beloved master, Reginbert' in the course of which they speak thus: 'Behold, we have sent you the rule of the great teacher Saint Benedict, which your heart has always with intense longing desired to have. Our copy lacks nothing, we believe, of the sentences and syllables and even of the letters that were set down by the aforesaid father; for it has been copied from that exemplar which was copied from the very codex which the blessed father took care to write with his own sacred hands for the welfare of many souls.' They add that they have supplied in the margin the readings of other texts corrected by 'modern masters', wishing their abbey to have both the original text and the current revision. Such is the very precise history of Sangallensis 914. It may be observed upon this history that the position of the Rule among ancient books is thus a unique one; of no other ancient book have we a copy which is separated from the original by only one intermediary. The text of Sangallensis 914 has been printed in a diplomatic edition by Dom Morin.[5] The manuscript itself bears out the claim made for it by its scribes; it is accepted by the critics as a very faithful

[5] *Regulae S. Benedicti traditio codicum manu scriptorum Casinensium* (Monte Cassino, 1900).

copy and as the necessary basis of any edition of the text of
the Rule. But this is not to say that Sangallensis is free from
all error; its scribes were very careful, but they were human
and have made a few obvious mistakes. Moreover, the manuscript has suffered a little in the course of the centuries. However, Sangallensis 914 does not stand alone; there are other
representatives of the Carolingian tradition. And, besides these,
there are the Cassinese manuscripts and the ancient representatives of the early revised version. Taking Sangallensis as his
basis and using these other manuscripts to control and correct
its text, the modern editor is able to reproduce St. Benedict's
Rule, as he himself wrote it, with reasonable certainty.

BIBLIOGRAPHY

The fundamental book for the history of the text of the Rule
is Ludwig Traube's *Textgeschichte der Regula S. Benedicti*
(1898, 2nd. ed. by Plenkers, 1910). Traube, starting from the
work of Dom Schmidt and adding his own researches, gave
the text-history an entirely new orientation and set the study
of the text on the lines which it has since followed. Dom
Schmidt had clearly discerned the existence (apart from the
Textus Receptus) of two main families of manuscripts. The
one family begins the Rule with the late Latin form OBSCULTA
and is marked throughout by late Latin forms and usages. The
other begins with the more correct form AUSCULTA and proceeds similarly; it has the prologue in a shortened form. Dom
Schmidt had concluded from his study that St. Benedict himself issued two editions of the Rule, the OBSCULTA class with
the full prologue being his second edition. He attributed most
of the vulgarisms of this text, not to St. Benedict, but to
the copyists, and he corrected these in his own edition.
Traube, however, proved to the satisfaction of scholars that
the OBSCULTA text represents St. Benedict's original and single
redaction and that the vulgar forms are his; whereas the other
text is an interpolated one, due to the editorial work of later
hands.

Other important contributions have been made by Heribert
Plenkers, Dom Morin, Abbot Butler, Abbot Chapman, Dom
Benno Linderbauer, Dom Bruno Albers, Prof. Otto Graden-

witz. References to this literature will be found in the editions of Linderbauer and Butler. The first-named scholar, Heribert Plenkers, was engaged up to his lamented death (1931) in the preparation of the definitive edition of the Rule, to be published by the Vienna academy; but that publication seems now to be postponed indefinitely.

A word may be added concerning the two most famous manuscripts. Sangallensis is the chief representative of the pure text. This MS. is now in the public library of the town of St. Gall in Switzerland. On the suppression of the abbey in 1798, its library was taken over by the town and is accommodated in part of the old monastic buildings. Besides the Rule this MS. contains Abbot Theodemar's letter to Charlemagne and the letter of the two Reichenau monks, Grimalt and Tatto, as well as other items. The original page measures 9¼ by 6½ inches.

Oxoniensis is the chief representative of the interpolated text and the most ancient manuscript of the Rule. The original page measures 12 by 8½ inches. In 1929, when Monte Cassino celebrated its fourteenth centenary, the Curators of the Bodleian Library sent an appropriate gift: a volume of reproductions from Oxoniensis accompanied by an expert palaeographical description. This volume, published by the Clarendon Press, has the following title: *Regula S. Benedicti. Specimina selecta e codice antiquissimo Oxoniensi elegit atque adnotatione instruxit E. A. Lowe, Palaeographiae apud Oxonienses Praelector.*

CHAPTER IX

THE CONTENTS OF THE RULE

Constituenda est ergo nobis dominici schola servitii
REG. PROL.

'BESIDES the many marvels which made Benedict famous', says St. Gregory, 'he was eminent also for his teaching. For he wrote a Rule for monks which is remarkable for its discretion and lucidity. And if anyone wishes to know his character and life more precisely, he may find in the ordinances of that Rule a complete account of his practice, for the holy man cannot have taught otherwise than as he lived' (*ch.* 36). In these words the biographer draws our attention to that which is certainly the most authentic source for our knowledge of the work of St. Benedict.

The famous Rule for Monks has come down to us in many ancient manuscripts. The oldest of these, which is preserved in the Bodleian Library at Oxford, was probably written by the Benedictines of Canterbury at the beginning of the eighth century, that is to say about a century after St. Augustine and his companions brought the knowledge of the monastic rule to this island along with the knowledge of the faith, and a century and a half after St. Benedict. The Venerable Bede was then living his life of fruitful monastic and literary labour in his peaceful Northumbrian monastery. Scholars have examined this and many other manuscripts and determined the pure text, over against the interpolated version which seems almost as ancient as the other, so that some have thought that St. Benedict issued two editions of the Rule. But, in speaking of this variety of text, we do not wish to give the impression that the variations are very great in number or substance. Only in one passage—the conclusion of the prologue—is there a considerable and substantial difference between the two traditions, and there the 'interpolated text' has abbreviated and not enlarged the original. We have already spoken of the history of the text as written elaborately by the palaeographer Traube and discussed by many scholars. There is no doubt about the authenticity of the Rule.

What were St. Benedict's sources? He is familiar of course with the Scriptures and with the writings of those whom he calls the holy Catholic Fathers. He quotes St. Augustine, St. Jerome, St. Cyprian, St. Leo. He displays an extensive acquaintance with monastic literature, including the Rules of St. Basil, St. Pachomius, St. Macarius of Alexandria, St. Orsiesius and other anonymous rules. He knew the lives of Eastern monks and their recorded sayings. But his chief debt is to the writings of Abbot John Cassian of Marseilles, who collected in his *Institutes* and *Conferences* a copious body of monastic theory and practice. St. Benedict used his sources industriously —he is very occasionally content to reproduce them verbally— but the Rule, though its composite character is plain, is not, for all that, an unoriginal patchwork. It is a complete whole, a structure with a genuine unity. A considerable portion may be borrowed from earlier writers, but the presiding spirit, the wisdom, sobriety and moderation which run through the whole, these are St. Benedict's own.[1]

[1] Much was written in the years 1929–31 about a short, anonymous rule which has been generally known as the 'Second Rule of St. Augustine' (Migne, *P.L.*, xxxii, 1499–52) but of which the more correct title is 'Of the Order of the Monastery' (*De Ordine Monasterii*). Dom Lambot first directed attention to it in the *Revue Liturgique et Monastique* (xiv, 1929, pp. 331–57), describing it as a precursor of the Benedictine Rule. The discussion would appear to have been settled decisively by Dom Germain Morin (*Revue Bénédictine* xliii, 1931, pp. 145–52). He puts the document well before St. Benedict, about the year 440, and believes that it was composed in southern Italy under African (Augustinian) influence. He suggests as a possible author an exiled African bishop, by name Gaudiosus, who founded a monastery at Naples about the year 440. The document is of great interest in regard to the monachism of Cassiodorus (see Chapter XII) for in its true text (the Migne text is faulty) it shows the same liturgical horarium as was used by Cassiodorus. For the debate of the last twenty years regarding the so-called *Rule of the Master* see the Appendix.

When was the Rule written? For this, as we have said already, no definite date can be assigned. It is believed—and the belief is very probable—that the saint did not compose his Rule at one time or in one effort. Portions of it may have been formulated even at Subiaco. There are sections such as the chapter on the 'Instruments of Good Works', and that on the 'Twelve degrees of Humility', which may very likely have existed independently, as useful summaries for purposes of instruction. Probably also the considerable section which deals with faults and their correction had a similar separate existence. And the liturgical *cursus* was doubtless custom long before it was set down as law. Indeed we must suppose that the whole Rule is the result of experience, of the application of old monastic principle and precept to the purpose which St. Benedict sought to realize, conditioned by the circumstances of locality and temperament. The Rule was lived before it was codified. It is supposed that the saint drew up the Rule, as we now possess it, at Monte Cassino and towards the end of his life, when he was about sixty years old and had had some forty years' practical experience of the life and government of monks. As we have it now it consists of a prologue and seventy-three chapters. Of these chapters the last seven would appear to be an addition by St. Benedict to his first codification, and it is probable that the prologue was written last.

The seventy-three chapters of the Rule cannot be made to conform to a clear-cut, logical sequence; indeed it would seem at first sight that St. Benedict did not attempt any logical order, but set his chapters down haphazard. However, it will be found that they fall into groups, united by similarity of subject. After the prologue there come three chapters which characterize the form of life which he is instituting and provide its main constitution, in the chaper on the abbot and the chapter on calling the brethren to Council. Then there follow four chapters of fundamental spiritual instruction (4–7). After that we have eleven chapters on the Divine Office (8–18), ending with one on the proper method of assisting at the Office (19) and another on prayer in general (20). After two chapters (21, 22) of particular ordinances (on Deans and Sleep) we have a large section devoted to the methods of correcting faults (23–30), of which the legislator has more to say later (43–6).

With Chapter 31 we resume particular ordinances for the life of the monastery (31–42, 47–57). The fifty-eighth chapter begins a section of the Rule which deals with admission into the monastery (58–61). Then we have chapters on the priests of the monastery, the order of the community, the appointment of the abbot, of the prior and gate-keeper. The last seven chapters, which are considered to be later than the rest, deal with certain particular points, and the Rule ends with an exhortation to zeal.

The abbot is the corner-stone of St. Benedict's monastic edifice. The polity which he creates might be described epigrammatically as 'autocracy tempered by religion', but the epigram would be misleading. A more accurate description would speak of paternal government. Roman law gave the father of a family very large authority over the members of his household. The government of the family was concentrated in his hands, and in the times of the Republic his power was so absolute that he could even inflict the punishment of death. By the imperial legislation, and especially by that of the early Christian emperors, the *patria potestas* was curtailed. Yet it remained considerable. Law and custom gave the father a status and an authority to which there is no parallel in modern times. St. Benedict conceived the abbot as exercising an authority which is similar to that of a Roman father. He has a paramount authority; but he must exercise it according to the law of God and the Rule, with the counsel of his monks, with prudence and equity, firmness and discretion, and with a constant sense of his accountability. The officials of the monastery are appointed by him and removed at his pleasure, while his own authority is for life. The whole life of the monastery hinges upon him, and there is no part of its activity but the direction and regulation of it appertains to him, though he may give others a delegated authority. The Rule recommends him to summon the community to advise him, but he is not bound by their advice. 'As often as any important business has to be done in the monastery let the abbot call together the whole community and himself set forth the matter. And, having heard the advice of the brethren, let him take counsel with himself and then do what he shall judge to be most expedient' (*ch.* 3). In the same way the *paterfamilias* of a Roman family might summon the members of the family to a *judicium domesticum* before exercising his supreme authority. For less important matters the abbot is advised to seek the advice of the senior monks.

St. Benedict has no qualms about entrusting this absolute power to one man. He is content to remind the abbot constantly of the responsibility of his position, of the account which he will have to render. For the rest this paternal authority seems to him the most natural thing in the world. And indeed it was entirely according to monastic precedent and contemporary secular practice. St. Benedict probably thought very little about the problem of authority, and it is even doubtful whether he was alive to the parallel between the authority of the abbot and the authority of the *paterfamilias*. He accepted the absolute abbot as he accepted many other elements of monastic tradition. Moreover, the secular government of his day was conceived in the same fashion. Therefore his institution would seem to his contemporaries natural and almost inevitable. And if abbot and monks were faithful to their ideals and lived up to the standard which St. Benedict requires of them, if the abbot were always such a wise and prudent ruler as the saint envisages, then certainly the system would be ideal. But, as in secular government, so here, it has been found that absolute authority is dangerous both for ruler and ruled. Benedictinism has in this point modified the Rule of its founder. The councils which St. Benedict prescribes now enjoy a legal status, and besides the consultative voice have also in important matters a right of veto.

The provisions of the Rule regarding the method of the abbot's appointment have given rise to much discussion, for they contain elements which seem strange to us in our more ordered times, when all is precisely regulated by long custom and definite law. It is quite clear, however, that St. Benedict expected the abbot to be chosen normally by the community and from among the community, as is now the standard practice. But this choice appears to fall short of a definitive election, for he provides for the case where the majority of a lax community might choose a too complaisant abbot, and in such a case he wishes the choice of the 'healthier' minority to prevail, by the intervention of external authority. He says expressly that if the community should even unanimously elect an unworthy abbot, he would wish the bishop of the diocese, or neighbouring abbots, or even devout layfolk to intervene to prevent such a consummation and to 'set a worthy steward over the house of God'. The history of the time—as revealed, for instance, in St. Gregory's correspondence—shows plainly that such a provision was not unnecessary. The lax monks of Vicovaro, who would have poisoned the saint when he tried to reform them, are not by any means a figment of the imagination.[2]

Besides the abbot, the chief officials of the monastery are the prior, deans, cellarer, novice-master, guest-master, infirmarian. St. Benedict would have them appointed by the abbot, and hold their authority in entire dependence on him. The chapter on the prior—an official whom St. Benedict does not care for—is instructive on this point. The saint speaks with vehemence of the evils that arise when the prior is appointed by external authority. Such a one is tempted to think himself the abbot's equal, for he has been appointed by the same authority, and there ensues a state of rivalry and dissension which is disastrous for the monastery. The saint is prepared to do without a prior altogether, and to entrust the subordinate governance of the monastery to deans. These *decani* had charge of ten monks each, over whom they were to exercise constant supervision under the general control of the abbot. The cellarer —to whom also a whole chapter is devoted—has charge of the material side of the monastery life. St. Benedict requires much of him. 'As cellarer of the monastery let there be chosen out of the community a man who is prudent, of mature character, temperate, not a great eater, not proud, not headstrong, not rough-spoken, not lazy, not wasteful, but a God-fearing man who may be like a father to the whole community' (*ch.* 31). He has to be a prudent manager, but also a kindly, affable man, whose administration shall be acceptable to his brethren. And he must ever keep a religious sense of his responsibility. So too with regard to the other officials, St. Benedict requires

[2] See the letter of Venerandus (pp. 175–6) for an illustration of the jurisdiction which the Rule expects the bishop to exercise in a monastery. The community normally *chooses*, the bishop always *appoints* the abbot. This is implied in St. Benedict's words about the prior.

such character and qualities as shall enable them to fulfil their duties to the corporal and spiritual benefit of those under their charge.

After the constitution of the monastery and careful provision for its administration, it is important to consider the sanctions with which the legislator supports his legal structure. The Rule is quite full and explicit on this point, devoting as many as twelve chapters to the subject of faults against the monastic discipline and their punishment, besides incidental references to the 'discipline of the Rule'. St. Benedict recognizes two main divisions of faults, slight and grave. The second class admits of degrees, running from the faults which submit to treatment up to those which resist all efforts to amend them and are to be cured only by expulsion from the community. We may classify the penalties recognized by St. Benedict as of three kinds, verbal rebuke, corporal punishment, spiritual punishment, with the fourth and extreme measure of expulsion. Verbal rebuke will be the natural preliminary in every case; in most cases it will perhaps suffice, and St. Benedict provides for its threefold application before sterner measures are called into play. Corporal punishment, under which we may include everything from small acts of humiliation to actual bodily stripes, operates throughout the whole range of faults, for its severer forms may be the only way of influencing those upon whom spiritual penalties have no effect. Spiritual punishment is excommunication, that is to say isolation from the life of the community in its common exercises. It may operate in the refectory only, or both in refectory and in oratory. This penalty comes into effect when rebuke has failed and when the offender is amenable to spiritual punishment. Its milder form, excommunication from the common meal, is the penalty for lighter faults, the double excommunication being reserved for grave offences. When all these measures have failed, St. Benedict bids the abbot resort to prayer—'his own prayers and those of all the brethren, that God, who can do all things, may effect the cure of the sick brother'. But if prayer too fails, then the abbot must use the 'knife of amputation' and expel the refractory brother 'lest one diseased sheep contaminate the whole flock'. Boys are to have special treatment, the normal punishments for them being fasting and the rod.

It would probably be a mistake to infer, from the prominence given in the Rule to this subject of the punishment of faults, that offences against the monastic discipline were very numerous and that the abbot and his officials were continually occupied in the business of correction. It is true that characters were ruder then and that Christianity and civilization have combined to produce an improvement in social behaviour, perhaps not without some loss of native vigour and spontaneity. There may have been some barbarians in the community at Monte Cassino. But we should remember at the same time that the faults dealt with are offences against monastic discipline, various degrees of disobedience to the law of the monastery, not offences against the law of God, except indirectly. The punishments prescribed are the natural safeguard of the monastic community, if it would preserve itself from dissolution. Therefore we find that St. Benedict is constantly severe on grumblers—he will not have 'murmuring' at any price—and that the worst offender, for whom expulsion is decreed, is one in whom disobedience has passed into absolute and obstinate mutiny.

In the first sentence of the Rule the saint speaks of obedience; to obedience he devotes a whole chapter; it is frequently referred to elsewhere; it is part of the vow taken by the novice; it is to be exercised in an heroic degree. There is no mistaking his meaning. He conceived the monk's life as the service of God by obedience to the monastic rule. The monk has to see God's will in the ordinances of his superiors. He has to realize the absolute surrender that is expressed in Our Lord's words: 'I came not to do my own will, but the will of Him that sent Me.' By this surrender and only so shall he achieve sanctity. Such surrender, it may be, is uncongenial to modern notions of the autonomy of the individual, but objection to it is generally based on a fundamental misunderstanding. It must be remembered that it is an obedience freely chosen and accepted, and further, that it is exercised within the ambit of a well-defined spiritual system, and as a means towards a definite spiritual end. It is an instrument which the individual elects to use, not for the destruction of his individual liberty, but for its strengthening, for the development of his spiritual life to a point that it would otherwise be unable to attain.

In fact, the purpose of all the ordinances of the Rule is the same, the purification of the soul and the development of its true life. The monk's aim is spiritual perfection. To this prayer and work, obedience, silence, fasting and every element of the monastic code are directed. Of prayer and work sufficient has been said already. Of silence it need only be said that St. Benedict does not seek to impose it in an absolute manner but allows some social intercourse. Of fasting, while recognizing the undoubted austerity of St. Benedict's regime, we may point out that, judged by the standard of contemporary monastic tradition, it is moderate. His regulations as to the normal allowance of food and drink are again austere in our eyes, but generous even to the point of laxity when judged by Eastern standards. A sentence that occurs in the chapter on the measure of drink deserves to be quoted as displaying the prudence and discretion of the saint, and also what seems like gentle humour: 'We do indeed read', he says, referring to the Book of the Sayings of Eastern monks, 'that wine is no drink for monks; but since nowadays monks cannot be persuaded of this, let us at least agree upon this, that we drink temperately and not to satiety' (*ch. 40*). And he allows his disciples a sufficient daily measure of wine.

The last considerable section of the Rule to claim attention may be said to be the first in order of historical incidence, the section, that is, which deals with the conditions and method of admittance into the monastic community. Four chapters (58–61) deal severally with four classes of postulants: the 58th with the ordinary applicant, the 59th with oblates, the 60th with priests, the 61st with monks. The last two, if they are granted admittance, receive it on simple terms: they accept the life and promise stability in it. The oblates are young boys who are not of an age to make their own profession; they are offered by their parents and this offering is regarded as a valid contract. The custom was common and ordinary then, but it has long fallen into desuetude. There remains the main class of ordinary adult postulants.

Their trial begins at the very gate of the monastery. We read in the life of Paul the Simple that St. Antony kept him waiting several days outside the door of his cell in order to test his resolution. In the same way St. Benedict ordains that no easy admittance shall be granted to the postulant. 'If such a one, therefore, persevere in his knocking, and if it be seen after four or five days that he bears patiently his harsh treatment and the difficulty of admission and persists in his petition, then let admittance be granted to him.' After a few days in the guest-house he enters the novitiate and is put under the care of the novice-master, a senior monk 'skilled in winning souls', who is to 'watch over him with the utmost care and to consider anxiously whether he truly seeks God, and is zealous for the Work of God, for obedience and for humiliations'. The difficulties, the *dura et aspera,* of the monastic life have to be put plainly before him. For twelve months his trial continues, and the Rule is formally read to him three times during this period with the monition: 'Behold the law under which you wish to serve; if you can observe it, enter; if you cannot, freely depart.' If he persevere to the end, then he shall be received into the community; but he is told that it is 'decreed by the law of the Rule that he is no longer free to leave the monastery or to withdraw his neck from under the yoke of the Rule, which it was open to him, during that prolonged deliberation, either to refuse or to accept'. Then St. Benedict proceeds to arrange the ceremony of the profession. The novice has to make a public avowal of his purpose, in the oratory before the community. He makes a formal promise of stability, conversion of life, and. obedience. This promise is not oral only; the monk must present a document embodying his promise and, having signed it, place it upon the altar. Then with his brethren he chants three times the words of the psalm: *Suscipe me, Domine, secundum eloquium tuum et vivam: et non confundas me ab exspectatione mea* (Ps. cxviii, 16). Finally he begs the prayers of all, and thenceforward is reckoned as a member of the community.

This solemn ceremony, so carefully conceived both spiritually and juridically, with the preliminary year of prudent trial, shows the master-hand, the wisdom and spiritual insight of the Roman and the saint. It has remained through all the centuries the form of the Benedictine initiation, and has served as a type for many subsequent religious foundations. In one respect only has it suffered substantial modification: the Benedictine does not now take *perpetual* vows until he has spent *four* years of life in the monastery, one as a novice and three under temporary vows.

St. Benedict's ritual for the profession ceremony distinguishes between the novice's verbal promise and the formal document which embodied that promise. At the present day—and such has been the practice for centuries—this document is itself the formula of the vows and the novice pronounces his vows by reciting it. But that was not the ancient practice; there were two distinct things, a short formula of the vows used by the novice and the longer petition embodying the same vows. Moreover, the manner in which the novice makes his promise has changed. Since the eighth century that promise has been made in the form of a direct statement of the vows: 'I promise stability, etc.' But this was probably not the method of the sixth century. Abbot Herwegen[3] has shown good reason for the view that the earliest form of profession followed the method of that standard contract in the Roman law, the *stipulatio*. This was a contract made by oral question and answer according to fixed verbal forms. (There is a good example of its method in the ritual for Baptism.) Now there is an ancient ritual for the Benedictine profession which is conceived in this manner. It is found in a ninth-century manuscript which derives from the diocese of Albi, and it was in that diocese that the first Benedictine monastery of Gaul was founded, at Altaripa. Traube[4] prints a letter which the founder of the monastery, by name Venerandus, sent to the bishop of Albi about the year 625 along with a copy of the Rule of 'Saint Benedict, Roman abbot' (*sancti Benedicti abbatis Romensis*), bidding him see that the monks of Altaripa followed that Rule without the least deviation. It cannot now be proved that the ritual of which we are speaking goes back to the foundation of Altaripa and the early seventh century, but the supposition is very plausible, both from the use of the ancient technique of the *stipulatio* and from the occurrence of the word *conversatio* in the correct primitive form. Leaving out eight words which Abbot Herwegen regards as a characteristic Frankish addition to the Roman simplicity of the original, we here give this profession ritual:

[3] *Geschichte der benediktinischen Professformel* (1912), pp. 38–9.
[4] *Textgeschichte der Regula S. Benedicti* (1910), p. 88.

Suscipiendus in oratorio frater coram omnibus sic interrogatur: Promittis de stabilitate tua et conversatione morum tuorum et obedientia coram Deo et sanctis ejus?

Ipse novitius respondeat sic: Promitto.

Credis ut, si aliquando aliter feceris, a Domino putas te damnandum quem irrides?

Et ipse respondeat: Credo.

However, this form of profession went out of use at a very early date and the Benedictine has since recited his vows in the form of a direct statement. Following the text of the Rule he vows 'stability, conversion of life[5] and obedience'. By the promise of stability he binds himself to permanence in the community of his profession. St. Benedict was keenly alive to the value of stability, which had been impressed upon him by the spectacle of the loose lives led by the roving monks of his time, the Gyrovagues, whom he castigates in his first chapter. He therefore exacts a precise promise of stability from his monks and from stranger monks or priests who wish to join his community. They shall promise to abide steadfastly in the monastery until death. Such was his meaning. In modern Benedictine practice stability in the monastery is generally extended to stability in the community and sometimes even to stability in the congregation. The effect is that a monk, though normally living in the actual monastery in which he pronounces his vows, may dwell in a dependency of that monastery or even in another monastery of the same congregation.

The second vow, *of conversion of life,* is a very general one. We propose to discuss it fully in the next chapter. For the present it will be sufficient to say that the monk in taking it promises to live his life according to the monastic programme. It is the most comprehensive of the three vows. Stability and obedience are particular conditions of the cenobitic life as St. Benedict conceived and regulated it; the second vow embraces the whole complex of the precepts and counsels which are involved in the profession of the monastic life.

The third vow, of *obedience,* like the first, emphasizes an element which St. Benedict regarded as essential to his monas-

[5] The form *conversio morum* is still in use and we translate that. See the next chapter.

tic institute, but which had not always been considered necessary to the monk. The hermit has no occasion to exercise obedience, and the depraved Sarabaite will have none of it. 'Their law is their own good pleasure: whatever they think of or choose to do, that they call holy; what they like not, that they regard as unlawful.' Thus it may be said that *stability* and *obedience* represent St. Benedict's criticism of contemporary monachism and are his reaction against its chief defects. They are to be characteristic of his cenobitical institute, to form the *differentia* distinguishing it from other forms of monachism and from degradations of monachism. On the other hand, the vow of *conversion of life* is the general monastic vow.

CHAPTER X

THE SECOND VOW

Promittat de . . . conversatione morum suorum
REG. LVIII

THE Benedictine monk makes his religious profession in this form: *Promitto coram Deo et Sanctis ejus Stabilitatem et Conversionem morum meorum et Obedientiam.* Premising that the word 'manners' is used in the archaic sense of 'morals', as in the Wykehamist motto 'Manners makyth man', we may translate the formula thus: 'I promise, before God and His Saints, Stability, Conversion of my Manners, and Obedience.' From this it appears that the second vow has the meaning of a general reformation of life, and the monk in taking it promises to aim at this moral reformation. It was thus that the first commentator on the Rule, Paul the Deacon (late eighth century), interpreted the vow, saying that it signified the 'rooting out of vices and implanting of virtues'. So, too, eleven centuries later, the Presidents of the Benedictine Congregations, in their congress at Rome in 1907, pronounced for the same interpretation: 'By it the monk binds himself to assiduous and unwearied labour at the reformation of his morals or habits according to evangelical perfection, rejecting what is worldly and directing his life according to the Rule of St. Benedict.' Such, in fact, has been the standard interpretation of the vow throughout the centuries, and it is an easily intelligible one. Eschewing paraphrase or verbiage we might fairly render the three vows in the simple English: Stability, Reformation of Life, Obedience. There is no difficulty, then, with this version of the vow and its meaning.

But it is now an established fact that St. Benedict did not

use the word *conversio* but the cognate *conversatio*, and the resulting phrase *conversatio morum meorum* is a more difficult one, so that there has been much discussion regarding its precise meaning. It would seem, indeed, to have presented difficulty at a very early date, for some of the earliest forms of profession which have survived either omit it altogether or combine it with the first vow of stability. In response to the Emperor Charlemagne's request for information regarding their monastic practice, Monte Cassino sent him about the year 790 just such a two-vow form:

> In nomine Domini. Promitto me ego ille in sacro monasterio beati martyris sive confessoris illius secundum instituta beati Benedicti, coram Deo et sanctis angelis ejus, praesente etiam abbate nostro illo, omnibus diebus meis in hoc sancto monasterio amodo et deinceps perseveraturum et in omni obedientia quodcunque mihi praeceptum fuerit obediturum.
>
> Ego ille hanc promissionem a me factam manu propria coram testibus scripsi et roboravi.

According to this formula the monk promises these two things:—lifelong perseverance in the monastery and complete obedience.

Such was the formula, not of sixth-century Monte Cassino, but of the eighth-century revival under Abbot Petronax. Paul the Deacon, who compiled the information required by Charlemagne, was himself the author of the first commentary on the Rule. In this commentary, in conformity with the text of the Rule, he gives a three-vow formula:

> Promitto de stabilitate mea et conversione morum meorum saecularium et obedientia coram Deo et sanctis ejus. That is: Stability, Conversion of Life, Obedience.

It will be noticed that Paul uses the word *conversio*. He was familiar with the authentic text of the Rule and indeed has a note on the rival words *conversio* and *conversatio*, but he chose to use *conversio*. No doubt it seemed to him to give an easier phrase and a better sense. From that time onward the use of a three-vow formula gradually became general, with the second vow in the amended form. And so it has continued down to our day and the primitive phrase *conversatio morum* has not secured wide acceptance.

What is the meaning of that phrase? It has been studied by a succession of Benedictine scholars, in particular by Abbot Butler, Dom Matthäus Rothenhäusler, Abbot Herwegen, Dom Benno Linderbauer, Abbot Chapman. The three German scholars, in effect, find no difference of meaning in the two expressions *conversio morum* and *conversatio morum* and consider that both denote the same monastic self-reformation. In his German translation of the Rule (1928) Dom Linderbauer wrote 'Bekehrung der Sitten', which is the same as the traditional 'Conversion of Manners'. Dom Rothenhäusler reached much the same result by a longer route, instituting a parallel between St. Benedict's teaching and the three renunciations of Cassian. According to Cassian the monastery is the proper place for the second renunciation, which he describes also as *actualis conversatio*, or as *actualis, id est, ethica disciplina*. But, argues Dom Rothenhäusler, this is the same thing as *conversatio morum* and the latter phrase means self-reformation.

On the other hand the English abbots (Butler and Chapman) were not disposed to accept this solution, believing that it did not do full justice to the authentic word *conversatio*. Both would find in the word a definite monastic note and would translate the full phrase *conversatio morum* accordingly. Abbot Butler taught that the monk, by the second vow, promised 'monastic life according to the Rule'; Abbot Chapman made him promise 'monasticity of behaviour'. They were, in fact, accepting the verbal noun in its most general meaning of 'conduct, behaviour, way of life', which meaning can be abundantly illustrated. It was in use for any way of life, the precise one intended being indicated by an adjective or merely by the context. There is a text of St. Benedict's period which fully illustrates the adaptability of the word.

The learned monk, Dionysius Exiguus, who holds an honoured position in the history of the Canon Law, was living and working in Rome in St. Benedict's lifetime. He was a fellow-student of Cassiodorus, who has an attractive eulogy of him in his *Institutiones*.[1] Cassiodorus tells us, among other things, that

[1] See the edition of R. A. B. Mynors (Oxford, 1937), pp. 62–4. Dionysius was a Scythian by origin, probably Greek-speaking. He

Dionysius had a complete mastery of Latin and Greek and could translate fluently from either tongue into the other. At some time early in the sixth century he made a Latin translation of a Greek life of St. Pachomius. This *Vita Pachomii*, published so near to him in place and time, did not fail to come into St. Benedict's hands. Abbot Butler notices two phrases from it in St. Benedict's Rule; I find several more and a great likeness of spirit and doctrine.[2] The *Vita Pachomii* is a text which may, without hesitation, be described as one of St. Benedict's books of predilection and must have been constantly in his hands. What is its testimony regarding the word *conversatio*? The evidence which it provides is so abundant in quantity as to be embarrassing, for the word occurs in it no less than thirty-seven times. It is obviously impossible to discuss all these passages and we must be content with a summary.

In the first place I find a series of passages in which *conversatio* is used in its general sense of 'behaviour', 'manner of life'. For example, a converted actor, by name Silvanus, was found to be guilty of frivolous behaviour so that he was an evil influence in the community. Pachomius admonished him to amend and to renounce his old ways: *ut se corrigeret et antiquae conversationi renuntiaret* (255). A woman was cured of diabolical possession and a secret habit of sin. She thanked God for her deliverance from the devil and from her abominable habit: *quod non solum daemone sed etiam detestabili conversatione caruisset* (255). There can be no question of translating *conversatio* in these and suchlike passages by 'monasticity'. So the word could still be used in a text of St. Benedict's time, which was used by him, in its general sense.

Apart from these clear passages I find *conversatio* used very frequently with an adjective or phrase which specifies its mean-

---

came to live in Rome early in the sixth century and is variously described as 'monk' and 'abbot'. His chief work was his collection of canons and papal decrees, at the instance of Pope Hormisdas. He wrote also about the calendar and is responsible for the Christian Era which we now use. His letters *De Paschae Ratione* are in Migne dated 525 and 526. He would appear to have retired from Rome during the Gothic War and joined Cassiodorus at Vivarium.

[2] The *Vita Pachomii* is printed (from Rosweyd) in the first book of the *Vitae Patrum* in Migne, *P.L.*, LXXXIII, 227–72. In citing it I shall give the column numbers of this edition.

ing. In the generality of these cases the natural rendering of
conversatio is again 'manner of life' or 'conversation' (in its
archaic sense). Examples are *sanctorum conversatio, sancta
conversatio, desidiosa conversatio, perfecta conversatio, sincera
conversatio, praeclara et fulgens conversatio, veri monachi
casta conversatio, singularis monachorum conversatio.* We are
told that among St. Pachomius' monks there was *magna conversationis diversitas.* The context in nearly every case being
monastic we may interpret these phrases of the monastic way
of life, or the monastic discipline; but has *conversatio* this
meaning of itself or in virtue of its context? Here is another
case: the text tells us (230) that at that time many converted
pagans began to follow the life and manners of the saints and
to become members of this institute: *sanctorum vitam con-
versationemque sectari et hujus institutionis esse.* In this triple
phrase *conversatio* would seem to be distinguished from mere
'life' on the one hand and from 'monasticity' on the other. I
should be disposed to translate 'regime' or 'discipline'. In many
other cases also I feel a transition of meaning from 'life' or
'behaviour' in general to 'system of life', 'ascetic regime', 'discipline'; but of this later. For the present let me record my
judgment that the fundamental meaning of 'behaviour', 'manner of life', predominates in the *Vita.* Here is one final example
of this usage: Pachomius' successor, Petronius, is described as
being of strong faith, *humble bearing*, great prudence, good
morals and perfect discretion: *potens in fide, humilis in conversatione, intellectu prudentissimus, bonis moribus, discretione perfectus* (271).

Let us look, now, for examples of *conversatio* used abso-
lutely for the monastic manner of life, the regime of a monk.
I do not find many examples of this usage, but there are some.
In one context the word appears to occur, so to speak, in transition to this meaning. Pachomius consents to have dealings with
his sister only if she will follow his manner of life: *si volueris
hanc conversationem sequi quam teneo* (248). Here 'regime'
or 'manner of life' is a sufficient translation. His sister agreed
and Pachomius then wrote rules for her and her companions:
quibus utentes jugiter conversationis suae momenta dirigerent
(248). I should translate 'by using which they might constantly govern the phases (or, details) of their observance'. But

'life' would still do. In another place Pachomius, looking into
the future, foresees the evils which may come to his institute
if the superiors be bad men who are ignorant of the very name
of 'religion': *ipsumque nomen sanctae conversationis igno-
rantibus* (262). But this would show that the name of the
monastic life is not *conversatio* simply, but *sancta conversatio*,
the 'holy life', the 'holy discipline'. Again, Pachomius gives as
his reason for not allowing stranger monks to mix freely with
his community that he had known some who were so ignorant
of the life itself that they did not even know the monastic
habit: *in tantum ipsius conversationis ignaros, ut nec monachorum habitum noverint* (253). The presence of *ipsius* seems
to make 'life' a more natural translation than 'monastic life',
but the latter would certainly be a good translation. I should
then leave out 'itself'. Finally, we are told that Pachomius did
not admit people into the community except after long training
in the life: *quos post longam conversationis experientiam
monachorum coetibus aggregabat* (243). Here I would not
hesitate to translate, considering the context, 'in the monastic
life'. I have said previously that the text uses the word *institu-
tio* when the author wishes to refer precisely to the monastic
institute. There is a case of this usage in the context regarding
the nuns. We are told there that, except that they did not
wear the *melota* (sheep-skin cloak), the nuns agreed with the
monks in the whole form of their institute: *omnis institutionis
earum forma* (248). From this inquiry I conclude that *conversatio* does occur, though not frequently, as a term for the
monastic life. Yet even here we are not compelled so to translate, but could be content with less definite words such as 'life'
or 'discipline'. However, it is obviously *the* life or *the* discipline
par excellence.

We come now to a third series of passages in which it would
appear that *conversatio* occupies an intermediate position, between 'behaviour' in general and 'monasticity' in particular. I
conceive that in these cases it means ascesis, ascetical regime,
moral discipline, self-discipline, and the life which is governed
by such ascesis. Just as the hagiographer may say of his saint
that 'his mortification was extreme' so could the Greeks speak
of a man's *ascesis* and the Latins of his *conversatio*. Abbot
Chapman gives many passages from the *Novels* of Justinian

in which the Greek has *ascesis* and the Latin version *conversatio*. He uses the texts to establish his own thesis that *conversatio* means 'monasticity'. I find 'discipline' alone in most cases a more natural rendering, for in the majority of cases *ascesis* is defined by some adjective or phrase to make its meaning more precise.

But to return to the evidence of the *Vita Pachomii*. I have said that there are passages in which the meaning of *conversatio* passes beyond that of 'behaviour' or 'manner of life', and would seem to be something more precise, such as: ascesis, moral discipline, self-discipline. I give now some examples, asking the reader to test them for himself with the three choices: behaviour, discipline, monasticity.

The *Vita* tells us that the hermit Palaemon had long led a life of strict discipline: *vitam rigidae conversationis* (233). Palaemon says of himself that he punished himself with the hardest and sternest self-discipline: *nimis ardua et durissima conversatione* (233). Pachomius, we are told, mortified himself with a strict and singular self-discipline: *arcta et singulari conversatione* (239). When the nuns required the services of the monks, Pachomius always put the brothers in charge of men of great discipline: *magnae conversationis viri* (249). In this last case 'monasticity' is a possible rendering, but not, I think, the natural one. I give one further passage of exceptional interest. We are told in the *Vita* (242) that Pachomius was instructed by the angel who gave him his rule to form his monks into twenty-four troops (*turmae*), assigning to each troop a letter of the Greek alphabet. The letters were to be assigned in such a way as to express the moral quality of each troop (*uniuscujusque turmae mores*). Thus the more simple and innocent monks would be distinguished by the letter Iota, while more difficult and tortuous characters would come under Chi: *ita ut pro modo conversationis et propositi singulis turmis litterarum elementa concinerent*: so that the letters should fit each troop according to its conduct and purpose.

This passage is of exceptional importance because the identical phrase *pro modo conversationis* occurs in the Rule of St. Benedict: *Lectisternia pro modo conversationis, secundum dispensationem abbatis sui, accipiant* (Cap. XXII. The editors of the Rule have not noted this). It is important also because this rule of St. Pachomius exists in several versions, Latin and Greek, and we may compare the corresponding passages. In Latin versions we have (1) *ut mores per eas significentur animorum;* (2) *convenienter institutis eorum et vitae et moribus.* And the Greek versions have similar 'non-committal' words. It will be seen from these passages that there is no trace of 'monasticity'. I think it is fair to interpret them all in the sense of 'character and conduct'. The conduct is the conduct of monks, but it cannot be said that *vita, mores,* etc., are monastic terms. The criterion in fact by which the monks are to be classified is a moral one. They were to be arranged according to the moral character of their lives.

Such is the evidence of the *Vita Pachomii.* I have tried to set it forth as completely as possible and to abstain from forcing it into the service of any theory. I think it shows abundantly that the predominant use of *conversatio* is in its standard meaning of 'manner of life', 'behaviour', 'conduct'. Yet it shows also—where the context is definitely monastic—that the word may fairly be taken to denote the monastic discipline or monastic manner of life.

But this conclusion does not settle the matter. We have still to explain the word *morum,* since St. Benedict's full phrase for his second vow is *conversatio morum.*

With the *medial* use of *conversatio*—which has been abundantly illustrated—it is very difficult to construe *morum.* How difficult it is may be judged from Abbot Chapman's desperate solution: 'monasticity of behaviour'. It is time, therefore, to consider another, recognized use of *conversatio.*

The Thesaurus Linguae Latinae distinguishes between the uses of the active and passive voices of the word *conversare,* finding that the active gives a *conversatio* which has an active meaning, and the passive a *conversatio* which has a medial meaning. The first *conversatio* is, in effect, equivalent to *conversio.* It signifies a 'turning' or 'turning round', whether literally or figuratively. It is used, for example, of the rolling of the eyeballs, or of a man turning over in bed. In its figurative sense it is used of repentance. And it is used of the specific monastic 'conversion', i.e., conversion from the secular to the religious life.

This 'active' *conversatio* is obviously the one that we need.

Like its fellow, *conversio*, it goes easily with an objective geni-tive, and the phrase *conversatio morum* now presents no diffi-culty but translates easily as 'conversion of manners' or 'con-version of life'. And the translation is supported by age-long tradition.[3]

[3] The present writer's Latin-English edition of St. Benedict's Rule has a good deal to say about *conversatio*.

CHAPTER XI

THE LIFE OF THE RULE

Deverte a malo et fac bonum; inquire pacem et sequere eam

PS. XXXIII

ALREADY, in the course of the previous chapters, many items of St. Benedict's spiritual teaching have been noted as occasion required; let us attempt now to consider that teaching as a whole and to inquire what is his conception of the life which he regulates by his Rule.

In the first chapter of his Rule St. Benedict describes four sorts of monks: cenobites, hermits, sarabaites and gyrovagues. He dismisses the last two kinds in emphatic terms and these obviously do not concern us. At the end of the chapter he announces his intention of legislating for one sort only, the 'strong sort' (*fortissimum genus*), namely cenobites. What, then, is his attitude towards the hermits?

'Anchorites or hermits', he says, 'are those who, not in the first fervour of their religious life, but after long probation in a monastery, having learnt in association with many brethren how to fight with the devil, go out well-armed from the ranks of the community to the solitary combat of the desert. They are able now to live without the help of others, and by their own strength and God's assistance to fight against the temptations of mind and body.'

This passage is based chiefly upon Cassian and reproduces Cassian's teaching without any substantial alteration. If we take it at its face value it would appear to show that St. Benedict accepted the standard conviction of ancient monachism that the hermit's life was the highest. It is possible, of course, that he is doing no more than reproducing his source, Cassian, and then dismisses the hermit from his mind as completely, though not so drastically, as he dismisses the sarabaite and the gyrovague. That is a possible view, and perhaps even the true one; yet the full description which he devotes to the evolution of the hermit's vocation would seem to be against it. St. Benedict's contemporary, Cassiodorus, in the institute which he established on his estate in Calabria, made exact provision for the two separate vocations of the hermit and the cenobite, in a passage which has often been thought to echo this paragraph of the Rule. It cannot be proved that Cassiodorus was a disciple of the Rule; indeed, such evidence as we possess goes to prove the contrary. Yet we may ask, as we consider the arrangements of Cassiodorus: Was this St. Benedict's mind? Agreeing with the tradition that the hermit's life was the highest, did he make provision for that life at Monte Cassino and allow his monks after due preparation to pass over to it? We have no evidence that there were hermitages at Monte Cassino. The poet Mark does, indeed, report a tradition that St. Benedict himself, even at Monte Cassino, used sometimes to retire into complete solitude, thus resuming intermittently the life which he had led in the cave at Subiaco. But this perhaps occurred only in his earliest days at Monte Cassino, before he had formed a community. St. Gregory tells us of a hermit, Martin, who lived near St. Benedict's monastery, but he does not represent him as a disciple of the saint's. We cannot, therefore, tell whether St. Benedict made any practical provision for the eremitical life for the benefit of trained members of his community. But it would appear reasonable to conclude from his words that in theory at least he accepted the tradition and regarded the eremitical life as higher than the life of the cenobite. May we argue from this that he conceived the life for which he actually legislates as a life which though good is a second best? Is that the meaning of those many passages in his Rule where he appears to be offering a gentle apology for his discreet and moderate requirements? Is that why he calls his own Rule a 'little rule for beginners'? He would then be regarding himself as choosing the good rather than the best, the practical rather than the ideal, a prudent compromise rather than the great adventure of the ancient monks.

Pachomius before St. Benedict had broken with the ancient tradition in order to establish the cenobitic life. But in the later narratives of his decisive step, where we are told that he was determined by angelic intervention and that his cenobitic rule was thus dictated to him, we may perhaps see evidence that the biographers felt that the step required more than ordinary justification. Yet Pachomius broke decisively with the tradition and even claimed for the cenobitic life a higher excellence. He had himself made trial of the eremitical life and knew to the full its character and its dangers. He wished to make provision for those who would be monks and yet could not safely give themselves to the life of solitude. They needed the support and encouragement provided by the society and example of many brethren. In and through this common life—such was Pachomius' teaching—they could reach a higher perfection, and reach it more securely, than could the hermit in his solitude.[1]

Very similar, it would seem, were the experience and the mind of St. Benedict. He chooses the cenobitic life decisively and legislates only for that life. He describes cenobites as the 'strong sort' of monks, in which phrase we may fairly see an allusion to the dangers of the solitary life. Though he appears to leave a loophole and not to exclude the possibility of one of his disciples passing to the hermit life, yet all his interest and

[1] St. Basil is an even greater exponent of the cenobitic life than Pachomius, and his institute, in so far as he legislated for a single monastery where the monks dwelt closely together and not, as with Pachomius, in separate houses, is nearer to St. Benedict's. But St. Basil was a bishop as well as a monk, and adapted his monachism very definitely to the service of the Church, contriving that his monks should teach the ignorant, nurse the sick, tend orphans. St. John Chrysostom, too, though originally a strong advocate of monastic seclusion, sought as bishop to use the monks for the needs of his apostolate. So also St. Augustine. So, and most effectively and decisively, St. Gregory the Great. I am not criticizing these great monk-bishops, far from it; but would only wish to say that such an application of monachism does not seem to have fallen within the horizon of St. Pachomius or St. Benedict. In later centuries, when monks became clerics and passed normally to the priesthood, the outlook and scope of monachism were greatly changed. But for St. Benedict, as for St. Pachomius, the institute was an institute of laymen and clerical members were the exception.

all his regulations are concerned with the cenobitic life. If he speaks modestly and in terms of gentle apology, it is not that he thinks poorly of the life which he has chosen or would exchange it for another, but because his regulations, within that life itself, were discreet and moderate beyond ancient example. He is in fact, like Pachomius, a convinced cenobite. What, then, we may ask, was his fundamental conception of the cenobitic life? To gain an answer to this question we may turn now to Cassian.

For Cassian, St. Benedict's chief teacher, interpreting Eastern monachism to the monks of the West, has much to say about the separate vocations of the hermit and the cenobite. Both forms of life, he says, are excellent; yet they are different, and so he endeavours to give to each its precise quality and function. In the passage of his eighteenth Conference which inspired St. Benedict's first chapter, he says that hermits are those who have chosen the solitary life after having first been trained in the coenobium and made perfect in the 'practical life' or 'practical discipline' (*in actuali conversatione*).[2] This phrase occurs frequently, and along with it are such expressions as *scientia actualis, disciplina actualis, disciplina ethica*. The main substance of the practical life being the purging out of vices and reformation of morals (*vitiorum purgatio, morum emendatio*), it is plain that he means by it a life which employs ascetic exercises in order to achieve moral perfection. And since *actualis* as he employs it is indistinguishable from 'moral'—he uses *ethica* as a synonym—we may call it briefly a moral discipline. Presiding over the process is the important virtue of prudence, which he calls 'discretion' and commends as the 'mother of the virtues'. And, though the life be conceived predominantly as a moral discipline, there must necessarily go with it, involved in its very nature, a discipline of the mind: the cenobite by constant prayer and the study of the Scriptures both directs his moral effort and attains an ever deeper understanding of God and divine things. Such is Cassian's standard conception of the 'active' or 'practical' life of the cenobite. As for the goal which this life seeks to attain,

[2] There enters here, from his Greek sources, the antithesis between the life of action and the life of contemplation. *Actualis* represents the Greek πρακτικός. More will be said of this later.

his favourite conception of its immediate aim is a negative one, 'purity of heart', though he speaks also positively of that perfect charity, or love of God, for which purity of heart is the disposition. As for the ultimate end, he is sure that the end of every monk, be he hermit or cenobite, is the same, viz., a close union of mind and will with God: *ut divinis rebus et Deo mens semper inhaereat* (Col. i. 8). Nor, though placing him in the 'active life', does he exclude the cenobite from the exercise of contemplative prayer, for he lays it down that 'the end of every monk and his soul's perfection is directed towards a continual and uninterrupted perseverance in prayer': *Omnis monachi finis cordisque perfectio ad iugem atque indisruptam orationis perseverantiam tendit* (Col. ix. 2).

If we turn now from Cassian to St. Benedict, we find the same doctrine, not indeed expressly set out in formal fashion, but tacitly assumed, and indicated by many a significant phrase. Apart from his use of the word *conversatio*, which echoes Cassian's use, we find St. Benedict also much concerned with the emendation of vices. 'Turn away from evil and do good' is the keynote of his prologue. The whole prologue is indeed a programme of the practical life. He has also Cassian's 'purity of heart' and his 'discretion'. We find him frequently coupling together the two aspects of the cenobite's progress: virtue and knowledge. But, not to weary the reader with a tedious comparison, the final paragraph of St. Benedict's chapter on humility (which itself is largely taken from Cassian) may be cited as one example for all. Cassian distinguishes two stages in the moral discipline of the cenobite: in the first it is a difficult struggle, in the second a pleasure and delight. So also St. Benedict: the monk will come to live his life for love, of a good habit and a delight in virtue. Cassian speaks of emendation of vices, of purity of heart, of charity. St. Benedict says that his monk having passed through the degrees of humility will presently come to perfect charity. That gift will be given him by the Holy Spirit when he has attained purity of heart. That purity of heart will be his when he is free from vices and sins. The agreement with Cassian's doctrine is certain and it holds throughout the Rule. Cassian conceived his *actualis conversatio* as a life of moral discipline directed to the end, negatively of purity of heart, positively of love of God. It may be asserted with confidence that St. Benedict conceived the cenobitic life for which he was legislating in precisely the same way.

But St. Benedict nowhere uses the phrase by which Cassian denotes the cenobitic life, the phrase *conversatio actualis*. Though he uses many other words of Cassian's, though he speaks with him of the monk's life as a warfare (*militia*), and of the spiritual craft (*ars spiritualis*), and of the tools to be employed in that craft (*instrumenta*), and so on, he does not use the phrase *conversatio actualis* or its equivalent *conversatio ethica*. He does use the word *conversatio*, ten times, but never with Cassian's adjectives. Yet in one place, and that the vital one of his second vow, where he is concerned to find a phrase to denote the life of his own institute, he uses the significant words *conversatio morum*. The inference is reasonable, and even necessary, that in these words we have nothing more nor less than an alternative expression for Cassian's *conversatio actualis*, for that life of moral discipline directed to a spiritual end which he conceived to be the proper life of the cenobite.[3]

But there is more than this in Cassian. For besides this 'practical life' which he conceives as the proper life of the cenobite, he has a further life, of contemplation, which he appropriates schematically to the hermit. In his third Conference the whole monastic life is set forth in terms of three renunciations. 'The first is that by which as far as the body is concerned we make light of the wealth and goods of this world; the second, that by which we reject the fashions and vices and former affections of soul and flesh; the third, that by which we detach our soul from all present and visible things and contemplate only things to come, and set our hearts on what is invisible.' The first of these renunciations is the common renunciation both of cenobite and hermit; it is just that renunciation of the world which a man makes when he chooses the monastic way of life. The second renunciation is the proper business of the cenobite; it is that 'practical life' of moral discipline of which we have spoken already; and it is the normal preparation for the third stage. This third stage, or third renunciation, is proper to the

---

[3] See for all this Dom Matthäus Rothenhäusler: *Zur Aufnahmeordnung der Regula S. Benedicti* (1912), where the pertinent passages of Cassian and the Rule are cited in full.

hermit and is characterized by the exercise of contemplation. Not that some sort of contemplation is not possible in the cenobitic life, but that in its highest form it requires for its exercise the complete freedom and isolation from distraction which is provided by the hermitage.

Is there any trace of this further doctrine of Cassian's in the Rule of St. Benedict? The answer must be in the negative. St. Benedict does not speak of any such exercise of contemplation in eremitical solitude as Cassian propounds. If the contemplative life be conceived in that fashion, it must be admitted that St. Benedict does not speak of it, for he does not legislate for hermits. There is no trace in his pages of that quasi-angelic life which Cassian attributes to the perfect solitary. Such a one, he teaches, having achieved perfect purity of heart and a deep union with God, enjoys a contemplation of the Godhead (*intuitus Dei solius*) which is a practical anticipation of the beatitude of heaven. His prayer is of the extremest simplicity and his life a continual prayer. He is frequently rapt in ecstasy. Isolated from human intercourse, taking the least possible thought for the needs of his body, he is barely any longer a man, but would almost seem to have escaped into another mode of existence. Cassian describes this vocation with deep reverence and enthusiasm, but he recognizes that it must needs be a rare one and that only few succeed in it. A man may even, after experience of its high graces, turn aside from the eremitical life, as did Abbot John, and seek perfection by the more secure road of the cenobite. If he does so, he is not changing the purpose of his life, but pursuing it by another and less ambitious path.

For the cenobite also aims at purity of heart and charity. He also is occupied with the thought of God. His end also is contemplation. But his contemplation—teaches Cassian—is normally a less sublime contemplation than the hermit's. He contemplates God rather in His works than in Himself. He follows Him in the mysteries of His human life. He loves and serves Him in His brethren, his fellow-men. It is in the practice of such service, in obedience and humility, that he will attain his proper perfection. That perfection is not conceived in terms of contemplation—he is not encouraged to expect the high contemplation of the anchorite—but rather as a moral perfection.

His way is affective rather than speculative. His end is charity. Yet he, too, has to study and meditate upon divine things. He, too, has to ponder the Sacred Scriptures, and by devout meditation upon them acquire a solid spiritual knowledge, no mere human learning but the science of the saints. If the circumstances of his vocation do not normally allow him or encourage him to attain the continual prayer of the hermit, yet his prayer too will be pure in proportion to his purity of heart, and, at least intermittently, will attain a special intensity and a fiery ardour (*Conf.* IX, 15). We might, to use other phraseology, denominate the way of the cenobite as portrayed by Cassian the 'illuminative way', while yet being prepared to admit that it is a way that verges upon and may easily pass into the unitive way. That certainly, in Cassian's eyes, is its end. And again, as before, this way of the cenobite, thus described, would appear to be the way which St. Benedict sets before his monks. Their life is a practical moral discipline in association with many brethren and a life which seeks its perfection in the exercise of humility, obedience and love. Its summit is not given as contemplation but as 'perfect charity'. It is nourished upon meditation of the Scriptures. St. Benedict would have his monks walk in the footsteps of Christ under the guidance of the Gospel (*per ducatum Evangelii pergamus itinera eius*) and to see Christ in their fellow-men. The monastery is to be a 'school for the Lord's service', where they are to learn to fight for their true King. They are given a full measure of public prayer, in the Divine Office, and they will also have their own private prayer. That prayer should be 'pure prayer', that is to say, according to Cassian's teaching, a prayer of the greatest simplicity and of a contemplative character. However, unless God's grace inspire them, this prayer should be 'short'. They are to pray with 'pure devotion', trusting rather to 'purity of heart and compunction' than to mere length of prayer.[4]

[4] To prevent misconception it should be observed that the argument does not say that Benedictine life is not contemplative, but only that it is not Cassian's contemplative life. It would seem to be clear already that the active life as described by Cassian and accepted by St. Benedict runs to contemplation, so that it would by modern standards be termed a contemplative life. The text attempts such a modern assessment immediately.

There is some peril in discussing St. Benedict's spirituality in our modern terms, for those terms have meanings which belong to another world than his. Such a one, for instance, is the word 'contemplation'. And yet, in spite of the obvious peril, we may feel a need to assess his life in modern categories. We may ask, for instance, in regard to his Rule: Is this an ascetical or a mystical document? We answer that if there be a sharp distinction between the ascetical and the mystical life and we have to choose, then the Rule is assuredly an ascetical document. Again, we may ask: Is the life designed by the Rule an active life or a contemplative life? We answer that according to the ancient notion of the contemplative life, as that was accepted by Cassian or St. Benedict, the Rule provides for the active life and not for the life of contemplation. But how does it appear according to our modern standards? That is a more difficult question and will need a longer answer. Let us seek to determine it thus.

The formula of two lives, the active and the contemplative, derives from Greek philosophy and according to its original Greek conception does not fit exactly on to the Christian life. For the Christian conceives the purpose of life in other terms than the Greek, and the end whether of his activity or of his contemplation being different, his life, whether active or contemplative, takes a different character. In particular, Christian contemplation is of its nature a very different thing from the speculation of the Greek philosopher. For not only is the object, God, very different from the object of the philosopher, but the approach to that object is differently conceived. There enters into the contemplative's life not only the energy of speculative thought but also the energy of will. It is in fact of the essence of Christian contemplation that it should comprise also this energy of will. For Christian perfection is not to be conceived as an intellectual achievement, but fundamentally as an achievement of the whole man, both mind and will. We have both to know God and to love Him. And so important is the element of will, that Christian perfection is summarily defined as the love of God above all things. It is divine charity. Along with that love and at its base goes the theological virtue of faith, whereby we are given an intellectual grasp of the God whom we love. In the development of our faith, by God's grace, we attain an ever deeper appreciation of that which we love; but our energy must not stop there, the soul has to go out to God with all the vigour of its will. And so doing, teaches St. Thomas, it comes into a more immediate contact with the object of its striving, for, as the author of the *Cloud of Unknowing* says: 'Love may reach to God in this life, but not knowing.' There is given to the soul that Gift of Wisdom with which St. Thomas especially associates the exercise of contemplation. It obtains a *sapida scientia* and an *instinctus divinus* which enhance the knowledge of faith, and bring a knowledge which is a far different thing from mere speculation. The soul penetrates into the secret things of God.[5]

It is to be noted further that this new element, the element of love, entering into the formula of the two lives, active and contemplative, crosses the division and so to say transcends it. For the Christian, whether his life be predominantly active or predominantly contemplative, has in either case the same end, the love of God above all things. And if that be so, if each life be directed to the same end of divine charity, then the division loses much of its absolute character and becomes of secondary importance. Moreover, it is recognized, as for instance by St. Thomas, that the same person may alternate between the two lives, exercising now one and now the other. His general life would be denominated active or contemplative according to its predominant character, but in either case he exercises throughout a single energy of soul directed to the one object of the love of God above all things.[6]

Our problem, then, reduces itself to this: Is the life which

---

[5] Here is a specimen passage from St. Thomas: *Sapientiae donum eminentiam cognitionis habet, per quamdam unionem ad divina, quibus non unimur nisi per amorem, ut qui adhaeret Deo sit unus spiritus cum eo* (1 Cor. vi). *Unde et Dominus* (Joann. xv) *secreta Patris se revelasse discipulis dicit in quantum amici erant. Et ideo sapientiae donum dilectionem quasi principium supponit, et sic in affectione est. Sed quantum ad essentiam in cognitione est; unde ipsius actus videtur et hic et in futuro divina amata contemplari.* III Sent., d. 35, q. 2, art. 1, sol. 3.

[6] *Dixerunt discipuli: Domine, ecce duo gladii hic. At ille dixit eis: Satis est* (Luc. xxii). *Dixit abbas Theophilus: Duo gladii duas vitas significant, activam et contemplativam. Si quis ergo has duas virtutes habeat, hic perfectus erit* (Migne, *P.L.*, LXXIV, 139). See the postscript to this chapter.

St. Benedict designed for his disciples such that it would allow of the grace of contemplation and promote its exercise? To this question we think the answer should be 'Yes'. His provision for his monks in the Divine Office, in private prayer, in sacred study, in silence and work, are the provisions of one who expects them to be constantly occupied with God. In his first degree of humility he bids them live constantly in a vivid realization of God's presence. He hopes that they will run in the way of God's commandments 'with an unspeakable sweetness of love'. He expects them to exercise the 'pure prayer' of the contemplative. He does not, indeed, make any reference to the Greek conception of the life of speculation as adapted to the monastic vocation, but he makes emphatic use of the genuinely Christian conception of the love of God. At the end of his chapter on humility he says that the monk, having passed through its twelve degrees, will presently come to that perfect love of God which casts out fear, and will henceforth serve, not out of constraint, but from love of Christ and a delight in virtue. From his whole Rule, in fact, it is plain that he is not conceiving the life of his monks in terms of mere activity, still less in terms of speculation, but according to the fundamental Christian conception of divine charity. And that being so, when he postulates 'perfect charity', we may venture to say that he postulates also, in whatever measure, the exercise of Christian contemplation. More than that, such a consummation may be said to be expressly indicated when he asserts that his disciples will reach the perfection of that life which he is proposing to them under the operation of God's Holy Spirit: *Quae Dominus iam in operarium suum mundum a vitiis et peccatis Spiritu Sancto dignabitur demonstrare* (*c.* vii).

Such then is St. Benedict's fundamental conception of the cenobitic life: It is a practical, moral discipline of which the goal is the perfect love of God in the full measure and with the accompaniments of that love. To this end he provides an ordered life of prayer, study and manual work and a regime of moderate austerity. Although he expresses the opinion in his forty-ninth chapter that a monk's life should always be lenten in its character, yet he does not seek to impose a lenten observance all the year round. In Lent itself he asks for special abstinence in food, drink and sleep; for a special purity of life; for more earnest prayer and devotion to sacred reading. These things are evidently constituent elements of his ideal; but he does not impose that ideal regularly in all its fullness. He is content with something less, and always he provides his monks with a sufficiency of simple fare and unbroken sleep. The details of his ascetical discipline have already been summarized, nor need we do more than refer to such a chapter as the fourth, which covers the whole range of the Christian precepts and counsels. But we should do less than justice to St. Benedict if some few words were not said about the important seventh chapter, which he devotes to humility.

Why did he choose out humility and set it apart for this apparently disproportionate treatment? The best answer is that it was an important part of the wisdom of the East and had been transmitted to him as such by Cassian. The Eastern monks had learnt by experience the dangers which beset a proud individualism. The solitary was a law to himself and not seldom pushed his effort towards an extravagant singularity. Sometimes the motive force was a quite unspiritual rivalry, and the resulting life, when it did not break down under the unnatural strain, one of a proud arrogance rather than of Christian meekness and charity. Against such an aberration humility was the true safeguard. So St. Benedict accepts it and proclaims its fundamental value. He will have no pride or individualism in his monastery. There is to be an absolute community of endeavour: in prayer, in work, in every part of the discipline. He allows of private prayer apart from the Divine Office, and bids his monks who would practise it in the oratory 'just to go in and pray', but he gives a whole series of chapters to the monastic prayer which is pre-eminently theirs, the common endeavour of the 'Work of God'. He allows also of special austerities in Lent; but those who would practise them have to get the express approval of the abbot, or they will be guilty of presumption and vainglory. He wants no individualism, no singularity, no least vestige of spiritual pride. His monks have to rid themselves of all wilfulness, of all self-love and self-seeking, and from every manifestation whether in their interior life or in their external behaviour which betrays the spirit of pride. So he tells them that their life is a ladder of humility and that by climbing its twelve rungs, and thus only, shall they reach their goal, that is, perfect charity.

There is, we may say, a special aptness in the prominence given by St. Benedict to the virtue of humility. For modesty is the mark of his whole Rule. St. Gregory the Great describes that Rule as 'conspicuous for moderation'. In all his regulations St. Benedict shows himself concerned to eliminate extremes or extravagances. He hopes to ordain nothing harsh or hard: *nihil asperum nihilque durum nos constituros speramus* (Prol.). To an Eastern monk his regulations for prayer, sleep, food, drink, clothing, would savour of weakness and laxity. But St. Benedict was determined to make the monastic life possible, not only for exceptional souls, but also for the generality, 'that the strong may still have something to long after and the weak may not draw back in alarm': *ut sit et fortes quod cupiant et infirmi non refugiant* (Cap. LXIV).[7] He was not afraid of the charge of laxity, but met it with a disavowal of all great pretensions. My purpose, he might say, is this modest one and humility is its badge.

We do not need to speak of the twelve degrees of humility in detail. Beginning with that profound humility which sets us as creatures before the majesty of God and under His constant gaze, he leads his disciples through the various phases of their life, teaching them under this rubric of humility the fundamental virtues of detachment from self-will, obedience, patience, candour, fortitude, modesty in thought and speech, and modesty finally in all outward behaviour. It is a comprehensive scheme, including the whole religious effort of his disciples within the framework of humility. Humility, as so conceived,

---

[7] The *Vita Pachomii* (243) tells us that Pachomius expostulated with the angel on the fewness of the prayers which he prescribed for the monks. The angel replied that he had prescribed what the weaker brethren might perform without distress; but the perfect, needing no such rule, would still be able to give themselves to the high exercises of contemplation. It seems to me that this passage represents St. Benedict's mind very truly and was perhaps present to him when he wrote the sentence in the text. In many places throughout his Rule St. Benedict addresses himself not only to the weaker brethren but also to the strong. His final chapter especially is an appeal to the strong, telling them where they may find the spiritual teaching that will lead them to the summit of perfection.

is something far different from that moral virtue which is a subdivision of a subdivision of the virtue of temperance. It transcends that classification and joins the virtue of religion itself. 'Be ye humbled under the mighty hand of God', says St. Peter (1 Peter v, 6). The Scriptures teach us constantly that same attitude before the Divine Majesty, for 'God resisteth the proud and giveth grace to the humble'. This is where St. Benedict's mind is moving; he is concerned with the fundamental attitude of the creature before the Creator, and it is with that profound humility that his ladder begins.[8]

We need say little more about St. Benedict's spiritual doctrine. It is not an abstruse or difficult system that he offers to his monks, but the plain and simple road of the love of God.[9] The many exercises of the life are all designed for this end, that the monk may be gradually purified from other attachment and established in the love of God. Along with the love of God and as part of it, he must practise also the love of his fellow-men, loving his abbot with a sincere and humble affection and his fellow-monks with a chaste fraternal love. The saint sets this forth eloquently in his seventy-second chapter: 'Of the good zeal which monks ought to have'. 'Just as there is an evil zeal of bitterness which separates from God and leads to hell, so is there a good zeal, which separates from vices

---

[8] St. Thomas in his *Summa* (II–II, Q. 161, A. 6) assembles and discusses St. Benedict's twelve degrees. He expounds them with his customary lucidity and brings out the special quality of St. Benedict's first degree by explaining that the root of true humility is reverence towards God. His exposition is, however, embarrassed by a curious accident. He took his list of St. Benedict's degrees of humility from a copy of St. Bernard's *Twelve Degrees of Pride* in which the degrees of humility were arranged in the inverse order, so that the twelfth became the first, and so on. St. Thomas is obviously troubled by the appearance of rules for external behaviour as the first degrees, but, patient as ever with his sources, he finds a good reason for it: A man may in his human efforts towards humility begin with the discipline of his behaviour and come later to the discipline of his soul. See the article by Dom Lambot in the *Revue Bénédictine*, XXXIX (1927), pp. 129–35.

[9] St. Benedict is very fond of representing life in terms of a road and a journey. One instance out of some twenty: *ut recto cursu perveniamus ad Creatorem nostrum* (c. 73). The last word of the Rule is *pervenies*.

and leads to God and to life everlasting. Let monks, therefore, exercise this zeal with the most fervent love. Let them, that is, in honour prefer one another. Let them bear with the greatest patience one another's infirmities, whether of body or character. Let them vie in paying obedience one to another. Let none follow what seems good for himself, but rather what is good for another. Let them practise fraternal charity with a pure love. Let them fear God. Let them love their abbot with a sincere and humble affection. Let them prefer nothing whatever to Christ. And may He bring us all alike to life everlasting.'

The final chapter (LXXIII) is very characteristic of the modesty of the saint. It is entitled: 'That the full observance of justice is not established in this Rule.' St. Benedict does not claim to have written the last work on the monastic life. 'This Rule has been written', he says, 'in order that by practising it in monasteries we may show that we have attained some degree of virtue and the rudiments of monastic observance'. He refers those who 'hasten to perfection' to the Scriptures, to the writings of the Fathers of the Church, to St. Basil and to Cassian. And he concludes: 'Whoever, therefore, thou art that hastenest to thy heavenly country, fulfil by the help of Christ this little rule which we have written for beginners. And then at length, under God's protection, shalt thou arrive at those loftier heights of wisdom and virtue.'

Hanc minimam inchoationis regulam: this little Rule for beginners. In the light of the subsequent history of the Rule, these words read strangely. Yet they are entirely characteristic of the man, and true in their historical perspective. There is no denying the fact that St. Benedict's fame—if we go beyond the circle of his immediate influence—was a posthumous one, that the great work so quietly and so unpretentiously achieved in the cloisters of Monte Cassino was not seen in its true perspective until time had set upon it the seal of an extraordinary success. The saint himself, in more than one modest phrase and self-depreciatory sentence of the Rule, makes it clear that he neither sought nor expected a world-wide result. He was doing what many had done before him, writing a rule for his monks, for that 'school of the Lord's service' which he was establishing, but he did not aspire to rival a Pachomius or a

Basil. He suggests and persuades, he is seldom imperious, and then only in matters of essential duty. He apologizes for the moderation of his regulations, as though he would seem to many to be doing an injury to the monastic ideal. He speaks of his Rule for Monks, which history has so abundantly justified and in which historians have recognized a 'monument of legislative art, remarkable alike for its completeness, its simplicity, and its adaptability', as 'this little Rule for beginners'. And yet that Rule has appeared to pure and noble souls in every one of some forty generations as the practical embodiment of their highest aspirations, a sure guide to a perfect life. That Rule stands, and apparently is destined to stand, as the finished expression of the monastic ideal.

POSTSCRIPT

In regard to the debate whether the Benedictine life is contemplative, I add that I agree profoundly with Abbot Theophilus (p. 134n.) and had intended to leave the matter there. But a friend tells me that he finds Abbot Butler's treatment of the point very misleading and mine only slightly better. I ought, therefore, to try to make my meaning clearer. I would say then, in the first place, that I regard the antithesis (active-contemplative) as one of those unfortunate simplifications which tend only to confuse thought instead of assisting it. Secondly, I would say that I do not believe that any Christian life, let alone a Benedictine life, can in practice be either purely active or purely contemplative. Thirdly, I would say that if the terms are taken, as they are commonly taken, as irreconcilable and mutually exclusive, then the Benedictine life as established by the Rule is fundamentally an active life and not a contemplative life. Whatever further perfection St. Benedict hoped that his disciples might attain, his main effort is directed towards establishing them soundly in the practical discipline of the cenobite. That discipline involves active work and a substantial quantity of active work. It does not much matter what that work is, but it matters very greatly that it should be there. It may be manual work or study; it may be the work of the teacher or the work of the apostle. Whatever it is, it will be inspired and consecrated by the fundamental purpose of the monk's life. The Benedictine schoolmaster, for instance, does not live in the presence of God and work for God when he is in choir, and then pass out of that Presence and work for himself when he is teaching mathematics to small boys. He does not live his life in compartments. His life is dominated and controlled by a single purpose. The ideal, says St. Thomas, is *contemplata aliis tradere*. So too the Benedictine monk is then truly living his Benedictine life when the purpose and inspiration of that life dominate and pervade his whole activity. And though his prayer may not help him to expound the integral calculus any better, his teaching is as much a part of his life as his prayer, and it will not be able to escape the influence of his single purpose. Nor will his pupils, whatever he be teaching them, escape the influence of his consecrated life. He must, in fact, as Abbot Theophilus recommends, have both lives and so will he be perfect. And that, after all, is what the debate comes to: the Benedictine life is both active and contemplative. And the two lives, so often put in an unreal opposition, are necessary each to the other and work together in the greatest harmony.

CHAPTER XII

UNDER JUSTINIAN

Proelia et opiniones proeliorum
MT. XXIV

THE date of St. Benedict's migration from Subiaco to Monte Cassino, as has been said already, is unknown. We have no means of determining it except by a calculus of probabilities. Abbot Chapman would say 'about 520', but he is otherwise interested in any early date; most writers would set it some ten years later. In any case we shall not be far wrong if we bring it into approximate relation with the advent to the throne of the Eastern Empire, in the year 527, of the Emperor Justinian the Great. Justinian, unlike his soldier-uncle, the Emperor Justin who preceded him, was a man of culture and intellectual parts; he was also ambitious and determined. His long rule (527–65) was to prove of vital significance for St. Benedict's Italy.

Opposed to him in the West, after the death of Theodoric (526), there is no figure of the first magnitude, unless we assign such quality to King Totila. The Goths, under a succession of ineffective leaders, saw their grasp on Italy loosening; their domestic feuds weakened them still further and the province would seem to have passed into a state of semi-anarchy. It invited that intervention for which Justinian was already disposed and eager.

Nor had the Church in the West at this time any great leader. After the ten years' pontificate of the efficient Pope Hormisdas (514–23) there follows a succession of short-lived pontiffs—six in fourteen years—until we come to Pope Vigilius

(537–55) who has achieved a dubious immortality in the pages of religious controversy. It was in his pontificate that St. Benedict died.

But we have no intention here of writing the history either of the Gothic War and Justinian's reconquest of Italy (535–55) or of the contemporary papacy. Our concern is with St. Benedict and his life at Monte Cassino. How was he affected by the fortunes of Italy at this time? Did civil disturbance and open war interrupt the peaceful tenor of his life, or did that go on untouched and unimpaired by secular trouble? In the next chapter we shall recount the story of the visit to Monte Cassino, not long before St. Benedict's death, of King Totila. Has St. Gregory anything to tell us, of an earlier date, which would bring St. Benedict into relation with the events of his time?

Procopius, the historian of the Gothic War, has something to say of the distress which the people of Italy suffered as a consequence of its destructive progress. The business of agriculture was often seriously interrupted and acute famine ensued. He tells us also that in the year 538 there was added to the influences of constant war a great drought followed by widespread famine. The Dialogues for their part provide us with several famine stories, which we cannot date exactly but which belong no doubt to this period.

At another time [writes St. Gregory], a famine fell upon that same region of Campania so that all the people were straitened by great lack of food. And already in Benedict's monastery all the wheat was spent and almost all the bread consumed, so that when dinner time came no more than five loaves could be found for the brethren. The venerable father, seeing the monks saddened by this circumstance, set himself to chide them gently for their faint-heartedness and again to comfort them with a promise. 'Why', said he, 'are you sad for lack of bread? There is want to-day, but to-morrow you shall have plenty.' And so it fell out, for on the following day two-hundred bushels of meal were found in sacks before the monastery gate, which Almighty God had sent them, but by what hands remains unknown to our day. When the brethren saw the meal they gave thanks to God and learned thereby not to doubt of plenty even in the midst of want (*ch.* 21).

Again he writes:

Moreover, at the time when famine was gravely afflicting Campania, the man of God had given away all the victuals in his monastery to various needy folk, so that there was scarcely anything left in the storeroom but a little oil in a glass vessel. Then there came a subdeacon, by name Agapitus, urgently asking that he might be given some oil. The man of God, having resolved to give away all things in this world so that he might keep all in heaven, gave orders that even the little quantity of oil that was left should be given to Agapitus. But the cellarer, though he heard the order, postponed its execution. And a little later, Benedict asking whether the oil had been given as he commanded, the monk replied that certainly he had not given it, for had he done so, there would have been nothing whatever for the brethren. Then Benedict was angry and bade other brethren take this very vessel, in which some oil still remained, and throw it out of the window, lest the fruit of disobedience should any way remain in the monastery. And so it was done. Now below that same window was a sheer cliff, rough and craggy. The glass vessel fell on the rocks, but remained as whole as if it had never been cast forth; the glass was not broken nor was the oil spilt. Then the man of God bade them recover it and give it whole and entire to Agapitus. And summoning the brethren he rebuked the disobedient monk before them all for his disloyalty and his pride (*ch.* 28).

To these narratives we may add one of a different interest which implies that Benedict, although no believer in roving monks, yet was accustomed himself to preach the Christian faith in his neighbourhood and to send his disciples to minister to the needs of his converts.

Not far from the monastery there was a village in which a great many folk had been converted from idolatry to the faith of God by the exhortations of Benedict. There were also in the same place certain nuns, and Benedict, God's servant, often took care to send his brethren to them for the

good of their souls. On a certain day as usual he sent one of
his monks to these nuns. When the monk had given them
their sermon, the nuns begged him to accept a gift of some
handkerchiefs, which he took and concealed in his bosom.
When he returned to the monastery, the man of God began
to rebuke him bitterly. 'How', said he, 'has evil entered into
your bosom?' The monk was astonished, and forgetting
what he had done could not understand why he was rebuked. Then Benedict said: 'Was I not present when you
took the handkerchiefs from God's handmaids and put them
in your bosom?' Immediately the monk fell at his feet, re-
pented of his foolish action and cast forth the handkerchiefs
which he had hidden (*ch.* 19).

And here is one final narrative, this time from the fourth
book of the Dialogues, which again shows us a monk journeying from his monastery. But the story has a further interest.
Not infrequently St. Benedict's monastery is conceived as an
assemblage of illiterate and uncultured folk, Roman peasants
or Gothic barbarians; but the conception is a false one. St.
Benedict makes it clear in his Rule that his monastery is open
to all alike, both noble and slave, rich man and poor, and all
are to receive identical treatment. The freeman shall not take
precedence of the slave. His community in fact was a mixed
one, but it must have contained a considerable, if not a preponderant, number of monks who derived their origin from the
more or less well-educated classes of that day. It was to such
people, in fact, that the life of prayer and study enjoined by
St. Benedict would make its readiest appeal. If the Rule
makes special provision also for the illiterate, that very fact
would tend to show that such, though certainly there, were
yet in a minority.

St. Gregory writes as follows:

By the relation also of those same disciples of Benedict
I have learnt the history of the two brethren, Speciosus and
Gregory, who were noblemen and scholars, and had sub-
mitted themselves to the holy discipline of his Rule. The
venerable father sent them to dwell in that monastery of his
which he had built near the town of Terracina. In the
world they had been men of great wealth, but they sur-

rendered all their possessions to the poor for the redemption
of their souls and abode in that same monastery. One of
them, namely Speciosus, had been sent to the city of Capua
on the business of the monastery, when on a certain day,
his brother Gregory, while sitting at table with the brethren
and eating his dinner, was raised up in spirit and saw that
the soul of his brother Speciosus, who was so far from him,
had gone forth from its body. At once he told the brethren
and hastened to Capua, to find his brother already in his
grave. He learnt that he had died at the very hour of his
vision (*Bk.* IV, *ch.* 8).

Apart from such narratives as these which connect St. Benedict with nameless or minor personages, is there any means
by which we can bring him into relation with some of the
greater figures of his time, with a Cassiodorus or a Dionysius
Exiguus? We have seen, in an earlier chapter, that he was
aware of, and made use of one important literary work of
Dionysius. Abbot Chapman believes that he was familiar also
with the other work of that studious monk, in particular with
his canonical collections. So far from it being unlikely, we may
say that it is even certain that St. Benedict was in touch with
the life of Rome and with the men who figured largely in that
life. Even at Subiaco he was well known to important people
in Rome, and that connection would not be broken at Monte
Cassino. St. Gregory depicts him as receiving a succession of
distinguished visitors, bishops and influential laymen. St. Benedict in his Rule assumes that his disciples are familiar with
the liturgical practice of the Roman Church, for when he
comes to prescribe the canticles of his Office, he is content to
tell them to follow the custom of Rome: *sicut psallit ecclesia
Romana* (Cap. XIII). We may be sure that there was constant intercourse between Rome and Monte Cassino; but the
records that have survived give us no precise evidence regarding such intercourse. There is no record, then, of any personal
contact between St. Benedict and such a kindred spirit as
Dionysius.

What of his other great contemporary, Cassiodorus? This
secretary of state to King Theodoric rose after that king's
death (526) to the great office of Praetorian Prefect (533). He

continued to serve the Gothic state during the early years of
Justinian's war of reconquest, while there still seemed some
hope for the kingdom which he had served so faithfully. But
he was now, about the year 540, some sixty years old and un-
equal to the task of restoring a desperate cause; so he broke
completely with his past, threw up his high office and retired
from the world, to become a monk on his ancestral property
in Calabria. There in the Gulf of Squillace (Scyllacium), between the mountains of Aspromonte and the sea, he founded
his monastery of Vivarium. He had already, in the midst of
his public cares, looked wistfully towards the monastic life. As
a man whose duties obliged him to survey the whole of Italy
and every phase of its social life, he must have been aware of
St. Benedict and his work. If we believe but a fraction of the
history which St. Gregory has transmitted to us, we must admit that St. Benedict would be a notable character, at least in
his own Campania. A man of a far different type, the Gothic
King Totila, marching through that territory, felt bound to
visit the saint. But Cassiodorus was often in Campania. As he
travelled from Rome to his estate in Calabria, he would pass
along that Latin Way which skirted the foot of St. Benedict's
mountain. Abbot Chapman has good reason for his contention
that Cassiodorus was personally acquainted with the great abbot of Monte Cassino. And if he knew him, what then? Has
the acquaintance nothing to do with Cassiodorus' own monastic vocation? We should like to believe that St. Benedict advised the Praetorian Prefect and helped to determine the subsequent course of his career.

Cassiodorus tells us in the preface to his Institutions that
he had once endeavoured to persuade Pope Agapetus (535–
6)[1] to found in Rome a Christian university, after the manner

---

[1] Pope Agapetus collected a library in his house on the Coelian
Hill *ad clivum Scauri*, the same house that afterwards came to his
relation, St. Gregory the Great, became, under him, St. Andrew's
monastery, and later sent forth St. Augustine and his companions
to England. The library also passed to St. Gregory and it was in this
library that he wrote his Dialogues. (See Traube, *Textgeschichte*,
1910, p. 95.) Cassiodorus in his Institutions (p. 149) speaks of
working in a Roman library, but it is not certain that he means the
library of Agapetus. He does not know, at the time he is writing,
that the library had not been destroyed by the Goths, i.e., by Totila

of the schools of Alexandria and Nisibis, wherein the faithful might study sacred theology and acquire also a sound literary training. But war prevented the accomplishment of his desire; there was no room for the business of peace amid the clash of arms. Now, however, he has found another way and in the security of his remote monastery feels himself obliged by divine charity to take up the office of teacher and to write his book of introduction to sacred and profane learning.[2] To the same end also, to fulfil the functions of that university which could not be established in Rome, he directed the labours of his monks. He provided them with the best library he could collect; he instructed them how to use it most profitably; he occupied them in the transcription of further books, for the welfare of the Christian people, teaching them that they could exercise no better or more profitable charity than this. Such were the occupations which he provided for his monks.

But what of their monastic life, how was that regulated? He nowhere tells us of any one particular monastic rule that was followed in his monastery of Vivarium. But he bids his monks read Cassian sedulously as their monastic instructor (p. 74), keep the rules of the Fathers (*Patrum regulas*, p. 79), and obey the commands of their superior (*praeceptor*, teacher, p. 79). Nowhere in his writings does he mention St. Benedict or allude to his Rule. It is true that some particular duties which he mentions are expressed in words which seem to echo St. Benedict's Rule, and there are other similar passages in other writings of his, which have been assembled by Abbot Chapman; but these passages are not such as to compel us to conclude that they derive from the Rule rather than from common monastic sources.

The Benedictine editor of the works of Cassiodorus, Dom John Garet, in setting forth his argument (against Baronius) for the Benedictinism of Cassiodorus, takes first a very interesting passage of the Institutions which appears to agree closely

in 546. From this it would appear reasonable to infer that of the various dates ranging from 551 to 560 or even later assigned by scholars to the Institutions, the earliest one is appropriate for at least a portion of the book.

2 *Cassiodori Senatoris Institutiones*, ed. R. A. B. Mynors (Oxford, 1937), p. 3. Further references will be to the pages of this edition.

with St. Benedict's sentences regarding hermits in the first chapter of his Rule.[3] The fact is that the institute of Cassiodorus was two-fold, providing for two quite different sorts of life. His estate at Squillace was of considerable extent, including even a river and a mountain, or mountainous district, which he calls Mount Castellius. On the lower ground, not far from the sea, he built the monastery of Vivarium, where his disciples might lead the cenobitic life; Mount Castellius, with its many caves and enclosure wall of an abandoned Greek settlement, he designed for the use of those who desired the eremitical life. He expected—as St. Benedict may appear to expect—that some of his cenobites might be called to that more austere life. And since he mentions two abbots, Chalcedonius and Gerontius—he does not appear to have taken the office himself—we may even speak, with Hodgkin, of two monasteries, 'one for the austere hermit and the other for the less aspiring cenobite'.[4]

This is how Cassiodorus conceives the relation of the two different vocations:

> For if, as is likely, God's grace assisting, you be adequately instructed by the discipline of the monastery and it happen that your purified minds desire something more sublime, then you have the sweet recesses of Mount Castellius where with God's help you may live happily as anchorites. For those recesses are apart and like unto desert places, and the ancient walls provide them with enclosure. Wherefore it will be fitting for you, when you are disciplined and completely proved, to choose that place for your dwelling (p. 74).

At first sight this passage might appear to describe the exact state of things envisaged in St. Benedict's words and to be a practical realization of St. Benedict's mind. But again, the two-fold vocation is clearly taught in the passage of Cassian which inspired St. Benedict, and the double institute was familiar in the East, so that we cannot press the passage to prove that Cassiodorus was a disciple of the Rule.

---

[3] Migne, *P.L.*, LXIX, 483–9.
[4] Thomas Hodgkin: *The Letters of Cassiodorus*, p. 54.

However, if the argument so far is an open one, incapable of conclusive determination, there is a further matter which tells very strongly against the Benedictinism of Vivarium. It is barely possible that a monastery should be following the Rule of St. Benedict and yet not observe the liturgical horarium prescribed by that Rule. But that is the case with Vivarium. They had Vespers, but called it *Lucernarium* (Lamplighting), the old name; the serious thing is that they had no Hour of Prime. In fact the horarium agrees with the horarium of the anonymous *De Ordine Monasterii,* which is considerably older than St. Benedict's Rule. So we seem compelled to conclude that the rule of Vivarium was not the Rule of St. Benedict.

Could we make Cassiodorus a Benedictine and put Vivarium under St. Benedict's Rule, then we should be able to forge another link between St. Benedict and the learned Dionysius Exiguus. For it appears that Dionysius too abandoned the turmoil of Rome for the peace of Calabria and became a monk at Vivarium. And there he spent the remainder of his days, in prayer and study and teaching, to die at the last about the year 550.

There are further points, concerning the relation of Cassiodorus to St. Benedict, which we must not forbear to mention. Cassiodorus lived on until the year 575 and died at the great age of ninety-six. The later fortunes of his beloved retreat are not certainly known. Calabria would appear to have passed soon under Greek influences and to have become dissociated from central Italy and Rome. Certainly his foundation, as he conceived it, did not long survive Cassiodorus, for the library which was its heart, and which he had been at such pains to collect, was transported early in the next century (600–12) to north Italy and passed to Bobbio and Verona. But his writings remained and transmitted his ideals and his teaching to the Middle Ages. Their influence was not inconsiderable, but we must be careful not to misconceive or exaggerate it.

From certain descriptions of Cassiodorus and his work it would be possible to derive the impression that he was concerned chiefly with the foundation of an academy of letters. But such was not his primary purpose. He, no less than St.

Benedict, conceived himself as establishing a 'school for the Lord's service', *Dominici schola servitii*. All the studies that he prescribed, secular as well as divine, were ordained to the primary purpose that his monks by means of them might obtain from the 'Father of Light', *a Patre luminum*, the gift of a profitable and saving wisdom (p. 70).

And, secondly, his work is sometimes put into too sharp opposition with that of St. Benedict. It is scarcely true to imply, as Hodgkin would appear to do, that St. Benedict's monastery was a place only of 'pious meditation', whereas Cassiodorus provided for serious and solid study.[5] That does not do justice to St. Benedict's ordinances for 'sacred reading' (*lectio divina*) to which he devoted an average of four hours daily. Moreover, he required his abbot to be a man of learning, 'able to bring forth new things and old' for the benefit of his monks. The provisions of the Rule would of themselves necessitate a considerable monastic library. Granted that St. Benedict conceived that library as essentially a spiritual one, yet it involves a further misconception to say that 'the Benedictines of later times might more truly be called Cassiodorians'; for to represent Cassiodorus as the founder of the later monastic culture is to exaggerate his influence beyond all measure. An examination of the medieval writers, of their libraries, and of the extant manuscripts of the works of Cassiodorus would appear to prove that the book of his Institutions was not the creative manual which it is assumed to have been, so that his influence in the development of monastic studies must be conceived after a more modest fashion. The monks of the West did not, in fact, need his example or encouragement in order to give themselves to humane as well as sacred studies. The Irish monks, in the same century as Cassiodorus, took such culture for granted. English monks, as the Venerable Bede informs us, went to school in Ireland and no doubt brought back with them the same ideals. The school of Canterbury, under Theodore and Adrian, reinforced the same wide conception of monastic studies. That same conception was carried to the Continent by Irish and English monks, and became firmly established in Western monachism. If those monks required any

[5] Thomas Hodgkin: *The Letters of Cassiodorus* (1886), p. 57.

justification for their studies, they had it in a greater than Cassiodorus, in St. Augustine himself, who in his *De Doctrina Christiana* advocates the spoiling of the Egyptians and the turning of the gold of pagan culture to the service of Christian wisdom. The writings of Cassiodorus were taken into the stream of this monastic culture and added their contribution to it; but they did not create it, nor does the evidence show that they exercised a predominant influence on its course.

But we would not wish to part with Cassiodorus on a note of criticism or disparagement. Indeed, we could wish that we were able, as did the Middle Ages, to regard him without question as a Benedictine, one of the earliest and greatest of St. Benedict's sons. Those ages even admitted him, as Saint Cassiodorus, to the monastic calendar; nor should that much surprise us. His ideal and lofty purpose are clear, but no less clear are his Christian faith and deep spirituality. We would liken him, in fact, to another monk of very similar habit and purpose, and dare to attribute to him the grave title of Venerable.

PRAYER OF CASSIODORUS
FOR THE FINAL VISION OF GOD

Grant us, O Lord, we beseech Thee, this most glorious and holy vision; let not those, whom Thou hast inspired with so great a longing, be cheated of that boon. May we see Thee alive for ever, who didst deign to die for us; may we see the glory of Thy majesty, who didst will to appear in the lowliness of our flesh. Already here in this present world Thou dost look with lovingkindness on Thy servants; but that they too should look upon Thee, that this world cannot give. Grant that grace to Thy faithful, O Lord, in which all Thy rewards are included (p. 162).

CHAPTER XIII

LAST YEARS AND DEATH

Laudabit usque ad mortem anima mea Dominum
ECCLUS. LI

ST. BENEDICT was past the prime of life when he left Subiaco and established himself on Monte Cassino. Ten years elapsed of peaceful but productive activity, in which the community was securely founded and the Rule written. The saint was then about sixty years old and within a few years of his death. As he looked around him on the fruits of his years of monastic labour, his thoughts may often have travelled back to the scenes of his early life: to Nursia, Rome and Subiaco. He may often have considered the way by which God had led him through those years and have reflected often upon the purpose which was revealed in that loving guidance. Nor would it be unnatural that his thoughts should travel forward also, into the mysterious future, and that he should speculate on the destiny which awaited his monastic institute. It was to be no smooth and unruffled progress from success to success, no calm, uninterrupted development, but a history full of storm and stress, of abrupt check and apparent destruction, until innate vigour and enduring strength rose superior to all obstacles, and Benedictinism spread with peaceful momentum and beneficent power over the provinces of the West.

St. Gregory tells us that St. Benedict was allowed to see some part of the trouble which awaited his monks.

A certain nobleman, by name Theoprobus, was a monk, having been converted by the exhortations of Abbot Benedict, with whom he enjoyed a very close familiarity because of his virtuous life. One day he entered Benedict's cell and found him weeping most bitterly. He waited for some time, but the weeping did not cease; and then, since the man of God was not weeping in prayer, as was his wont, but from sheer grief, he inquired what was the cause of that great lamentation. The man of God at once replied: 'All this monastery that I have built, and all that I have provided for the brethren, are by the decree of Almighty God delivered to the barbarians. And I scarce was able to secure the lives of my monks.' Such was the prophecy that Theoprobus heard; we in our time have seen its fulfilment, in the destruction of his monastery by the Lombards. A short time ago [St. Gregory is writing in 593] the Lombards attacked by night, when the brethren had gone to rest; they plundered the whole place, yet failed to capture so much as one monk. So did Almighty God fulfil the promise which He had made to His faithful servant Benedict (*ch.* 17).

Another and more famous prophecy is recorded in the narrative of the meeting of Benedict and the Gothic King, Totila, which probably took place late in the year 542. St. Gregory narrates it as follows:

In the time of the Goths their king Totila, hearing that the holy man had the spirit of prophecy, made towards his monastery and halting at some distance from it sent word that he was coming. An answer was returned to him forthwith, bidding him come. But Totila, being of a cunning disposition, thought to try whether it was true, as he had heard, that the saint had the spirit of prophecy. He took one of his guards, by name Riggo, gave him his own shoes, had him clad in the royal robes, and bade him go in his place to the man of God. He assigned him three counts of his bodyguard, Vultheric, Ruderic and Blidi, to walk by his side and make it appear to Benedict that he was King Totila himself. Moreover, he gave him other servants and a bodyguard, so that from his train as much as from his purple robes he might be thought to be the king. Now when Riggo with his gorgeous robes and splendid train entered the grounds of the monastery the man of God was seated at

some distance; he saw Riggo approaching and waited until he was within hearing. Then he cried out: 'Put off those
robes, my son, put off those robes; they are none of thine.'
Riggo at once fell to the ground and was in great terror
because he had dared to mock such a man; and all those
who had come with him fell likewise to the ground. When
they rose they would not venture to come near him, but returned to their king and with fear told him how quickly
they had been detected.

Then King Totila came in person to the man of God.
When he descried him sitting some distance away he would
approach no nearer, but cast himself on the ground. Again
and again did the man of God bid him rise, but he would
not; so that Benedict, the servant of Jesus Christ, deigned
to go up to the prostrate king, and himself raised him from
the ground. Then he rebuked him for his deeds and in a
few words foretold all that was to happen to him.

> Much evil art thou doing,
> Much evil hast thou done:
> Cease now at length from iniquity.
> Thou shalt enter Rome,
> Thou shalt cross the sea,
> Nine years shalt thou reign,
> In the tenth thou shalt die.

At these words the king was greatly terrified and begging
his prayers departed; and thenceforth he was less cruel. Not
long after he went to Rome, and thence to Sicily. In the
tenth year of his reign, by the judgment of Almighty God,
he lost his kingdom and his life (*ch.* 15).

This narrative of the saint's encounter with King Totila is
almost the only narrative in the Dialogues to which we may
assign a definite date. The encounter, as we have said, probably took place in the year 542 when Totila was marching
through Campania and preparing for his assault on Naples.
It is by another reference to the same Gothic king that it is
possible to determine with some probability the year of St.
Benedict's death.

The traditional date for the saint's death is March 21st,

543; but this date rests ultimately on nothing better than the assertion of a twelfth-century chronicler (Leo of Ostia) corrected by later inferences. It is unnecessary to discuss its credentials. But the Dialogues provide material that gives a result which we may accept with some confidence.

St. Gregory tells us that the bishop of Canusium, by name Sabinus, was in the habit of visiting St. Benedict, who loved him much for the worthiness of his life. On one such visit they fell to talking of Totila's entrance into Rome and the destruction of the city. Sabinus said: 'That city will be destroyed by this king, so as not to be inhabited again.' St. Benedict replied: 'Rome will not be destroyed by the barbarians, but will be worn out by tempest, lightning, whirlwind and earthquake and will decay in itself' (*ch.* 15).

Of what entrance of Totila's into Rome were they speaking? The Gothic king occupied Rome twice, in 546 and in 549. On the first occasion he had proposed to destroy the city and actually began the work of destruction, but then suddenly changed his mind and withdrew his troops, leaving Rome in a ruinous and deserted condition. In 549, on the contrary, his purpose was to establish himself in Rome and make it the seat of his government, so that there was then no question of destroying the city. It is obvious, therefore, that the conversation of Sabinus and St. Benedict has reference to the first occasion, that is to the destructive occupation of 546. Rome fell into the hands of Totila and his Goths on December 17th, 546. The news would take a little time to reach Monte Cassino, so that the conversation must be put at the earliest towards the end of that December. On the other hand, it must have taken place before the spring of 547, when Rome was recaptured by Belisarius and ran no further risk of destruction. We may say, therefore, with some confidence that St. Benedict was alive at the end of the year 546.

How long did he live after that date? Paul the Deacon tells us that between his death and the destruction of Monte Cassino by the Lombards, which took place at the latest in 589, there were four abbots. From 546 to 589 is a period of only forty-three years. It is not likely that the combined rule of the four abbots occupied a period of much less than forty years.

We may say, therefore, with some confidence that St. Benedict died in the year 547 or soon after that date.[1]

As the days of Benedict's earthly course draw near their end St. Gregory takes us back again in his narrative to the thought of his home at Nursia. Many years had passed since he left it to go as a young student to Rome, and, for all that we know, Benedict did not revisit the home of his childhood during his monastic career. We know nothing of his relations with his parents, though it is not improbable that he preserved some measure of intercourse with them, and that they on their part were not ignorant of the fortunes of their saintly son. The biographer tells us only of his sister, Scholastica, who like Benedict had consecrated herself to God from an early age in the monastic life. Nothing is known of the character of the life which she led, whether it was solitary, or in a convent, or in the bosom of her family; St. Gregory speaks vaguely of her 'cell'. If we assume that Scholastica remained at Nursia in the home of her parents, then it follows from St. Gregory's narrative that there was at any rate one permanent link between Benedict and his family. But it is more probable, from St. Gregory's language, that Scholastica was living, at least at this time, in some community of nuns.

St. Gregory tells us that Scholastica used to visit Benedict once a year and that their meeting used to take place in the domain of the monastery, not far outside the gate. In the last of these visits they spent the day as usual in prayer and conversation and towards evening took food together.

While they were still sitting at table and the hour grew late amid their spiritual converse, the nun, his sister, said to Benedict: 'Leave me not, this night, my brother, so that we may talk till morning of the joys of the heavenly life.' But Benedict replied: 'Nay, nay, sister, ask me not this, for I may not remain out of the monastery.' Now the sky was clear and cloudless. When the holy nun heard her brother's refusal, she joined her hands and putting them on the table

[1] I owe this argument to Dom Philibert Schmitz, whose essay, 'L'année de la mort de S. Benoît' (*Revue Liturgique et Monastique*, 1929, pp. 123–6), I have followed closely. Abbot Chapman would put St. Benedict's death some six years later.

bowed her head upon them in prayer to Almighty God. Then she raised her head, and at once there broke such a storm of lightning, thunder and rain, that neither the venerable Benedict nor his monks could stir a foot from the place in which they were . . . Then the man of God, amid the flashes of lightning, pealing thunder and torrents of rain, seeing that return to his monastery was impossible, complained sorrowfully to his sister: 'May Almighty God forgive thee, my sister. What is this thing thou hast done?' She answered: 'I asked thee and thou wouldst not listen to me; I asked my Lord and He has heard me. Go now, if thou canst; leave me and go back to thy monastery.' But Benedict, being unable to leave the house, having refused to stay willingly remained now against his will. And so they spent the whole night in vigil and comforted each other with holy converse of spiritual things (*ch.* 33).

St. Scholastica had not much longer to live. Three days after the final meeting Benedict saw from his cell a vision of the soul of his sister going up to heaven in the form of a dove.

Rejoicing at her great glory he gave God thanks in hymns and psalms of praise, and told the brethren of her death. Then he sent them at once to bring her body to the monastery and bade them place it in the grave which he had prepared for himself. So it happened to these two, whose minds had ever been united in the Lord, that even in the grave their bodies were not separated (*ch.* 34).

Benedict did not long survive his sister. As the time of his death approached he warned his disciples, both near and far, and gave those who were distant from Monte Cassino a sign by which they should know that he had departed this life. Six days before his death he gave orders for his grave to be opened. Presently a fever attacked him and gained upon him daily.

On the sixth day he had himself carried into the oratory by his disciples and there strengthened himself for his death by receiving the Body and Blood of the Lord. Then supporting his feeble limbs by the help of his disciples, he raised his hands to heaven and standing breathed forth his

last breath amid words of prayer. On that same day two of
his monks, the one in his monastery, the other far away,
saw the selfsame vision. They saw a path strewn with rich
coverings and flashing with innumerable lamps, stretching
eastwards from his monastery to the sky. And beside it
above stood a man in venerable garments who asked them
whose path it was that they saw. When they confessed that
they knew not: 'This', said he, 'is the path by which Benedict, the beloved of the Lord, ascended to heaven.' And so,
while the disciples who were present saw the death of the
holy man, those who were absent knew of it by the sign
which he had foretold them. He was buried in the oratory
of St. John which he had himself built when he destroyed
the altar of Apollo (*ch.* 37).

Thus does his biographer recount the death of St. Benedict.
There is no reason for us to quarrel with the circumstances
in which he has invested it. That erect and fearless death, in
the oratory where he had served so faithfully and with the
familiar words of prayer upon his lips, was an end entirely appropriate for the great Father of Monks.

Thus ended the long years of his monastic effort, begun in
severest isolation from his fellow-men, consummated in close
communion with them of love and service. The material structure that he had erected was to be destroyed; but his ideal,
the union of many souls in a common and convergent effort,
each resting on all and deriving strength from that union, this
remained, and was destined to bear abundant fruit. The Rule
in which he enshrined his purpose and defined with generous
wisdom the conditions for its attainment, was to be the most
lasting achievement of his life and to secure him in the world
of men an undying influence.

CHAPTER XIV

THE TRANSLATION OF SAINT BENEDICT

Ossa apud Francos, cineres penes suos Casinenses
MABILLON

To THE story of St. Benedict's life we add now a brief account of an event of some importance in his posthumous history, namely the translation of his bones from Monte Cassino to the abbey of Fleury in France, in or about the year 673. This translation, as is notorious, has been the subject of very keen controversy between the monks of Italy and France since the twelfth century and the matter is admittedly a thorny one. As Baronius says: 'Refugit animus tam densum controversiae hujus spinetum adire, quod horret vel e longe spectare' (*ad annum* 664). However, we shall not pursue the controversy into all its complexities and ramifications, but shall be content to give the early records of the eighth and ninth centuries. For the fact is that the thickets and thorn bushes do not properly belong to the matter; they have been added to it by unscrupulous controversialists, in particular by a master-forger, Peter of Monte Cassino (*d.* 1140). But all these spurious documents have now been discredited and the matter greatly simplified. It is quite plain, here as elsewhere, that we must dismiss all records which make their first appearance several centuries after the event, and retain those only which stand near to it in time. Following this rule we shall cite four documents of the eighth and ninth centuries—the translation occurred at the end of the seventh—which are as simple and direct as we believe they are conclusive.

St. Benedict died in the year 547 or thereabouts and was buried, as he had provided, in the same grave as his sister

Scholastica. About the year 581 the Lombards sacked Monte Cassino and the monks fled to Rome, leaving St. Benedict's body behind them in its grave. From the year 581 to the year 717 (136 years) Monte Cassino was deserted. In the latter year Petronax of Brescia came to the mountain to begin his work of restoration, in which he was helped by the contemporary popes. When he died, in 747, Monte Cassino was again a flourishing monastery. But his successor, Abbot Optatus, evidently found one thing wanting to the complete rehabilitation of the monastery, namely the body of its founder. For, two years after his election, in the year 749, he sent a deputation to Pope Zachary begging him to use his influence in France so that Monte Cassino might recover the body. The deputation was headed by Pepin's brother Carloman, who had taken the monastic habit at Monte Cassino. Pope Zachary granted the abbot's request and the deputation went to France taking with them a letter from the Pope in which he asked Pepin and the bishops of the Franks that they would

> without hesitation, according to the petition of the monks, God's servants, send back the body of St. Benedict to its proper place; so that they may rejoice for their father who is thus given back to them, and you may have lasting reward and commendation because you have justly brought about his restoration to his tomb from which he was secretly taken.

This letter is printed in full in Migne, Mansi, etc., and is quite authentic. It is conclusive evidence for the belief, even at Monte Cassino itself, in the middle of the eighth century.

Later in the same century (c. 790) we have the direct testimony of a reputable historian who was himself a monk of Monte Cassino, Paul the Deacon. He writes thus in his *History of the Lombards* (VI, 2), with the chapter heading 'Quomodo corpus beati Benedicti ad Gallias delatum est'.

> About this time, when on the mount of Casinum, where the sacred body of St. Benedict rests, there had been for many years a deserted solitude, some Franks, coming from the regions of Le Mans and Orleans and pretending to keep vigil at the venerable body, took away the bones of the same

venerable Father and likewise of his reverend sister Scholastica and carried them to their own country. Two monasteries were built there to their honour, that is to the honour respectively of St. Benedict and St. Scholastica. Yet it is certain that that venerable mouth, sweeter than all nectar, those eyes which ever contemplated heavenly things, and other members also, though decomposed, remained with us.

Such is the testimony of Paul the Deacon: the bones of St. Benedict are in France, the ashes remain with us at Monte Cassino. It is clear from the terms of his narrative that he does not like the fact, but he reports it nevertheless. Coming from a monk of Monte Cassino and such a one as Paul, the testimony is very important and deserves to be regarded as decisive. Those who have not accepted the translation have been under the necessity of rejecting Paul's testimony off-hand, a desperate course.

So far we have adduced two eighth-century documents of certain date and authorship and of unquestioned authenticity. And both are of Italian provenance. But there exist also non-Italian records which tell the story of the actual translation and tell it, so to say, from the side of those who effected it. The first of these is an anonymous narrative which is believed to have been written in Germany at a date very near to that of the translation itself (c. 673). It was printed by Mabillon (*Vetera Analecta*, IV, 453) from a manuscript of St. Emmeram (Ratisbon) which he judged to be of the end of the eighth century. That manuscript has since disappeared, but the same record is extant in a palimpsest of the same date which is at Munich. It has been printed in *Palimpsesttexte des Codex Latinus Monacensis* 6333, with a careful study of the whole matter of the translation by Dom Emmanuel Munding (Beuron, 1930). This early narrative of the translation is a brief one and may be given in full. It is as follows:

In the Name of Christ. There was in France by the forethought of a loving father a learned priest. He was to go to Italy in order to discover where the bones of St. Benedict lay buried, uncared for by men. He came at length to a desert place, seventy or eighty miles from Rome, where formerly the monastery of St. Benedict had been built and his monks had lived in stable concord. Nevertheless the priest and his companions were at first at a loss to find the place, discovering no trace of the monastery nor any grave. But at length, having hired the services of a swineherd, the priest recognized and determined exactly the site of the monastery. Yet he could not at all discover the tomb until he and his companions had fasted for two days and for three days. And then it was revealed in a dream to their cook, and the matter became fully known to them. In the morning the tomb was pointed out to them by the cook, that is to say by him who seemed the least among them, so that the words of St. Paul were fulfilled: 'God hath chosen the foolish things of this world' and despiseth the high things of men; and the words of our Lord: 'Whoso would be greater among you shall be your minister'; and again: 'Whoso would be first among you shall be your servant'.

Then they examined the spot and came upon a marble gravestone which had to be broken through. So they broke the stone and found the bones of the abbot St. Benedict, and in the same tomb the bones of St. Scholastica his sister, lying underneath St. Benedict's and separated from them by a marble slab. For, as we must believe, the almighty and merciful God chose to unite them in the grave whom He had previously joined in fraternal love and Christian charity.

Then, having collected the bones and washed them, they placed them in a most clean linen sheet, keeping the two bodies apart, so that they might carry them to their country without the knowledge of the Romans. For, if they had known, they would certainly not have allowed such holy relics to be taken from them without struggle or war. And God illustrated these relics then and there with a miracle, so that men might understand how great is the reward of piety and holiness. For the linen sheet in which their bones were wrapped was afterwards found to be red with their blood, as though flowing from living bodies, so that Our Lord thereby showed that they are verily living with Him for ever, whose bodies are here distinguished by miracles.

And then the bones were put upon a horse, which, for all that the journey was a long one, bore them so easily that it seemed as though he felt no burden. Even when their way led through forests or narrow passes, neither trees nor difficult roads proved any obstacle or impediment to their travel, so that the bearers fully recognized that it was due to the merits of St. Benedict and blessed Scholastica his sister that their journey was so prosperous until they reached France and the monastery which is called Fleury. There they are now buried in peace, and, being to rise again at the last day to glory, they there bestow benefits on those who ask the Father by Jesus Christ, the Son of God, who liveth and reigneth in the unity of the Holy Spirit for ever and ever. Amen.

Such is the primitive account of the translation. The writer does not appear to have known the names of the principals in the affair, nor to have heard of the separate destination (Le Mans) of the bones of St. Scholastica. Her bones did remain at Fleury for a short time after their arrival and were not taken immediately to Le Mans. It is suggested, therefore, that this early record was written in the very year of the translation, before St. Scholastica's bones passed on to Le Mans.

Finally, there are the records which come from Fleury itself. The chief documents are: (1) a history of the translation by a monk of Fleury, called Adalbert, who died in 853; (2) an account of miracles wrought at St. Benedict's shrine at Fleury written by Adrevald and other monks of that house in the period 869–88. These documents contain undoubtedly an element of legend, but there are no grounds for disputing their historical framework. The documents are too long to be cited *in extenso* and we must be content to give their story in its barest outlines. It is as follows:

An abbot of Orleans, by name Leobodus, founded a monastery at Fleury-sur-Loire and in the year 646 gave his foundation its first abbot, by name Rigomar. This abbot died in 651 and Leobodus appointed in his place Abbot Mummolus, who ruled Fleury for thirty years. At the time of his appointment St. Gregory the Great had been dead only forty-seven years and his Dialogues, with their account of St. Benedict, was a book eagerly read throughout the monastic west. Mummolus, reading in that book the account of the destruction of Monte Cassino, meditated much upon it and finally conceived the idea of sending one of his monks to search for and recover the body of St. Benedict. [A similar plan, to recover the body of St. Scholastica, was conceived at the same time at Le Mans, a hundred miles to the west. But we may ignore this collateral expedition.]

He had the man he wanted for the task in the person of one of his monks, a well-instructed and intelligent priest, by name Aigulf. Aigulf and his companion monks set out for Italy about the year 673. They went through Rome and arriving safely at Monte Cassino found the ruins of the monastery but could not at first locate the grave. Help came to Aigulf in the shape of a venerable old man who told him to keep vigil in a certain part of the ruins and to mark a ray of light which would indicate the exact spot where he would find what he sought. Aigulf obeyed these instructions and discovered the grave. The next morning he possessed himself of the precious relics and put them all together in a basket, 'which', says Adalbert, 'we still possess'. [Some dispute arose with the emissaries of Le Mans and there was difficulty afterwards in separating the two bodies and satisfying the rival mission. We omit this part of the story.] The party then made all haste to get out of Italy and safe home, for the Italians had got wind of their doings and prepared to pursue them. However, they brought their precious burden safely to Fleury, arriving there either on July 11th or December 4th. There were two churches at Fleury, one dedicated to St. Peter and the other to St. Mary. The second church was rebuilt and made into the shrine of St. Benedict. The relics of St. Benedict were translated to it from the Church of St. Peter either on December 4th or July 11th. Fleury became a great centre of pilgrimage and innumerable miracles were worked at St. Benedict's shrine.

Such, in outline, is the Fleury account of the translation. It will be noticed that it differs, in some small particulars, from the primitive narrative, but adds the names of the principals and allows us to supply some sort of a chronology.

The story of the translation of St. Benedict's relics was accepted very generally in the centuries which followed. Throughout the West we find that besides the feast of St. Benedict's death (March 21st) there is also a feast of his translation to France, usually kept on July 11th. [There is a third feast also, December 4th, and the liturgists suppose that two translations were celebrated, the second being the translation of the relics from their temporary resting-place in the Church of St. Peter to their final shrine. It is not certain which were the original respective dates, but July 11th became generally accepted as the feast of the translation proper.[1]]

And, meanwhile, what of Monte Cassino? We have seen that a mission was sent to France in the year 749, with Pope Zachary's help, in order to recover the relics. Although the mission received the countenance and help of Pepin, it did not succeed in its object; Fleury retained its treasure. But it is probable that out of its abundance Fleury gave something to the Cassinese monks, and indeed Adrevald tells us that Abbot Medo of Fleury did make them such a gift. So, when they returned to Monte Cassino, about the year 757, they did not come back empty-handed. A confirmation of the gift may be found in the circumstance recorded by the ninth-century chronicle of Leno (near Brescia) that when Leno was being founded in 759 by Cassinese monks they brought with them a relic of St. Benedict. So, after all, Monte Cassino possesses in their original resting-place some relics of St. Benedict besides the ashes claimed for it by Paul the Deacon.

Of the later history of the relics and of the fierce controversy which has raged over the fact of the translation nothing need be said. We may sincerely regret that the saint's body was ever removed from its original grave, and yet feel obliged by the evidence to admit the removal. At Fleury, so we believe, in the massive crypt of the noble Romanesque basilica, rests the treasure of Mummolus and Aigulf, a veritable legacy from Merovingian times.

NOTE

It will probably appear to the reader that the above account of the translation is a very one-sided account, giving only the case for Fleury; we ought, therefore, to add a note about the case for the opposition. Apart from considerations

1 Another and more likely view is that one of these dates has reference to a later translation, when the relics had been removed temporarily from their shrine to escape raiders.

of probability and national feeling, that case rests on certain Cassinese documents of the twelfth century which whether by implication or directly impugn the translation. There is first the *Chronicon Casinense*, begun by Leo of Ostia and continued by Peter the Deacon, both monks of Monte Cassino. And secondly there is a whole series of essays in historical forgery produced by the latter writer, as follows: *De viris illustribus archisterii Casinensis; Historica relatio de corpore S. Benedicti; Ortus et vita justorum coenobii Casinensis; Epitome chronicorum Casinensium; Translatio S. Benedicti*. These documents had already been subjected to much adverse criticism, but Peter's credit as an historian was finally destroyed by E. Caspar in his *Petrus Diaconus und die Monte Cassineser Fälschungen* (1909). Caspar's conclusions are generally accepted, as by Dom Morin (*Revue Bénédictine*, 1910, p. 251). Leo of Ostia (*Chronicon Casinense*, II, 43–4) narrates a visit to Monte Cassino in 1022 of the Emperor St. Henry. The emperor had been sceptical regarding the presence of St. Benedict's body at Monte Cassino, but after being cured of a sickness at the shrine ceased to disbelieve and thereafter made a point of burning every copy of the translation record that he encountered. This story, if true, might account for the extreme rarity of the primitive record.

POSTSCRIPT 1957

I have allowed the above account to stand much as it was written in 1937; but I confess that I am now much less confident about the truth of this matter. My scepticism embraces both the Italian claims and the French, though I still think the latter more plausible than the former. And it extends, I fear, to the claims very recently put forward by the abbey of Monte Cassino.

CHAPTER XV

BENEDICTINISM

*Multiplicabo semen tuum sicut stellas caeli et velut arenam
quae est in litore maris*

GEN. XXII

ST. BENEDICT died towards the middle of the sixth century.
Some forty years after his death his monastery of Monte Cassino was destroyed by the Lombards and the monks fled to
Rome, taking with them the precious Rule. They were kindly
received at Rome and established in a monastery next to the
Lateran basilica. In this migration to Rome historians have
agreed to recognize an event of great moment in the propagation of St. Benedict's institute. His monks were not in any remote and unfrequented solitude while they remained at Monte
Cassino—their monastery lay close to the Latin Way—but at
Rome they would be in close contact with the centre of
Church life and under the observation not only of the leaders
of the Church, but of all who came from every quarter to visit
the city of the apostles.

Their monastery was not the first to be established in Rome.
As early as the first half of the fourth century—after the visit
of St. Athanasius—many, both men and women, had been
stimulated with a desire to imitate the life of the Fathers of
the Egyptian deserts. But we know little, or nothing, of their
efforts and the success which attended them, though we may
infer that there was from this date a continuous monastic
tradition in the city. Some time before the year 575, that is
after St. Benedict's death but before the destruction of Monte
Cassino, Gregory, the future Pope and biographer of St.
Benedict, became a monk in the monastery of St. Andrew on
the Coelian Hill, which he founded out of his own patrimony.

It is not certainly known what rule was observed in this monastery; and, indeed, considering the conditions and character of monachism, not only then but for more than a century afterwards, the inquiry is inevitably difficult. There were, it is true, certain great collections of monastic precepts, such as the Eastern Rules and the writings of Cassian. But often the individual monastery would not confine itself to any one code; it would select and combine; and, more than written law, the abbot's authority was its guide. St. Gregory proclaims in the Dialogues the excellence of St. Benedict's Rule, from which and from certain passages in his correspondence, it is inferred by such cautious critics as Grützmacher[1] that the Rule of St. Benedict was introduced by him into his own monastery of St. Andrew's and became the main standard of its life. When did St. Gregory first make the acquaintance of the Rule? He tells us that he got his knowledge of St. Benedict's life from certain of his disciples, and among others he specifies Constantinus, who succeeded Benedict as abbot of Monte Cassino and Simplicius who succeeded Constantinus. The names of the abbots of Benedict's monastery until its destruction by the Lombards are given to us by Paul the Deacon, a reliable authority. In that brief period of some thirty or forty years there were four abbots. If Gregory was personally acquainted with Constantinus and Simplicius, as his words may imply, we are justified in inferring that he knew the Rule at least very soon after the death of its author, and before the foundation of St. Andrew's. And nothing that we know excludes the possibility that Gregory was aware of St. Benedict and his achievements at an even earlier date. But he is reticent in all that concerns himself; while he is eloquent in praise of St. Benedict's monastic work, he has nothing to say of his own and we cannot speak with complete certainty of the Rule by which St. Andrew's was governed.

However, there is another method of approach which provides clear evidence for the observance of the monastery. It is now regarded as certain that St. Augustine and his fellow-monks took with them on their mission to the Anglo-Saxons the

[1] *Die Bedeutung Benedikts von Nursia und seiner Regel in der Geschichte des Mönchtums* (Berlin, 1892), pp. 19, 54–61.

Rule of St. Benedict. They were monks of the monastery of St. Andrew, of which Augustine had been prior. It would therefore follow that St. Andrew's, in the year 596, was using the Rule of St. Benedict.

So, in the first half-century of its existence, the period from St. Benedict to St. Gregory, the Rule was observed in the monasteries of St. Benedict's foundation—Subiaco, Monte Cassino, Terracina—and had come to Rome. The history of its progress during the next two centuries, the seventh and eighth, that is to say during the period from St. Gregory to Charlemagne, is obscure and uncertain, from lack of precise historical evidence. We may say, however, in general terms, that the note of the seventh century is variety and not uniformity of monastic rule, whereas in the eighth century the opposite had become true and the Benedictine Rule rapidly acquired a position of unquestioned predominance.

This consummation was reached by slow stages and as the result of a gradual development. It was greatly assisted by the action of St. Gregory and some of his successors in the Roman See. The correspondence of St. Gregory displays him as a consistent advocate of the Rule in the monasteries which came under his notice; but his greatest service to it was performed in the book of his Dialogues, wherein he made known the saintly life of its author and commended the Rule emphatically for its moderation and lucidity. With the direct approval of papal authority, and that given by such a Pope as St. Gregory, the Rule was sure of a welcome in the monastic circles of the West; and, once known and studied, it made its way by those inherent qualities of good sense and orderliness which the Pope had praised. In contrast to such a monastic rule as that of St. Columbanus, it provided a discipline which was austere without being extravagant. And, in its precise regulations for prayer, study and work, it supplied a clear and comprehensive system that could be adopted and practised in its entirety. Monachism had been waiting for just such a Rule. Previous Rules had been little more than collections of religious precepts; St. Benedict was the first to write a true monastic code. His Rule presented itself as such, as a 'master rule' which was to be observed by everyone in the monastery, from the abbot downwards. Both its form and content justified its pretensions.

But the claims of the Rule were not immediately recognized; at first it was but one Rule among several and had yet to prove its superiority to its rivals. However, when the monasteries of the seventh century extended hospitality to this new-comer, welcoming it as they welcomed every monastic writing, they presently found that it offered something which was to be found nowhere else, so that they inevitably gave it a position of special honour and authority. But this position was not for some time yet an exclusive one, for along with the Rule they maintained their own older observances. We find, for instance, the Rule of St. Benedict coexisting in the same monastery with the Rule of St. Columbanus. We find a monastic founder such as St. Benet Biscop supplementing its regulations from his own experience of monastic observance. What are we to make of such cases? It is not easy in the circumstances to determine whether the Rule held such a predominant position that we may securely regard such houses as Benedictine monasteries. In favour of such a conclusion we might plead that, considering its nature, the Rule wherever accepted would be likely to provide the main structure of the monastic observance. We may observe further that the Rule is not so complete and exhaustive that it has not needed—always, throughout its history—to be supplemented by further regulations. It is possible, therefore, that many of these eclectic monasteries were in substance Benedictine, though not with that conscious and deliberate Benedictinism that was of later growth.[2]

The most flourishing monachism of the West in the seventh century was that of Gaul, deriving from such great monks as St. Martin of Tours (d. 397), John Cassian of Marseilles (d. about 435), St. Honoratus of Lerins (d. 429) and St. Caesarius of Arles (d. 542). To this Gallic monachism had been added in the sixth century the vigorous impulse of the Irish monks under St. Columbanus, with their centre at the abbey of

[2] I ought to say that by 'Benedictine' I mean 'observing the Rule of St. Benedict'. I do not mean that the monks of these early centuries called themselves, or were called, Benedictines, still less that they were specifically distinguished as such by canonical legislation. I conceive that the word was not generally so used until much later, when after the emergence of other Orders distinction became necessary.

Luxeuil. We do not know when St. Benedict's Rule first became known in Gaul, but we may surmise that the monks of Gaul heard of it first through the pages of the Dialogues.[3] Very soon after the publication of that book, St. Augustine passed through Gaul on his way to England, stopping on his way at Lerins and Arles. No doubt his hosts would hear from him about the Rule which he himself observed and which he was taking with him to England. The earliest precise evidence for the use of the Rule in Gaul is for the convent of Jussamoutier in the year 620 and it is characteristic of the times. The founder of the convent, St. Donatus of Besançon, a monk of Luxeuil, gave his nuns a Rule compiled from the three Rules of Caesarius, Columbanus and Benedict. On the other hand, at almost the same date (about 625), the monastery of Altaripa in the diocese of Albi was specifically obliged by its founder, one Venerandus, to the exact observance of St. Benedict's Rule. To make sure that it would be faithful he sent a copy of the Rule to the bishop of Albi and asked him to keep a vigilant eye on the monastery. His letter is extant and is of such interest that we venture to subjoin a translation of the relevant portions:

Venerandus to the Right Reverend Lord and most worthy Bishop Constantius. We have sent Your Beatitude the Rule of Saint Benedict, Roman abbot, which is contained in this present volume, to be put and kept in the archives of the holy church of Albi for this object, that if at any time any of the monks, or any abbot of the monks, whom we have assembled with God's help in our little monastery (*monasteriolum*) of Altaripa, should venture to act otherwise than you shall find written and said in it, or to contravene it in any point, they may be corrected by the holy admonitions of yourself and your successors . . . For this request we specially make of Your Holiness, that if any monk or abbot prove to be a despiser of the present Rule or shall have neglected to fulfil it [his phrases here echo the text of the Rule], if he be abbot he shall be immediately expelled from the

[3] If the *Vita Mauri* could be believed, we should have to add the direct influence of St. Benedict's favourite disciple. But see the Appendix, Note 4.

monastery with the utmost disgrace, nor ever be appointed superior there again, but if there be another in the community who is worthy to rule the rest, he shall be appointed in his place.[4]

This letter, it will be admitted, lacks nothing in precision; Altaripa may without hesitation be denominated a Benedictine monastery. Perhaps there were other such in Gaul even in this first half of the seventh century, but we know nothing of them. The evidence, such as it is, testifies rather to the same state of things as at Jussamoutier. The Rule of St. Benedict was frequently conjoined with that of Columbanus, and that even in the monasteries, such as Luxeuil, which had been founded by Columbanus himself.[5] Towards the end of the seventh century the Council of Autun (670) mentions only the Rule of St. Benedict and expects it to be observed by all abbots and monks. Not long after occurred the famous and much-disputed Translation of St. Benedict's relics from Monte Cassino to Gaul; and the abbey of Fleury, where they were enshrined, became

[4] The full Latin text may be found in Traube: *Textgeschichte der Regula S. Benedicti* (1910), p. 88. Constantius was bishop of Albi during the period 620–30.

[5] It appears to be an established fact that the great propagators of St. Benedict's Rule in seventh-century Gaul were the monks of St. Columbanus. Abbot Waldebert of Luxeuil (629–70) from the beginning of his government accepted the Rule and welded it into a single instrument with the Rule of Columbanus. His policy had an enormous success. Luxeuil presently numbered as many as six hundred monks and with the willing assistance of powerful laymen, to whom Abbot Waldebert and his monks would seem to have been very acceptable, made foundations throughout Gaul and even beyond. The histories of the foundations repeat the phrases: *Regula beati Benedicti et beati Columbani, Regula Benedicti ad normam* (or, *ad modum*) *Luxoviensis Coenobii.* Already we can see which was the dominant partner, destined in the end to rule alone. See the thesis of A. Malnory: *Quid Luxovienses monachi discipuli S. Columbani ad regulam monasteriorum atque ad communem ecclesiae profectum contulerint* (Paris, 1894), especially pp. 20–42: *De regula Benedicti a Waldeberto adscita, et de mira instituti Luxoviensis propagatione sub hoc abbate.* Malnory records sadly the ultimate eclipse of the great figure of the dauntless Celt and continues: Quare tunc ejus regula illi Benedictinae cessit, cui simul et major prudentia, et comptior dispositio atque nescio quid Romani roboris atque majestatis insitum erat.

a great centre of pilgrimage. Whatever opinion we may hold regarding the facts of the Translation, we must allow that this shrine is evidence of an interest in Benedictinism and would exercise a profound influence in its propagation.

In England, during the same seventh century, the Rule of St. Benedict, having started with the advantage of St. Augustine's mission, was the single monastic rule in the kingdom of Kent. As for the north of England: that was being evangelized at the same time by the monks of St. Columba and had its own Celtic monachism to which it long remained faithful. It is true that St. Wilfrid, himself a monk of Lindisfarne, established his monastery of Ripon (about 660) under the Benedictine Rule; and St. Benet Biscop in his foundations of Wearmouth (674) and Jarrow (680) would appear to have given the Rule a preponderant though not an exclusive position.[6] The Rule itself allows the individual abbot a wide discretion and its observance has always been compatible with difference of detailed custom. So, as we are told specifically by the Venerable Bede, St. Benet Biscop modelled the observance of his

[6] I am not sure that I do not in this context make too little of the Benedictine character of Wearmouth and Jarrow; but I am far from the opinion of those who would, how I know not, state positively that they were not Benedictine. The *Lives of the Abbots* both in the old, anonymous text, and in the Venerable Bede's recension, provide evidence which would allow us rather to assert roundly that they were in essence Benedictine. What was the important matter of the election of the abbot governed by? By the ordinances of the Rule of St. Benedict confirmed to them by a privilege of Pope Agatho. This is three times reported in explicit terms. (*Baedae Opera Historica*, ed. Plummer, 1896, pp. 375, 381, 393.) And this is how St. Benedict is mentioned: *regula magni quondam abbatis Benedicti; regula sancti abbatis Benedicti; regula sancti patris Benedicti; magnus abbas Benedictus.* In the same context we have the precise words of the Rule that the abbot should be chosen for his virtue and wisdom: *secundum vitae meritum et sapientiae doctrinam,* and the exact method which the Rule envisages with further use of the Rule's words. But even more significant than such explicit citations are the casual, unacknowledged borrowings from the Rule. I give two plain cases: *vero Regi militans* (p. 365); *in pistrino, in orto, in coquina* (p. 371). In the face of all this evidence such an assertion as that the Venerable Bede was not a Benedictine needs vast qualification. For myself I regard that position as untenable and unreservedly call St. Bede a Benedictine.

houses on the practice of no less than seventeen different monasteries. These monasteries would be those which he had visited in his journeys to Rome, and if not fully Benedictine would
certainly display the strong contemporary trend to Benedictinism.[7] The result of the labours of himself and other such
pioneers was that England by the end of the seventh century
possessed a number of powerful Benedictine houses, centres of
observance and study and the promoters presently of a great
apostolate. The Venerable Bede (d. 735) is the very type of
the monk-scholar, content to pass all his days in the discipline
of the cloister and in study. On the other hand, we have a
striking series of monk-apostles. Benedictinism had come to
England in the first instance as an apostolate, and it would
seem that the English Benedictines of the eighth century were
determined in their turn to take their part in spreading the
Catholic faith. St. Wilfrid had been already, in the seventh
century, a great missionary both in Frisia and among the
South Saxons. He had worthy successors in such men as Saints
Willibrord, Wicbert, Suitbert, Adalbert, and, greatest of all,
in St. Boniface, the apostle of Germany.[8]

So the seventh century closes with the Rule known throughout the West and winning a predominant position as the 'Rule
for Monks'. This position was consolidated in the eighth century. Pope Gregory II (715–31) assisted Petronax of Brescia
in the restoration of Monte Cassino, which had lain waste since
its destruction by the Lombards (581), a period of more than
one hundred and thirty years. Pope Gregory III (731–41) rebuilt the Lateran monastery. Pope Zachary (741–51) restored
the autograph of the Rule to Monte Cassino, and was the author of a Greek translation of the Dialogues of St. Gregory the

[7] He was himself originally (666) a monk of Lerins and Lerins
had certainly adopted the Rule before he founded Wearmouth.
I am confident that he visited this monastic sanctuary on every
one of his many visits to Rome. I believe that what he sought,
there and elsewhere, was not any modification of the Rule, still less
any rival rule, but the best tradition of Benedictine observance.

[8] It is a noteworthy fact that an English Benedictine, St. Willi-
bald, played an important part in the restoration of Benedictine
observance at Monte Cassino under Abbot Petronax. See Abbot
Chapman, *Revue Bénédictine*, xxi (1904), pp. 74–80, and *St.
Benedict and the Sixth Century*, p. 131.

Great. Thus it may be inferred that these Popes seconded and encouraged the development of Benedictine monachism. That development had already taken the direction of securing a monopoly for St. Benedict's Rule. In the eighth century we find such an object deliberately aimed at by the apostle of Germany, the English Benedictine St. Boniface. But it would seem to have gone on spontaneously throughout the West, doubtless because of the intrinsic excellence of the Rule. In England Benedictinism was securely established; in Italy, France, and Germany it had practically ousted all other rules; only in Spain, which was somewhat isolated from the rest of Christendom, does it seem, at this time, to have made but small progress. It may be fairly asserted that St. Benedict's Rule was then, at the end of the eighth century, the law of Western monachism. Charlemagne and Louis the Pious, with their assistants, especially St. Benedict of Aniane, pushed this success further. It is significant to note certain questions which were set before the Chapter of Aachen in 817. The assembled bishops and abbots were asked: 'Can there be any monks besides those who observe the Rule of St. Benedict? Were there monks in Gaul before St. Benedict's Rule came thither? And if there were, as there seem to have been (e.g., St. Martin), what Rule did they follow?' The interrogatories prove the success of Benedictinism, a success which was by this time so complete, that all memory of the stages by which it had been accomplished had perished.

The end of the eighth century—the year A.D. 800—may serve as a useful landmark in the history of Benedictinism, as fixing the point when the Rule had attained an unquestioned predominance. From this date onwards we have to consider not so much the growth and expansion of Benedictinism, as its internal aspect and the growing consciousness of Benedictine unity. In effect the notion of a unity to which the name of a Benedictine Order might be given now first clearly emerges.

According to St. Benedict's provisions each monastery is an independent, autonomous family. The Rule makes no provision for the federation of monasteries, still less for the subordination of many to one central authority. As a consequence of this principle of autonomy the now numerous Benedictine monasteries of the West were so many discrete units, observing the same Rule, agreeing in the main lines of their life, but not forming any sort of organic whole, and admitting of considerable variety in minor points of observance. This was only natural, for the Rule itself leaves a large, undefined power to the abbot, and envisages the adaptation and application of its provisions to the variety of circumstances. The autonomous Benedictine monastery has been compared to the Roman colony—a citizen outpost in conquered territory—and undoubtedly it was well adapted to the circumstances of those unsettled times. But independence and isolation had their disadvantages. It was possible for peculiarity and laxity to invade monasteries that were deprived of the assistance of some measure of co-ordination.[9]

The Emperor Charlemagne, in pursuit of that general effort towards organization and uniformity which characterized his government, turned his attention also to the monasteries of the Empire. He saw variety and difference where he desired uniformity and agreement; but he had hope in that common Rule to which all claimed to give their allegiance. He had visited Monte Cassino, and in that sanctuary of Benedictinism

[9] I do not conceive it to be my duty in the course of this brief sketch to dwell upon the recurrent phenomenon, as inevitable as human nature itself, of monastic relaxation. I do not for a moment wish to deny that Benedictinism sometimes suffered from such relaxation. The reforming movements which characterize the history of the Order are a witness to it, as they are a witness also to the innate soundness and vitality of the institute. Yet, even so, we are too often inclined to think of relaxation and reform as of great and catastrophic things; whereas the whole history of monachism would be more truly conceived as a constant tension between observance and relaxation, as a conflict in which the ideal struggled incessantly with opposing forces and was on the whole decisively victorious. It seems to me that the historians—I do not speak of the controversialist, who must needs do his scavenging—sometimes do less than justice to the monks. They make too little allowance for the constant invasion of monastic rights and monastic observance by secular force, for the influence of anarchic social conditions, for the crippling exactions of princes and lay lords. The Benedictine monasteries were of their nature specially open to such attack and could with difficulty defend themselves against it. They were open also and sensitive to the influences of their age, both good and bad. A just estimate of an institute with a life of fourteen centuries should take account of all these things.

he had proba
was so advise
sible to realize
this end he p
to its dissemin
the Pious, the
a vigorous eff
Benedict of A
servance in all
reaching and b
ing to propaga
its underlying
any systematic
remained what
units.

The next ce
Cluny (founde

ily. The scattered monasteries were to
tions, which naturally conformed t
litical divisions. They were to ho
intervals and to provide for t
But it is important to n
formed for mutual hel
to supplant the inde
words Congregati
ern ears a high
elaborately
alien to B
union
sum

gregation of a highly centralized form of organization, by which many monasteries (to be counted ultimately by hundreds) were included in one system and subordinated to the rule of the mother-house. The Congregation of Cluny was immensely efficient, and while it flourished did great service to religion and civilization; moreover, it certainly familiarized Benedictines with the idea of some sort of union and organization; but the majority of Benedictine monasteries were, as before, independent families enjoying complete autonomy. And so they remained until the end of the twelfth century.

Both before and after this date (A.D. 1200) there sprang from the great main family several offshoots, representing new or reformed interpretations of the Benedictine life. Of these the Cistercians, with their great figure St. Bernard, are the best known. The beginning of the thirteenth century witnessed a movement from the centre of Christendom itself, not in the direction of a radical change in the Benedictine ideal, but towards co-ordination and co-operation. The ordinances of the Fourth Lateran Council of 1215, though in their own time scarcely effective save in England, are represented in spirit and substance in the Congregations of the present day. At last Benedictinism at large had achieved a common polity, and that without sacrificing the basic principle of the autonomous fam-

be united into Congrega-
to existing national and po-
d General Chapters at regular
he ensuring of good observance.
te that these Congregations were
and support, and were not intended
endent government of the monastery. The
on and Order naturally suggest to our mod-
ly centralized form of government with parts
organized and subordinated; such government is
enedictinism. A Benedictine Congregation is a federal
f independent monasteries; the Benedictine Order is the
total of such federations.[10]

Passing quickly over the period from the thirteenth to the
sixteenth century, a period marked here and there by decline
and yet by several vigorous reforms—no doubtful sign of the
innate vitality of Benedictinism—we come to the great disaster
of the Reformation. In the countries which passed over to
Protestantism the monasteries were suppressed and despoiled.
And even in Catholic countries the Order suffered partial
eclipse, losing a great deal of its old power and influence. There
were, however, some notable revivals. Italy produced the Cassinese Congregation with such great monasteries as that of St.
Justina of Padua. In Spain there was the Congregation of Val-
ladolid. These two played a decisive part in the revival of English Benedictinism. France, on its part, had two such Congregations, of which the Congregation of St. Maur won for itself
a lasting fame for scholarship and learning. But disaster came
again. The French Revolution and parallel secularist movements caused the suppression of nearly every monastery in Europe, so that at the beginning of the nineteenth century a mere
handful survived. But again revival came.

In France and Germany new Congregations sprang into being and have had a vigorous growth. In Austria, Italy, Spain,
Portugal and Switzerland many of the ancient abbeys still survive. America and Australia have seen the foundation of mon-

[10] I ought here to refer to the *General Chapters of the English
Black Monks* (3 vols. London, 1931–7) by Mr. W. A. Pantin of
Oriel College, Oxford. The value of this work for English Bene-
dictine history can hardly be overestimated.

asteries which promise a great development. In Great Britain itself the English Benedictines, no new Congregation but the lineal descendants of the pre-Reformation monks, have six abbeys for monks and four for nuns. The statistics of the whole Order at a recent date (1955) give an aggregate of 572 monasteries and convents with 31,980 religious. And these figures do not include such offshoots as the Cistercians, Trappists, etc.

The history of the fortunes of the English Benedictines during the troubled period of the Reformation is singular and deserves record. They had held in this country a commanding position, which is indicated still by many a noble cathedral or ruined abbey. Coming first as the pioneers of Christianity among the Saxons, they were largely responsible for the establishment and organization of the Church in England. Many of the cathedral churches came to be served by Priories of Black Monks. At the time of the Dissolution of the Monasteries under Henry VIII it is estimated that there were close on three hundred of their houses in the country, and there were others in Scotland and Ireland. These were closed and the monks were cast adrift. The abbots of Glastonbury, Reading and Colchester, with some of their monks, were put to death. Of the rest a few sought refuge abroad, while the majority accepted pensions or preferment and adapted themselves to the ecclesiastical order which they had already accepted, before the dissolution of the monasteries, by subscribing to the oath of supremacy. When Queen Mary came to the throne an attempt was made at a revival, and a few of the surviving monks were brought together under Abbot Feckenham at Westminster (1556). But the revival lasted only three years, and with the accession of Elizabeth the monks were again dispersed. But Englishmen did not abandon St. Benedict so easily. Of the Catholic refugees who fled to the Continent in Queen Elizabeth's reign a considerable number became Benedictines in the monasteries of Spain and Italy. When it became clear that no immediate return of England to the ancient Faith was to be hoped for, some of these monks sought and obtained permission to return to England and to work (at the risk of their lives) as missionary priests. Two of them, Dom Thomas Preston (a Shropshire man who suffered many imprisonments and finally died in the Clink) and Dom Anselm Beech (of Manchester), both of the Italian Congregation, found still living on their arrival in England a monk of Westminster Abbey, by name Sigebert Buckley, one of those professed during the brief Marian revival. They saw the importance of this fact and were not slow in making use of it. In concert with these fathers Dom Sigebert Buckley arranged to secure the transmission of all the rights and privileges of the old English Congregation, which were now vested in him as the sole survivor. Two secular priests, Robert Sadler and Edward Mayhew, who wished to become Benedictines, were clothed with the habit by Dom Thomas Preston, Dom Sigebert Buckley assisting. After the year's novitiate had been completed, on November 21st of the year 1607, the feast of the Presentation of Our Lady, they took their vows in the presence of the aged Westminster monk, and were by him affiliated to the old English Congregation. Thus was that Congregation perpetuated and its ancient line preserved; to this day the English Benedictines keep the memory of the act sacred among them, and the day is to them the *Dies Memorabilis*.

The work of the Benedictines in the world during the fourteen centuries of their existence cannot be comprised within the space of a brief summary. But some points may be indicated. The mission of St. Augustine has already been mentioned and it is not necessary to speak of its results. After the conversion of England, English Benedictines went forth to evangelize Friesland and Holland. St. Boniface and his companions evangelized central Germany; the Benedictine, St. Anschar, first preached to the Scandinavians. Nor were these the only peoples who owed their Christianity to the devoted labours of Benedictine missionaries. Their monasteries were soon to be found throughout north-western Europe; they reached even to Iceland and Greenland; and wherever a Benedictine monastery was planted, there was set a centre of religion and civilization. By example, that most potent of influences, as well as by direct instruction, they taught the barbarian peoples the methods of agriculture and the arts of civilized life.[11]

[11] I must be content to refer the reader to the masterly survey of Dom Berlière's *L'Ordre Monastique* (1921), especially ch. 2, *L'apostolat monastique,* and ch. 3, *L'oeuvre civilisatrice.*

And here we may be allowed to quote a page in which Cardinal Newman gives his conception of the spirit of Benedictinism. 'When the bodily frame receives an injury, or is seized with some sudden malady, nature may be expected to set right the evil, if left to itself, but she requires time; science comes in to shorten the process, and is violent that it may be certain. This may be taken to illustrate St. Benedict's mode of counteracting the miseries of life. He found the world, physical and social, in ruins, and his mission was to restore it in the way, not of science, but of nature, not as if setting about to do it, not professing to do it by any set time or by any rare specific or by any series of strokes, but so quietly, patiently, gradually, that often till the work was done, it was not known to be doing. It was a restoration, rather than a visitation, correction, or conversion. The new world which he helped to create was a growth rather than a structure. Silent men were observed about the country, or discovered in the forest, digging, clearing, and building; and other silent men, not seen, were sitting in the cold cloister, tiring their eyes, and keeping their attention on the stretch, while they painfully copied and re-copied the manuscripts which they had saved. There was no one that "contended, or cried out", or drew attention to what was going on; but by degrees the woody swamp became a hermitage, a religious house, a farm, an abbey, a village, a seminary, a school of learning, and a city' (*The Mission of St. Benedict*, §9).

In a well-known chapter of *Italy and her Invaders*, Hodgkin thus characterizes the achievement of St. Benedict:

If we ask why has the fame of St. Benedict so entirely eclipsed that of all other Western monks, the answer is undoubtedly furnished to us by the one literary product of his life, his *Regula*. This Rule, extending only to seventy-three short chapters (many of them very short), and not probably designed by its author for use much beyond the bounds of the communities under his own immediate supervision, proved to be the thing which the world of religious and thoughtful men was then longing for, a complete code of monastic duty. Thus by a strange parallelism, almost in the very year when the great Emperor Justinian was codifying the results of seven centuries of Roman secular legislation for the benefit of the judges and the statesmen of the new Europe, St. Benedict on his lonely mountain-top was unconsciously composing *his* code for the regulation of the daily life of the great civilizers of Europe for seven centuries to come. The chief principles of that code were labour, obedience, and a regulated fervour of devotion to the Most High . . . It is, however, the man himself rather than the vast system almost unconsciously founded by him that it has seemed necessary at this point to bring before the mind of the reader. St. Benedict died only ten years before the extreme limit of time reached by this volume (553). Later on, when we have to deal with the history of the Lombard domination in Italy, our attention will be attracted to the further fortunes of Monte Cassino, ruined, restored, endowed with vast wealth, all by the same Lombard invaders. For the present we leave the followers of the Saint engaged in their holy and useful labours, praying, digging, transcribing. 'The wilderness and the solitary place shall be glad for them, and the desert shall rejoice and blossom as the rose.' The *scriptorium* of the Benedictine monastery will multiply copies not only of missals and theological treatises, but of the poems and histories of antiquity. Whatever may have been the religious value or the religious dangers of the monastic life, the historian at least is bound to express his gratitude to these men, without whose life-long toil the great deeds and thoughts of Greece and Rome might have been as completely lost to us as the wars of the buried Lake-dwellers or the thoughts of Palaeolithic Man. To take an illustration from St. Benedict's own beloved Subiaco, the work of his disciples has been like one of the great aqueducts of the valley of the Anio—sometimes carried underground for centuries through the obscurity of unremembered existences, sometimes emerging to the daylight and borne high upon the arcade of noble lives, but equally through all its course bearing the precious stream of ancient thought from the far-off hills of time into the humming and crowded cities of modern civilization (*Vol. IV, pp.* 496–8).

Such was the service which the monks rendered to the world. Amid the disruptive forces at work over the whole face of the Western world they represented the stable tradition of an older time; they seized the torch of literature and learning, and though, amid those warring elements, in the gusty currents of a barbarous world, its light at times burnt very low, yet they passed it on still burning, and made possible the glories of the thirteenth century and the renaissance of the fifteenth. It was in the monasteries that men found, in quiet and peace, the retreats in which they could study and write. It was here that they found the treasures not only of scriptural and patristic learning, but also of the learning of classical antiquity. The monasteries were the libraries of Europe, and enriched the stores which they possessed by the labour of assiduous transcription. Whence do the great libraries of the present day, in Paris, Munich, London, Oxford and Cambridge derive the greater part of their manuscript collections? Their most precious possessions are the remains of the monastic libraries and the fruit of the monastic labours of the Middle Ages. And what memories of study and fruitful learning are aroused by such names as Monte Cassino, Bobbio, Corbie, Cluny, St. Denis, St. Amand, Fulda, Hersfeld, Lorsch, St. Gall, Reichenau, Murbach, Werden, to mention only a few of the great continental abbeys? In our own England we have Wearmouth, St. Albans, Westminster, Glastonbury, Worcester, Durham, Bury St. Edmunds and many others. The names of the great abbeys are inseparably associated with the political and social history of the countries to which they belonged; they are even more deeply associated with their civilized culture. It is not too much to say that for the early Middle Ages, the period of their greatest influence, the Benedictine monasteries were the chief cultural centres of Europe.[12]

But to enumerate only these lasting benefits to mankind, to record only the external and tangible aspect of their activities, is to do the monks a serious injury and to betray a misunderstanding of their lives. For in truth these various human activities, social and educational, were but the 'limbs and outward flourishes' of a deeper interior life, and it was for this

[12] Again I refer to Dom Berlière, especially to his third chapter.

deep inner life that the monk lived and worked. That life has been described already, in its quiet round of prayer and work. It is simply the service of God, and its chief activity the daily Office of praise. *Per singulos dies benedicimus Te:* day by day we bless Thee and we praise Thee, world without end. There is a beautiful fancy that the very birds in the woods that surrounded those old monasteries, from long hearing of the strains of their daily psalmody, copied the rise and fall of the monastic chant and perpetuated in their unconscious song the melodies of the monastic praise. But, though this be fancy, what may we not suppose was the effect on the people who lived round those sanctuaries, what the influence of this daily spectacle of lives wholly devoted to the praise of God? It has been said (by Harnack) that the monks preserved for the world spiritual Christianity: saved the faith from the corrupting influence of secular interests and secular ambitions. But there is no calculus by which we can measure their pervading spiritual influence.

There is one beautiful life which, out of the vast array of Benedictine saints, both famous and unnamed, we may select as an example of the monk's peaceful yet fruitful existence. The Venerable Bede, an English monk of the monastery founded at Jarrow by St. Benet Biscop, left after him in his *Ecclesiastical History of the English People* a work of inestimable value for the early history of England. More than this, by his commentaries on Sacred Scripture he has won for himself the position of a Doctor of the Church. Even during his lifetime his homilies were read in the churches of Western Christendom, and tradition says that it is to this fact that he owes the title of Venerable. This great English monk at the end of his *Ecclesiastical History* speaks thus of himself: 'This have I written, I Bede, the servant of Christ and priest of the monastery of Saints Peter and Paul. I was born in the domain of the same monastery and when seven years old was given by my parents to the most reverend the Abbot Benedict and thereafter to Ceolfrid, to be educated. From that time forth I have spent my whole life in the same monastery, devoting myself to the study of the Scriptures; and with the observance of regular discipline and the daily service of the church, I have ever taken my delight in learning and teaching and writing.' Then, after giving a list of his works, he concludes with this prayer: 'And

I beseech Thee, good Jesu, who of Thy grace hast granted me to drink the sweet fount of Thy knowledge, that of Thy kindness Thou wouldst grant me too to come to Thee, the fountain of all wisdom, and to abide in Thy presence for ever.'

It would be possible to adduce many another famous name, to speak of St. Augustine, the apostle of England, of Pope Hildebrand, of St. Anselm, of Mabillon, and so to represent more fully the fecundity of Benedictinism. But let the instance of St. Bede suffice; for such as we see that his life was, so too must have been the lives of the unnumbered multitudes who throughout long centuries lived and died in the monasteries of Europe. Of most of them we may say that their lives made no display and passed almost unnoticed of men; their names are known only to God.

Such, in briefest summary, is the issue of the work begun at Subiaco and so quietly and characteristically achieved at Monte Cassino. There was never plainer fulfilment of the Gospel promise: 'Seek ye first the Kingdom of God and His justice, and all these things shall be added unto you.' St. Benedict sought God and the perfect service of God: to this every precept of his Rule was directed, in this his life was absorbed; but, because of this single-minded pursuit of the one thing necessary, that life and Rule have been blessed with singular fruitfulness, and Christendom has agreed to recognize in the unassuming abbot of Monte Cassino the quality and the style of Patriarch of the Monks of the West.

APPENDIX

NOTE I

SHORT BIBLIOGRAPHY

THE Notes which follow deal with certain special points and will contain some bibliographical references. To give a complete bibliography of the literature which concerns St. Benedict and Benedictinism would add considerably to the length of this book and seems unnecessary. The reader may be referred to the general repertories, such as Chevalier, to the bibliographical supplement published regularly by the *Revue Bénédictine*, and to the appropriate articles in the encyclopaedias. Special reference must be made to the comprehensive *Histoire de l'Ordre de St. Benoît* of Dom Philibert Schmitz.

A short list of informative books for the English-speaking reader would contain the following volumes:

BUTLER, ABBOT CUTHBERT: *Benedictine Monachism*, 2nd ed., 1924.

CABROL, ABBOT FERNAND: *St. Benedict*, Eng. trans. 1934.

CHAPMAN, ABBOT JOHN: *St. Benedict and the Sixth Century*, 1929.

DELATTE, ABBOT PAUL: *The Rule of St. Benedict*, Eng. trans. 1921; reprinted 1950.

HERWEGEN, ABBOT ILDEFONS: *St. Benedict, a Character Study*, Eng. trans. 1924.

MCCANN, ABBOT JUSTIN: *The Rule of St. Benedict, in Latin and English*, 1952.

THE DIALOGUES OF ST. GREGORY
THE GREAT

THE Dialogues are printed in the general collections of St. Gregory's works, as in Migne, *P.L.*, LXXVII. The latest and best edition is that of Umberto Moricca (Rome, 1924). The second book has frequently been printed separately as the *Life of St. Benedict*. Translations are very numerous. Pope Zachary translated the whole work into Greek in the eighth century and St. Gregory became known in the East as 'Gregory of the Dialogue'. The ninth century saw a translation into Anglo-Saxon by Bishop Werferth of Worcester under the auspices of King Alfred. The best-known English translation is that made by Fr. Philip Woodward and published at Paris in 1608. It was reissued (with modernization) by Fr. H. J. Coleridge, S.J., in the Quarterly Series in 1874. A new (illustrated) edition, edited by Prof. E. G. Gardner, was published by the Medici Society in 1911.

The question of the historical value of the Dialogues has exercised the minds of all modern writers on St. Benedict. The non-Catholic critic is disposed to reject the book *in toto* as containing little more than pious legend. Such is the attitude, for instance, of Dr. Dudden in his *Gregory the Great*, 1905 (Vol. I, pp. 321–56). Moricca's introduction supplies a valuable analysis of the book and a reply to some of Dr. Dudden's criticisms, but he does not rate its historical value much higher. On the Catholic side Abbot Chapman in his *St. Benedict and the Sixth Century* stoutly defends the historicity of the Dialogues. St. Gregory's picture of St. Benedict must be true, St. Benedict must have been the miracle-worker that he depicts him to have been; otherwise the impression which he made on his times is inexplicable. Other Benedictine writers claim for the Dialogues a 'substantial accuracy', with more or less scepticism about details. Abbot Herwegen considers that the stories of the Dialogues are at the very least true to character and as such can be used for a character study if not for a life. But even this moderate claim has been severely criticized. However, it may be said that the general tendency among Benedictine scholars is to maintain that St. Gregory has given a picture of the outlines and general course of St. Benedict's life which should be accepted as substantially true. We may be allowed to add to what we have said in the Introduction the following more particular account of the Dialogues.

The book was written in the winter of 593–4, in the fourth year of Pope Gregory's pontificate. The full title is: 'The four books of the Dialogues of St. Gregory the Pope, concerning the life and miracles of Italian Fathers and concerning the eternity of souls.' St. Gregory tells us that he wrote it at the request of 'brethren who live familiarly with me', and the same letter (III, 50) is an appeal for material, which he collected from very various informants. The East had produced several striking books on the lives and deeds of the saints of Egypt and Syria, by Palladius and others; Sulpicius Severus had told the story of St. Martin of Gaul; the book of the Dialogues was to do for Italy what those books had done for their respective regions.

The work is cast in the form of a dialogue—the same form had been used by Palladius and Sulpicius Severus—between the author and a certain ingenuous Peter, who is eager to hear all that Gregory can tell him about the doings of the holy men of Italy. Peter criticizes and raises objections, so that Gregory is given the opportunity of discussing theological points arising out of the narratives. Of the four books of the Dialogues only one concerns us here, viz., the second, which is devoted entirely to St. Benedict. This is a summary of its contents:

> PROLOGUE. Benedict born at Nursia. Sent to Rome, he flees from the world.
> 1 Enfide. The broken sieve. Subiaco. Romanus.

II The temptation of the flesh.

III Vicovaro; the poisoned cup. Twelve monasteries built.

IV The monk who could not stay at prayer.

V The miraculous spring.

VI The iron floats on the lake.

VII Maurus walks on the water.

VIII The poisoned loaf. An attack on his disciples. Departure for Monte Cassino. He purges the sanctuary.

IX A huge stone raised by prayer.

X The fantastic fire in the kitchen.

XI Healing of the monk crushed by a wall.

XII Benedict sees the doings of monks on a journey;

XIII and what Valentinian's brother did on his way to him.

XIV The trick of King Totila.

XV The prophecy of Totila's fate and of the fate of Rome.

XVI Of a cleric possessed by the devil.

XVII Benedict foresees the destruction of his monastery.

XVIII A detected theft.

XIX Of the monk who concealed a present.

XX Benedict reads the thoughts of a proud monk.

XXI Of the miraculous supply of meal.

XXII Benedict designs a monastery by a dream.

XXIII Of the contumelious nuns and their punishment.

XXIV Of the boy monk who could not be buried.

XXV Of the fugitive monk and the dragon.

XXVI The healing of a boy.

XXVII The miracle of the solidi. A strange disease cured.

XXVIII The miracle of the oil flask.

XXIX The miraculous supply of oil.

XXX A possessed monk delivered.

XXXI The countryman and the Goth.

XXXII The raising to life of a dead child.

XXXIII The miracle of his sister Scholastica.

XXXIV Benedict sees her soul going to heaven in the form of a dove.

XXXV He sees the whole world in a ray of light and the soul of Bishop Germanus being carried to heaven.

XXXVI That Benedict wrote a Rule.

XXXVII He prophesies his death. The manner of it.

XXXVIII A mad woman is cured in his cave.

The third book gives the story of Martin the hermit and Benedict's message to him; the fourth tells of the two learned brethren, Speciosus and Gregory.

In the prologue to the first book St. Gregory announces his intention of giving his authorities: 'To remove from my readers all occasion of doubt, I set forth in each case the authorities from whom I learnt what I report.' In accordance with this promise the second book contains the following indications of his sources and method. 'I have not learnt all his deeds, but the few that I narrate I have got from the report of four of his disciples, viz., from Constantine, a most venerable man, who succeeded him in the rule of his monastery; from Valentinian, who was for many years superior of the Lateran monastery; from Simplicius, who governed his community second after him; and from Honoratus, who is now still superior of that monastery in which he had previously lived.' (*Prologue*.) 'The brother of Valentinian, the monk I mentioned before, was a layman but a pious one'; from which we may infer that Valentinian is the authority for the narrative which follows (*Chap.* 13). After reporting the saint's prophecy of the destruction of Rome, he says: 'Although his disciple Honoratus, by whose report this is known to me, does not say that he heard it from his own lips, but testifies that the brethren told him that he (Benedict) said this' (*Chap.* 15). 'Nor do I think this should be passed over, which I learnt from the account of the noble Antonius' (*Chap.* 26). 'Nor may I omit the story that his disciple Peregrinus used to tell . . . But to return to the matters that I learnt from the report of his disciples mentioned in the exordium of this book' (*Chap.* 27). 'I should like, Peter, to narrate yet many things concerning this venerable father; but I purposely pass over some of his deeds, because I hasten to the exposition of the deeds of other men' (*Chap.* 36). 'And now we must cease a while from talk, in order that, as we are going to narrate the miracles of others, we may meanwhile by silence repair our powers of speech' (*Chap.* 38).

It will be seen from this that the account of St. Benedict rests mainly on the evidence of four of his disciples, and this fact is very much in its favour. Two questions have been raised about this testimony: (1) It has been suggested that St.

Gregory did not get his information directly from the informants he mentions, but at second-hand. In support of this it is pointed out that he says 'referentibus', not 'mihi referentibus'; and several of the informants were dead when St. Gregory was writing the Dialogues. (2) It is questioned whether his informants, supposing them to have been such in the fullest sense, were themselves eye-witnesses of the events to which they testified. These questions do not now admit of a definite answer, but we may attempt a partial one by seeking to determine the probable relation of St. Gregory's authorities to the events which they reported. St. Benedict died about the year 547; his monastery was destroyed about 581, the monks escaping to Rome where they took up their abode near the Lateran basilica. During this period there were four abbots. The first, Constantine, is said to have died in the year 560; he was succeeded by Simplicius, to whom we may perhaps give a ten years' rule (560–70). Valentinian had been abbot of the Lateran monastery for 'many years' and was dead when St. Gregory was writing; let us suppose that he ruled from 581 to 590. Honoratus alone of the four was alive in 593, being then abbot at Subiaco. All these dates are necessarily more or less conjectural, but they show the probable relation of the abbots to St. Benedict. They could quite well have known him, if only in his old age. But did they witness those deeds of his to which they testify? This question is hard to answer. In one case, the Subiaco narratives, there is difficulty in supposing so. For these we may suppose that Honoratus was the chief witness and that he sent his material to St. Gregory in or about the year 593. But it was then about a century since St. Benedict left Enfide for Subiaco (by the common reckoning), and we may not suppose that Honoratus witnessed any of these early events. It must be concluded that he reported the tradition that was current at Subiaco in his time. And perhaps a similar inference is permissible with respect also to other parts of the work. On the whole it would be safer to say that the Dialogues present us with the tradition about St. Benedict which was believed at Monte Cassino, at Subiaco, and finally in the Lateran monastery, in the period closely following his death, rather than that they contain what may be safely regarded as direct ocular testimony. As to St. Gregory's relation to this tradition it may be pointed out that he was born about the year 540, i.e., a few years before the probable date of St. Benedict's death. He would be twenty when Constantine died, and in his forties when the fugitive Benedictines came to Rome. He had himself become a monk in the monastery of St. Andrew in Rome, into which it appears certain that the Rule of St. Benedict was afterwards introduced, perhaps when St. Gregory was elected abbot (586). There is no questioning his acquaintance with the Rule and admiration for it when he was Pope (590–604). And as Pope, if not before, he would be in close relation with the Benedictines of the Lateran monastery. So that, when he wrote the book which had an immense influence in the propagation of the Rule, we may say that he was intimately acquainted with the institute of St. Benedict. We are justified, therefore, in claiming for the account of the Dialogues a substantial accuracy.

But there remains the question as to the particular value of some of the narratives contained in the book. The critics who reject the miraculous as of itself incredible make short work of the Dialogues, for the book is almost professedly concerned with miracle. But, while refraining from this summary procedure, one may yet hold that it is hard to require belief in all that is recounted in the book. In brief these reasons may be mentioned: (1) The age of St. Gregory was an uncritical one. Both he himself and his informants seem to have accepted stories on what we should regard as insufficient evidence. (2) Moreover, there was a strong disposition to believe even the most extraordinary things of holy men. The literature of sanctity which was then current and very popular exercised an immense influence upon general belief. (3) There is a sameness in the records which suggests that some stories were treated as commonplaces which might be attached to any man who was conspicuous for sanctity. We find in the second book of the Dialogues that certain of the narratives have prototypes in Sacred Scripture and previous hagiography.

It seems, therefore, that it must be allowed that there is a legendary element in the Dialogues. But how determine the extent of it? There is no sure criterion. In default of any independent source by which to test the book, we are thrown back on general principles and subjective considerations, and these may be very misleading. The only course would seem to be, while insisting on the general accuracy of the picture of the saint which is given in the book, to suspend judgment as to circumstantial detail. There is a considerable substratum of historical fact; for the rest we cannot be entirely certain.

St. Gregory, it will be noticed, says that he has not learnt 'all the deeds' of St. Benedict, and again that he does not report all that he has ascertained. An examination of the summary already given will show that the biographer does not concern himself with the ordinary routine of the saint's life so much as with the extraordinary events by which it was distinguished. Actual biographical material of the common kind occupies relatively a very small place in the record, and there is a notable absence of chronology, so that only one of the events narrated (the visit of King Totila) may be dated with any certainty. These characteristics, which make the book a difficult one for the historian, are yet quite consistent with St. Gregory's purpose. For he was not writing an historical biography—it is somewhat misleading to allude to the book as his 'Life of St. Benedict'—but rather a series of scenes from the saint's life, which should illustrate especially the supernatural power of the Catholic faith. The whole work may be described as Catholic apologetic. St. Gregory himself sent a copy to Theudelinda, the Catholic queen of the Arian Lombards. And it is probable that its attractive and deeply spiritual pages had a great influence in the conversion of those heretical or pagan barbarians to the Church.[1]

[1] There is a convenient modern edition of the second book of the *Dialogues*, translated by the present writer, which is published at Stanbrook Abbey, Worcester.

MARK THE POET

PAUL the Deacon, in his *History of the Lombards* (1. 26), reports the testimony of a certain poet Mark for some few details not mentioned by St. Gregory. 'All these things', he says, 'I have taken from the poem of the poet Mark, who coming hither to the same Father composed some verses in his praise.' The poem is one of sixty-six lines of what is on the whole graceful and correct verse. There are reminiscences of Virgil, Avienus and Sedulius; a non-classical tendency to rhyme is noticeable in a few of the lines. The additional information about St. Benedict is not of much importance. Mark says nothing about the saint's early life and very little about Subiaco. He is interested in the migration to Monte Cassino, concerning which he reports (1) that Benedict was divinely called to Casinum, (2) that all Subiaco mourned his departure, (3) that he was accompanied by three ravens, (4) that two youths appeared to guide him at cross-roads, (5) that another monk then living on the mountain was bidden make way for him. At Monte Cassino he tells of the abolition of the pagan worship of Jupiter (St. Gregory says Apollo) and has much to say of the transformation of the mountain under St. Benedict's rule. He alludes also to the saint's retiring from men into strict retreat in preparation for the feast of Easter. None of these items occurs in the Dialogues, and St. Gregory's account of the saint's departure from Subiaco 'taking a few monks with him' is perhaps in conflict with Mark's story of the same departure.

Who was Mark and when was his poem written? It is com-

monly supposed that he was a monk of Monte Cassino not
very long after the death of St. Benedict and practically a contemporary of St. Gregory's. Traube accepts this view and
would put him at Monte Cassino under the third abbot,
Simplicius, that is to say about 560. Very different and even
revolutionary is the view of Abbot Chapman. According to him
Mark was not a monk of Monte Cassino, but only a pilgrim-
visitor to the sanctuary of St. Benedict. And he would date his
visit in the eighth century, some time after the restoration by
Petronax (c. 720) and before the time when Paul was writing
his history (c. 790). It is a very considerable difference of dating, some two centuries. But we very much doubt if the chief
argument, St. Gregory's silence about Mark, will bear all the
weight that is put upon it. Mark's apparent ignorance of the
Dialogues may fairly be used, in exactly the same way, to
prove the opposite conclusion, viz., that he wrote before St.
Gregory. And, as for the opinion that Mark was not a monk
of Monte Cassino, it would seem to be in conflict with the
words of the poem itself. However, in default of more precise
evidence, the question of date does not appear to be capable
of exact determination. Here is an English rendering of Mark's
poem:

BENEDICT

When the blind folk their impious idols sought,
Holding them Gods whom human hands had wrought,
With deadly altars here they raised their fane,
Where bloody victims to foul Jove were slain.
Then Holy Benet came, called from far cell,   5
And purged this ground of all the filth of hell:
The idols smashed, the carven gods o'erthrew,
To living God the temple raised anew.
O ye, who long to see the saints' abode,
Hasten with faith undaunted by the road.   10
By hardship is the highest ever won,
The blessed life in narrow way is run.
Hither came I with load of sins oppressed:
My load is gone, my heart is now at rest.
Henceforth I trust the life of heaven is won,   15

Dost thou but pray, O Benet, for thy son.
Folly of old called this its Citadel,
Devoted it to marble gods of hell;
For here the blind and errant rustic strove
To pay his vows to soul-destroying Jove.   20
But had one truly marked its evil fame,
Foul Tartarus had justly been its name.
Yet 'Citadel' foretold the cloister's tower,
Designed the sacred castle and its power,
Whereby eternal hell is overthrown,   25
And tower of death life's tower henceforth is known.
Here is the gate of starry heaven stormed
By blessed throng in choir angelic formed.
Here prayest, Benet, to a Thunderer higher,
Mount-dweller, hermit leader of the choir.   30
When thou wert called from other mount one day,
Christ was thy Guide, and through the waste thy Way;
For ever, where the roads apart did lead,
Two youths appeared to guide thee in thy need.
And to the saint that once had lived hereby   35
Was said: 'Give place, another friend is nigh.'
Lo, at thy going fell a darksome cloud,
And pallid mist the mountain did enshroud,
And all its caves did mourn and weep amain,
And every beast in mouldering den complain.   40
Thee with true grief the lucent waters mourned,
For thee the woods their leafy vesture scorned.
Yea, that I speak the truth this sign will show:
Three ravens came lest thou shouldst lonely go.
Here too the people sought thee, thou didst say,   45
When thou wouldst wait apart for Easter Day,
Like orphans loud lamenting at thy door,
With tears, that thou wouldst live with them no more.
Lo! at thy coming, rock, lo! thornbush goes,
The arid earth a wondrous fountain shows.   50
Christ's mount art thou, thus to command the rest:
Beneath thy feet Cassino lowered its crest.
To let thee find a dwelling on its crown,
It bows its head and smooths its roughness down;
Lest men should tire who seek thy high abode,   55

Winds round its sides a gently-sloping road.
Yet justly does the mountain honour thee,
For thou hast made it rich and fair to see.
Its barren sides by thee are gardens made,
Its naked rocks with fruitful vineyards laid,   60
The crags admire a crop and fruit not theirs,
The wild wood now a bounteous harvest bears.
E'en so our barren deeds to fruit thou trainest,
Upon our arid hearts pure waters rainest.
Turn now to fruit the evil thorns, I pray,   65
That vex the stupid breast of Mark alway.

The Latin text may be found in Migne, *P.L.*, LXXX, 183 sqq.;
in the *Acta Sanctorum O.S.B.* (1668), Vol. I, pp. 28, 29; in
Abbot Tosti's *St. Benedict*, Eng. Tr., pp. 237–8; and in the
Enchiridion Benedictinum, pp. 231–43. Commentary is given
by Traube: *Anzeiger für deutsches Altertum*, XVIII (1892), pp.
211 ff., and *Textgeschichte der Regula S. Benedicti* (2nd ed.
1910), p. 95; by Manitius: *Geschichte der christlich-lateinis-
chen Poesie* (1891), pp. 388, 389, and *Geschichte der lateinischen Literatur des Mittelalters* (1911), I, pp. 91, 92; and by
Chapman, *St. Benedict and the Sixth Century* (1929), pp.
173–5.

NOTE IV

PAUL THE DEACON

PAUL the Deacon, also called Paul Warnefrid, was born at Friuli in Northern Italy about the year 725 of Lombard parents. He was educated at the court of King Ratchis at Pavia and when that king laid aside his crown to become a monk at Monte Cassino (A.D. 749) Paul probably served his successor, Desiderius. In the year 774 the quarrel between Desiderius and Charlemagne ended in the destruction of the Lombard kingdom and the exile of its king. But it seems that Paul had withdrawn from court life before this disastrous blow to his people, and was at that time a monk at Civate in the diocese of Milan. From Civate he moved, some time after 779, probably for political reasons, to Monte Cassino. In the year 782 we find him making supplication to Charlemagne on behalf of his brother Arichis, who for his share in a revolt at Friuli against Frankish authority had lost all his property and had been taken away into France (776). He followed up this petition by going in person to Charlemagne. There is extant a letter written by him from France (783) to the Abbot of Monte Cassino (Theodemar) in which he expresses his affection for his abbot and brethren and bitterly laments his separation from them and the peace of his monastery. It appears that Charlemagne was unwilling to part with such a man as Paul, whose services he required for the educational revival which he was promoting. So Paul stayed four years, serving the emperor and enjoying a close intimacy with him. During this period he travelled through the kingdom and probably visited the chief

Benedictine monasteries, among them Fleury. In the year 786-7 he was allowed to return to Monte Cassino where he continued his literary and educational work. Here he wrote the first commentary on the Rule of St. Benedict and an account of the saint which is for the most part a versification of the Dialogues. He was the writer of the letter which accompanied the important copy of the Rule which Theodemar sent to Charlemagne. His last years were spent on his greatest work, the *Historia Langobardorum*, which he did not live to complete, dying about the year 799.

In his writings Paul frequently expresses his devotion to St. Benedict, and he inserted his account of the saint, with little alteration, into his History of the Lombards. But he gives nothing that is not in Mark and Gregory, to whom he refers his readers. It is noteworthy that he puts most of what he has to say into two metrical versions of the Dialogues. This is his preface to the verses:

'In these days also the most blessed father Benedict, first in the place which is called Sublacus, forty miles from Rome, and then on the hill of Casinum, which is called the Citadel, shone with the merits of a great life and with apostolic power. His life, as is known, has been written in graceful prose by the blessed pope Gregory in his Dialogues. And I too, so far as my poor wit would allow, have written in honour of that great father, embodying each of his miracles in a couplet of an elegiac poem as follows.'

After this poem Paul adds a hymn in iambic dimeters. With the exception of a line in the first, which alludes to the restoration of Monte Cassino with the generous help of the descendants of those Lombards who had sacked it, the two poems do not go beyond the data of the Dialogues. In conclusion, Paul speaks thus:

'I may report briefly what blessed Pope Gregory has not recorded in his life of this most holy father. While he was travelling, by divine command, from Sublacus to this place where he now rests, a distance of about fifty miles, three ravens, which he had been wont to feed, followed circling round him. And at every cross-road, until he reached this place, two angels appeared in the shape of young men and showed him which way he should take. Moreover, in this place there then dwelt a certain servant of God, to whom there came the divine command: "Do thou give place, another friend is nigh." Now when he came here, that is to the citadel of Casinum, he kept himself always in great abstinence. But especially in the time of Lent did he abide enclosed and separated from the turmoil of the world. All this I have taken from the poem of the poet Mark, who coming hither to the same father composed some verses in his praise, which for fear of being prolix I have not written down in this book. However, it is certain that this glorious father was divinely summoned and came to this fertile spot overlooking a rich plain for this reason, that there might be here a community of many monks, as now by God's help there is. Having thus briefly narrated a matter that was not to be omitted, I will resume the course of my history' (*Hist. Langobardorum*, I, 26).

In the fourth book of his History (Chap. 17) Paul records the sack of Monte Cassino by the Lombards (about A.D. 581) and gives some important details.

'About this time the monastery of St. Benedict, which is situated on the hill of Casinum, was attacked in the night by the Lombards. They plundered everything, but were unable to take so much as one of the monks, in order that the prophecy of the venerable father Benedict, which he foresaw long before, might be fulfilled; in which he said: "I have scarce been able to obtain from God that the lives of my monks should be granted to me." Moreover, the monks, fleeing from the same place, made for Rome, taking with them the book of the holy Rule which the aforesaid father had written, some other books, the weight for bread and the measure for wine, and what furniture they could get away. Now, after St. Benedict this community was ruled by Constantine, after him by Simplicius, after him by Vitalis, and finally by Bonitus, under whom this destruction took place' (IV. 17).

In the sixth book (Chap. 2) occurs the famous reference to the translation of St. Benedict's body to France (Fleury) at the end of the seventh century. This has been given in Chapter XIV.

In the same book (Chap. 40) Paul records the restoration of Monte Cassino under Petronax of Brescia (about A.D. 720) in the pontificate of Gregory II. The next Pope but one,

Zachary, who translated the Dialogues into Greek, was a considerable benefactor of Monte Cassino; for, as Paul tells us, he gave Petronax 'many helps, namely books of Holy Scripture and other things useful for a monastery, and moreover of his fatherly love granted him the rule which the blessed father Benedict wrote with his own holy hands (regulam quam beatus pater Benedictus suis sanctis manibus conscripsit).'

This then is the evidence of Paul the Deacon. It is given in full because Paul is a trustworthy writer and his record has great value; but it will be clear that he does not add to our knowledge of the facts of St. Benedict's life.

MON. GER. HIST., *Scriptores Rerum Langobardicarum* (1878), pp. 1–187.

MIGNE, *P.L.*, XCV, 419–672.

TRAUBE, *Textgeschichte der Regula* (1910), pp. 105–7.

MANITIUS, *Geschichte der lateinischen Literatur des Mittelalters* (1911), I, pp. 257 ff.

NEFF, K., *Die Gedichte des Paulus Diaconus* (1908).

ALONGSIDE the consistent fidelity of tradition to the history sketched by St. Gregory the Great there appear, chiefly in the ninth and twelfth centuries, certain records of doubtful origin which add to the data of the Dialogues. One of these is the *Vita Mauri* of which an account shall now be given.

St. Gregory's account of St. Maurus may be found in his narrative of St. Benedict's life at Subiaco (Dialogues, II, 3–8). We learn from him that Maurus was the son of a Roman named Evitius (or Equitius) who brought him to St. Benedict. St. Gregory tells us that he became the saint's assistant (adjutor) and gives three narratives in which he figures. It seems clear from the Dialogues that he did not accompany St. Benedict to Monte Cassino, but was left behind at Subiaco. He passes out of St. Gregory's narrative at that point and we learn nothing as to the time or manner of his death. Such is the information of the year 594.[1]

But two centuries and a half later, about the year 860, this meagre account of St. Maurus was replaced by an elaborate history from the pen of Odo of Glanfeuil. It is not impossible that his abbey had had an abbot of the name of Maurus; but Odo is responsible for the identification of this Maurus with

[1] Dom Lambot has argued very plausibly from St. Gregory's narrative and the faint indications which it contains that Maurus was left by St. Benedict in charge of Subiaco as his successor. *Revue Liturgique et Monastique*, 1931, pp. 101–4.

St. Benedict's disciple and for the whole history of the travels of St. Maurus of which St. Gregory knows nothing.

Odo was abbot of the monastery of Glanfeuil (St.-Maur-sur-Loire), about half-way between Tours and Nantes, in the year 860; this being, as he says, the monastery 'which blessed Maurus built and which he ennobled, not only with his life and virtues, but also with his grave'. A friend asked him for an account of the miracles of St. Maurus, which he wrote, sending at the same time a life of the saint which purports to have been written by one Faustus, a contemporary and companion of Maurus in his mission to France. This is the famous *Vita Mauri*. The story of its origin, as told by Odo, is as follows:

'Northmen came up the Loire and drove him and his monks from Glanfeuil. Taking with them the body of St. Maurus they fled into Burgundy, and there they fell in with some pilgrims returning from Rome. From one of these, by name Peter, Odo bought at a considerable price a small manuscript (quaterniunculos antiquaria conscriptos manu ac nimia paene vetustate consumptos) which contained a life of St. Benedict and lives of five of his disciples (Honoratus, Simplicius, Theodore, Valentinian, Maurus). Odo spent twenty days on the Acts of St. Maurus and then published his corrected version "salva fide dictorum et miraculorum inibi repertorum". At the end of his prefatory letter he says: "Haec omnia . . . utilia legentibus fore, nostrisque potissimum arbitratus sum. Quos per eam quae est in Jesu deprecor veritatem ut veris et absque fuco a me prolatis fidem adhibentes religiosioris vitae studiis sollicite operam dare non negligant; quatenus fructum laborum suorum in die retributionis a pio Domino recipientes perennis vitae praemiis cum eo, cujus et audiunt et legunt virtutes, participari mereantur."'

The narrator of the life is Faustus who, when a boy of seven, was entrusted to St. Benedict at Monte Cassino. He tells us that he became a loving disciple and imitator of the saint, who made trial of his virtue and found him strong. Now when St. Benedict was disconsolate for the future destruction of his monastery (as told in the Dialogues) he received some divine consolation which St. Gregory does not mention. He was told that his institute would survive this disaster and spread through the West. Presently there came an embassy from the bishop of Le Mans begging him to send some of his monks to Gaul. St. Benedict consented and chose five: Maurus, Simplicius, Antonius, Constantinianus, and Faustus. Of these five Faustus and Simplicius returned in old age to Monte Cassino. Faustus was prevailed upon to write the history of their mission, especially by Theodore, abbot of the Lateran monastery, and his work was approved by Pope Boniface the Third (607). He asks indulgence for his style and then proceeds to his narrative, beginning with the early life of Maurus.

Maurus was of senatorial birth, his father being Eutychius and his mother Julia. When he was twelve years old he was entrusted to St. Benedict and soon became a model monk, conspicuous for his austere life, so that the abbot used to hold him up as an example to the rest. After reproducing the narratives of the Dialogues which concern St. Maurus, Faustus enlarges on the intimacy of Benedict and Maurus. Then he tells of the arrival of the embassy from Le Mans, of its success and of the sweet sorrow of the consequent parting. St. Benedict comforted the emigrants in an affectionate address and gave Maurus a copy of the Rule and the measure for the bread and wine. They spent the first night of their journey at a farm belonging to the monastery, and here they had their final communication from St. Benedict, a messenger bringing a box of relics and a letter in which the saint prophesied his death. On their way Maurus worked miracles at Vercelli and Agaunum. They had left Monte Cassino about the feast of the Epiphany, and they spent Easter with Romanus (the monk who had assisted St. Benedict at Subiaco) near Auxerre. Having arrived there on Good Friday, Maurus held converse with Romanus, in the course of which he told him that St. Benedict was to die on the next day. So they spent the night in vigil and prayer. The next morning, at the third hour, Maurus was praying in the church when he saw the vision of the saint's triumphant death as it is recorded in the Dialogues. They kept Holy Saturday and Easter Sunday in great joy, and on the Monday the travellers said good-bye to Romanus.

When they reached Orleans they learnt that the bishop who had invited them to Le Mans was dead, and found that his successor was not disposed to carry out the project. They were at a loss what to do when they found a zealous and powerful patron in one Florus. He gained them the favour of Theodebert, king of the Franks, and made them a grant of land at Glannafolium. Maurus at once began to build and in eight years had completed a monastery with four churches (dedicated to SS. Peter, Martin, Severinus, Michael). During its building Maurus worked several miracles. Florus himself became a monk there and the king and his nobles assisted at the clothing (Theodebert was dead at the reputed date of this event). Faustus then tells of the munificent gifts of Theodebald and Clothair. In the twenty-sixth year of the foundation the monks of Glanfeuil numbered 140, and this number was fixed by Maurus as the proper one for his monastery. In the thirty-eighth year Maurus, feeling his end approaching, made himself a hermitage near the church of St. Martin, and Bertulf took his place as abbot. Two and a half years after this, as was foretold to Maurus in his hermitage, a great pestilence attacked Glanfeuil and 116 monks died in five months. Then Maurus himself fell ill. In the forty-first year after his arrival there, on the fifteenth of January, he died before the altar in the church of St. Martin and was buried there. Faustus and Simplicius, the survivors of the original band, then prepared to return to Monte Cassino (as Maurus had bidden them), but were prevailed upon by Abbot Bertulf to remain until his death, which took place two years afterwards. 'Then', writes Faustus, 'we returned to you, O most holy fathers, and obeying your command wrote the life and miracles of blessed Maurus.' His life is summarized thus: When he was twelve years old he became an oblate at Subiaco. He was thirty-two when St. Benedict sent him to Gaul. He lived at Glanfeuil forty years and fourteen days.

Such is the *Vita Mauri*. It contains many errors of chronology, which could not have been made by a contemporary such as Faustus represents himself to be. These have usually been attributed to the editing of Odo and the rest of the document defended as a genuine record. Such, for instance, is the attitude of Ruinart in his *Apologie de la mission de St. Maur* (Paris, 1692). But the view which now obtains is that the whole is a ninth-century forgery, that is to say of no earlier date than Odo's preface and that Odo himself is the author. Apart from the very serious errors in chronology which occur throughout, it is hard to explain the complete silence of St. Gregory who gives no hint of this remarkable history. Nor is it mentioned by Gregory of Tours, though he was a contemporary of the supposed events, near at hand and especially interested in monastic matters. It is ignored likewise by the early Carolingian authors, although they show devotion to the memory of St. Maurus. It is apparently quite unknown to Paul the Deacon at the end of the eighth century, at the very fountain-head of Benedictinism. That great Benedictine, Rabanus Maurus (*d.* 856), was educated at Tours under Alcuin and took his second name out of veneration for St. Benedict's disciple, in whose honour he wrote some verses; but he, too, knows nothing of the history. Nor does the martyrologist, Ado, although he made every effort to make his work complete. (It was published in 858.) The first trace of the story occurs in the martyrology of Usuard (finished in 868) who gives the notice: *In territorio Andecavensi Sancti Mauri abbatis*. But Usuard was a contemporary of Odo and the *Vita Mauri* was now published.

Furthermore, Giry has shown that the author of the *Vita Mauri* based his work closely on a life of St. Severinus of Agaunum, from whom he borrowed Faustus, many phrases and incidents, and the general lay-out of his narrative. But the *Vita Severini*, as its preface tells us, was published at the request of Bishop Magnus of Sens (801–18) and dates therefore from the beginning of the ninth century. Nor is the *Vita Severini* itself an authentic story. It is based in its turn on the writings of Ennodius of Pavia (474–521), from which its author took Faustus and most of the other characters of his history.

There would seem, therefore, to be no course but to regard the *Vita Mauri* as a ninth-century forgery, and to conclude that we have no certain information concerning St. Maurus beyond what is given by St. Gregory in his Dialogues.

The relics of St. Maurus, located by the *Vita* at Glanfeuil, were, as Odo relates, removed from there under stress of the invasion of the Northmen. In the year 868 they were brought to the 'coenobium Fossatense', a monastery on the Marne near Paris which became known as St.-Maur-des-Fossés. Odo was present at the translation and writes its history. The translation was not accomplished without difficulty, and Odo records the many miracles which were wrought through the intercession of the saint. He ends the whole work with these words: 'At nos optato tandem fine narrationis gaudentes, Christi misericordiam per beati Mauri imploramus suffragia, ut qui incultiori licet stylo, fide tamen integra, seriem hujus historiae prosecuti sumus, vinculis peccatorum solvi ab eodem mereamur Redemptore aeternorumque gaudiis perfrui valeamus praemiorum, juncti in caelestibus consortiis angelorum. Amen.'

The relics of St. Maurus were translated in the year 1750 from St.-Maur-des-Fossés (the monastery had become extinct in 1553) to the abbey of St. Germain-des-Prés. In the year 1793 the revolutionaries broke into the church, destroyed the reliquary and scattered the relics. They were collected and taken to the curé; but his sister, in dread of the revolutionary authorities, destroyed them by fire. Minor relics, obtained from the original shrine, are still extant.

ACTA SANCTORUM, January 15th.

ACTA SANCTORUM O.S.B., I (1668), pp. 274–98; VI (1680), pp. 165–84.

MALNORY, A., *Quid Luxovienses monachi . . . ad regulam monasteriorum . . . contulerint* (Paris, 1894), pp. 21–6.

GIRY, A., *Moyen Age*, IX (1896), pp. 62–4; *Bibliothèque de l'école des chartes*, LVII (1896), pp. 149–52.

SAINT PLACID

INVENTION has been busy also with the life of that other disciple of St. Benedict's, St. Placid. The original source is again the early part of the second book of St. Gregory's Dialogues. From St. Gregory we learn that Placid was the son of the patrician Tertullus and that he was taken to St. Benedict at Subiaco while yet a boy. He appears in two narratives belonging to the Subiaco period of St. Benedict's life, the first telling of his presence when St. Benedict prayed for the miraculous spring, the second of his rescue from drowning. And that is all. There is no hint from St. Gregory as to any later history, nor indeed from any other source until after more than five centuries.

The earliest liturgical mention of St. Placid is in litanies of Italian provenance which perhaps go back to the tenth century, and in these he appears among the Confessors. Strangely enough this evidence does not come from Monte Cassino, and in the four most ancient calendars of that abbey (8th and 9th centuries) there is no mention of St. Placid. In the Cassinese breviary of about the year 1100 the litany has SS. Benedict, Maurus, Placid, Paul, Antony, Romanus, above the general invocation 'Omnes sancti monachi et eremitae'. In general the conclusion is plain that until the twelfth century the cult of St. Placid, such as it was, was confined to Italy and that he was venerated as a Confessor.

But with the end of the eleventh century there came a change. The first indication of a development is in the record

of Leo of Ostia in the *Chronicles of Monte Cassino* (1, 1): 'It is
believed that the man of God, Benedict, then also sent blessed
Placid to Sicily, where the patrician Tertullus, father of the
same Placid, had granted the man of God eighteen farms of
his patrimony.' But Leo says nothing of a martyrdom. At
about the same time (the end of the eleventh or the beginning of the twelfth century) October 5th was marked as his
feast day.

Now the ancient martyrologies have on October 5th some
such entry as the following: 'In Sicilia Placidi, Eutici et
aliorum triginta. Et alibi Barici, Victorini, Fausti, Pelagi. In
Gallia, civitate Valentia, Apollinaris episcopi. In Gallia, civitate
Antissiodorensi, Firmati diaconi et Flavianae virginis Deo
sacratae.' The later names of this record, which may be dated
with some certainty, do not come down beyond the beginning
of the sixth century, and those first in order are earlier in
time. Liturgists believe that St. Placid, the Sicilian martyr, was
universally admitted into the martyrologies before the time of
St. Benedict. But the opinion reported by Leo of Ostia con-
necting St. Benedict's disciple with Sicily combined with the
record of the martyrology to win for St. Placid of Subiaco this
date in the calendar, and finally the status of martyr. The
chief agent in promoting the identification of the Benedictine
saint with the ancient martyr was Peter the Deacon. He took
the small seed, so tentatively dropped by Leo, added the data
of the martyrology and from this exiguous substance produced a complete Life and Passion of St. Placid and his Companions. (It is to be noted that he picks the names of his
characters from the martyrology without reference to the fact
that some of these are specifically attached to places very far
from Sicily.)

Peter the Deacon was archivist and chronicler of Monte
Cassino in the twelfth century and died about the year 1160.
Peter tells us that he was sprung from the noble family of the
Counts of Tusculum, but this must be regarded as doubtful.
He became an oblate at Monte Cassino in the early years of
the twelfth century (*c.* 1115) when he was five years old. He
was a man, it appears, with much vanity, a very lively imagination and a zest for writing, but lacking in patience and
judgment. As a consequence he composed a large amount of

very questionable history. For some centuries his work was accepted without criticism; but since Abbot Angelo della Noce (seventeenth century) Peter has met with severe treatment from his editors. The most charitable judgment has already been given, and perhaps it is reasonable not to adopt a severe standpoint in dealing with his work. Indeed, if it were not for the influence which it has exercised on subsequent writers, it would be better to ignore it altogether. For Peter had no severe view of historical method; he is an historical novelist rather than an historian; he considered himself at liberty to treat facts much as he pleased, and he had a flair for the manufacture of documents to support his narrative. It is estimated that in the course of his various works Peter cites forty-three spurious instruments, some being absolute forgeries, others genuine documents falsified, viz., ten imperial decrees, twenty-five papal pronouncements, and eight deeds of less important persons. The general purpose of all Peter's writings was to exalt his monastery, and in furthering this end he would appear to have been entirely unscrupulous. So he devoted special attention to the history of St. Placid, returning to it at different times until he had constructed a complete and interesting legend.

His first biography of St. Placid is in the book *De ortu et vita justorum coenobii Casinensis,* written about the year 1133 when he was twenty-three. This is a brief account—still extant in his own hand, as are the others—on the lines of the *Vita Mauri.* The Dialogues are used; the 'opinio' reported by Leo as to the Sicilian mission is put down as definite fact. But he has very little miracle to report and for this he apologizes: 'De signis porro ejus superfluum est quaerere; non enim signa sanctos viros faciunt, sed vita potius Deo placens et recta sanctificat hominem.' This biography as we now have it contains a reference to Gordian (the next biography) and an account of St. Placid's martyrdom; but both passages are written in Peter's hand over erasures. It is probable that Peter interpolated his own manuscript after he had composed the second life.

For, apparently, this first life did not satisfy its author and he set about the composition of another, which for fullness and interest might compare more favourably with the *Vita*

Mauri. So he took up the work again and chose the method of his model, finding for it a contemporary author 'Gordian', who is thus the counterpart of 'Faustus'. And in this second attempt he copied more closely the system and even the language of the *Vita Mauri*. To it he added a continuation, or appendix, bringing the history down to his own century and narrating the fortunes of the manuscript of Gordian's life. And finally he composed a third life which he attributed to an unknown 'Stephanus Aniciensis'. This is substantially identical with 'Gordian' and purports also to be a translation of the Greek original.

Besides the Pseudo-Gordian with its appendix and the life by 'Stephanus Aniciensis', Peter's 'Register of St. Placid' contains a remarkable series of spurious documents which were intended to support the history. Among these are the donation of Tertullus (an amazing document containing many historical blunders), two letters of Gordian, the one to Pope Vigilius, the other to Maurus ('Prior' of Monte Cassino), a letter of the Emperor Justinian to Pope Vigilius and the Pope's reply.

Neglecting this subsidiary matter and the life of 'Stephanus' we may review the work of Pseudo-Gordianus. The story of the provenance of this account is thus given in the appendix which has already been mentioned:

In the year 1115, when Peter was five years old, the Greek text was brought to Italy by one Simeon, a priest of Constantinople, aged 110 years, who, after visiting Sicily and satisfying himself that the Acts were true, landed at Salerno. He took up his residence at the Benedictine monastery of St. Laurence in that town, and while there spoke about the life and martyrdom of St. Placid, adducing the testimony of the Acts which he had with him. But his audience found his story hard to believe and were particularly puzzled that the Acts should have been written at Constantinople and that they had only just heard of the remarkable history after the lapse of so many centuries. Simeon, distressed at their incredulity, burst into tears and laid his hand on the crucifix with these words: 'Per istam sacratam Domini crucem et per sacrosanctam imaginem Salvatoris, quae ibi depicta est, quia haec, quae locutus sum ad vos de B. Placido martyre, vera sunt, et hanc cartam, quam de martyrio ipsius et Sociorum ejus in manibus teneo,

Gordianus famulus descripsit, et in domo parentum meorum reliquit juxta relationem eorum.' Some of the monks then believed the story and persuaded Simeon to translate the Greek Acts into Latin. Prior John, however, remained sceptical, and roundly calling Simeon a Constantinopolitan swindler (delusorem Constantinopolitanum) refused to transmit the document to Monte Cassino. Simeon then departed, leaving the translation with a monk who engaged to convey it to Abbot Raynald. But instead of going to Monte Cassino this monk went to Sardinia, and it was not till his death that Gordian's life reached Monte Cassino. Then Raynald handed the work over to me, says Peter, and bade me amend it diligently and so preserve it for posterity: which I have done. This is a summary of the Life and Passion of St. Placid as written by 'Gordian', translated by 'Simeon', and edited by Peter:

After telling us that he writes by command of the Emperor Justinian, Gordian narrates the birth of Placid. His father, Tertullus, a patrician of illustrious fame, married a noble wife of the gens Octavia and by her had four children: Placid, Eutychius, Victorinus and Flavia. When Placid was seven years old Tertullus took him to Subiaco where St. Benedict was then acquiring a great reputation and where he had built twelve monasteries (A.D. 522). After copying out the narratives of the Dialogues in which St. Placid figures (though he is writing before St. Gregory) Gordian tells of the revelation which bade St. Benedict go to Monte Cassino: 'Proficiscere idolorum ad pugnam, confortare et esto robustus, quia castrum tibi tradam, et illic sedes nominis tui in perpetuum erit.' St. Benedict addresses his disciples and then sets out for Monte Cassino. Gordian tells us of incidents of the journey and says that the hermit who made way for St. Benedict was the Martinus of Monte Marsico who occurs in the third book of the Dialogues. Arrived at the mountain, St. Benedict, after a retreat of forty days, began with the assistance of Maurus and Placid to demolish the pagan sanctuary, and with their constant help founded his monastery, 'illudque in sua corporali requie regulaeque descriptione caput omnium monasteriorum constituit'. Some of the narratives of St. Gregory are here inserted with the addition of the names of Maurus and Placid. The name of the monk who was crushed

by the wall is Severus. Then Tertullus, rejoicing at the news
of what had been achieved at Monte Cassino, which was on
his property, wrote to Placid to learn if he might be allowed
to pay a visit to the monastery. St. Benedict consented and
Tertullus came, bringing many distinguished friends, among
them being Boethius and Symmachus (then both dead). The
whole company was admitted into fellowship with the monks,
and Tertullus before leaving made over the mountain to St.
Benedict by a formal deed. At the same time, on the request
of Placid, he made St. Benedict a gift of land in Sicily,
eighteen farms. Meanwhile a certain Gordianus, a Roman well
versed in Greek, became a monk at Monte Cassino. Not long
afterwards messengers came from Sicily to say that the property was being despoiled by intruders. St. Benedict called the
community together and on their advice sent Placid to defend
his rights. With him went Gordian and Donatus. The date of
their departure was May 20th, A.D. 536.

On the journey to Messana, via Capua, Calatia, Furcae
Caudinae, Beneventum, Canusium and Rhegium, Maurus was
very hospitably received by the respective bishops and worked
very many miracles. Having arrived in Sicily he dealt with the
intruders and then commenced to build a monastery. He
worked an immense number of cures (omnes totius Siciliae
aegrotos curat), and his virtues inspired the greatest veneration: unde factum est ut per beatum Placidum et discipulos
ejus Patris Benedicti et Casinensis Coenobii veneranda religio
per totum orbem terrarum diffusa sit et diffamata. Four years
after their arrival in Sicily the monastery was finished and its
church was dedicated to St. John the Baptist. The community then numbered thirty monks. At this point Placid's
brothers and sister came to visit him, and at first—so emaciated
was he by his austerities—did not recognize him. They decided
to stay with him for a few days, but their stay was rudely
interrupted by an invasion of Saracen pirates. ('En errorum
labyrinthus', says Mabillon, who remarks on the 'supina in-
scientia' of calling them Saracens.) It appears that Spain was
occupied by these pagans under a king named Abdala, who
had sent out Mamucha with 100 ships and 16,800 men
'against the Roman Empire'. Landing in Sicily, they attacked
the monastery while the monks were at Vigils and captured

the whole community and the guests, Gordian alone escaping. There follows a long account of repeated interrogatories and tortures, ending with the beheading of Placid, Eutychius, Victorinus, Flavia and thirty monks on the sea shore. The date was October 5th, 541. Mamucha and his Saracens then embarked; but a storm arose and the whole expedition was utterly lost in the straits. The bodies of the martyrs lay for four days at the place of their martyrdom, when Gordian came and buried them: Placid and his brothers and sister in the church (which the pagans had failed to destroy), and the rest where they were martyred. The church became a great shrine where many miracles were worked 'down to this day'. The writer then praises St. Placid and says: 'Nam per hunc facta est Casinensis ecclesia purpurea, quae antea in P. Benedicti operibus exstiterit candida.' These are the dates of his life: He was seven when Tertullus took him to Subiaco, twelve when he moved with St. Benedict to Monte Cassino, twenty-one when he was sent to Sicily, and twenty-six when he was martyred (515–41).

Gordian then relates how the Sicilians sent a letter to St. Benedict telling him what had happened and asking him to send more monks. The letter is thus addressed: 'Universali monachorum institutori atque doctori benedicto servi filii ejus desolati et destituti pastore cum subjectione debita obedientiam.' St. Benedict rejoiced at the heroic death of his disciple and granted their request. Shortly after, having presided over Monte Cassino for fourteen years, he died in the year 542. Pope Vigilius confirmed to him all his possessions in Sicily, and his successors to the number of forty-nine did the same. (This last detail would bring the writer down to the year 882 or thereabouts.) After burying the martyrs Gordian sailed for Constantinople, where he spent the greater part of the remainder of his life and wrote in Greek the Acts of St. Placid and his Companions. After some years, leaving the Acts behind him, he sailed to Syracuse where he died piously. The church of St. John became the church of St. Placid. Thus far 'Gordian'.

The monastery is said to have lasted for about three hundred years, until Sicily was devastated by the Saracens. When Roger, first Count of Sicily, drove out the Saracens he gave the church to the knights of St. John of Jerusalem (A.D. 1087). Finally, as described in a book of the year 1591, the relics of the martyrs were discovered and translated, A.D. 1588.

This 'Invention' was accepted generally as establishing the substantial accuracy of the Acts of the Pseudo-Gordian, and the cultus of the martyrs received formal papal sanction. The feast of SS. Placid and his Companions was inserted in the Benedictine breviary published by the authority of Pope Paul V in 1612. But the Acts have not ceased to suggest difficulties and doubts to those who have studied them. Mabillon describes the writer as no mere interpolator but a forger. Many attempts have been made to disentangle a nucleus of genuine fact from the mass of fiction, but with no great success. And now the effort is regarded as necessarily hopeless. In the last few years the Holy See, in its partial revision of the breviary Office for St. Placid, has taken what is doubtless the first step towards his reinstatement in his true rank of Confessor.

MIGNE, *P.L.*, CLXXIII, 1067 sqq.: *Ortus et Vita justorum coenobii Casinensis.*

ACTA SANCTORUM, October 5th: *Passio B. Placidi*, etc. Appendix, *auctore Petro. Stephanus Aniciensis.*

RERUM ITALICARUM SCRIPTORES (Muratori) IV (1723), pp. 151–602, *Chronica Sacri Monasterii Casinensis;* VI (1725), pp. 1–62, *De viris illustribus Casinensibus.*

CAJETAN, A.: *Vitae SS. Siculorum* (Palermo, 1657), I, p. 181 sq.

The Acts are printed also by Mabillon in the *Acta SS. Ordinis S. Benedicti* (1668), I, 45–81 with some severe criticism. The latest and most complete study of the work of Peter the Deacon is by Erich Caspar: *Petrus Diaconus und die Monte Cassineser Fälschungen* (Berlin, 1909). The whole matter is considered by Dom Berlière in the *Revue Bénédictine*, XXXIII (1921), pp. 19–45. He accepts Caspar's conclusions.

THE MASTER'S RULE

THIS Note is concerned with an anonymous monastic Rule of unknown provenance which goes by the name of *Regula Magistri*: The Master's Rule. For twenty years now this Rule has been the focus of a controversy which closely concerns the origins of St. Benedict's Rule. RM (*Regula Magistri*) is a good deal longer than RSB (*Regula S. Benedicti*), perhaps three times as long. RM is a verbose Rule, containing many odd regulations and some legendary material. Its Latin has little of the concision and general simplicity of the Latin of RSB, being not seldom cumbrous in its syntax and outlandish in its vocabulary. But the crucial point is this, that RM and RSB have a good deal of material in common. The prologue and the first seven chapters of RSB appear in RM with a close similarity of text. And for the rest of RSB, until the end of the sixty-sixth chapter, there is much likeness of a minor character. It should be noted that RM ends at that point in RSB where the latter Rule is supposed to have terminated in a first draft.

This correspondence of the two Rules was no discovery of yesterday but a fact that had long been known to scholars. They had observed the textual agreement of RSB and RM, and had taken it to mean that the author of RM had copied RSB. This is the assumption, for instance, of the Maurist, Dom Ménard, in the seventeenth century, and of the palaeographer, Ludwig Traube, in more recent times. Both regarded RM as partly copy, partly paraphrase of RSB, and took little interest in it. The Maurist, for his part, dismisses RM with some contumely. In comparison with the passages which it shares with RSB, he condemns the style of RM as by contrast 'rude and scabrous'. That is a severe judgment and yet a fair one. For RM is of heterogeneous quality, and when the reader comes to the parts which it shares with RSB, he has a distinct feeling that he is leaving a semi-barbarous region and entering civilized country.

Such until the year 1938 was the general opinion regarding the relation between RSB and RM, viz., that RM was a later Rule and owed a good deal of its substance to RSB.

Then, in the year 1938, came the revolutionary thesis that the roles of RSB and RM should be reversed. It was argued that RM was certainly the older Rule, and that much of the substance of RSB had been taken from it.

It was to be expected that this thesis would stir controversy, for it appeared to diminish greatly the credit of St. Benedict's Rule. There has been a steady stream of articles in the learned reviews—chiefly on the Continent of Europe—both for and against this thesis. To date their number is approximately a hundred. The greatest variety of opinion has been expressed, but this is not the place to attempt a complete account of the debate. We may be allowed, however, to mention some few points of special importance.

The supporters of RM make much of two points: 1. The passages common to RM and RSB contain material that derives ultimately from Cassian, who flourished in the early fifth century. A close comparison of the texts as they appear in RM and RSB shows that RM reproduces Cassian more faithfully, and is therefore probably the earlier copy. To this it has been answered (a) that St. Benedict's first draft (a hypothetical document) may have copied Cassian more exactly; (b) that the author of RM possessed a copy of Cassian in his extensive library and got his text at this point directly from the original.

2. The liturgical cursus of RM is more primitive. Whereas RSB has a hebdomadal psalter with the 150 psalms neatly spread throughout the week and each psalm assigned to its definite Hour of the Office, RM has no such arrangement. The

psalter is recited straight on and the Rule gives no particular determination of the quantity or positions of the psalms. This is certainly a more primitive type of Office, but it need mean no more than that the author of RM was a staunch conservative or lived in some provincial backwater. St. Benedict, on the other hand, was close to Rome and—as we learn from his Rule—was prepared to model his Office on Roman practice.

The supporters of RM are embarrassed by the heterogeneous character of that document but have found a way out of their embarrassment. They allege that the text of RM, as we have it, is a text that has suffered a great deal of interpolation. They hope to identify and discard the interpolations and so produce the pure text of the Master's Rule.

This operation will be a task of great delicacy. In default of external evidence the 'interpolations' will have to be identified by subjective considerations, and the final product must be of doubtful value.

It may be mentioned, furthermore, that the extended debate has produced various suggested dates for RM and has supplied that text with a variety of authors. We do not propose to report the suggestions regarding date and authorship, except for one odd view, viz., that St. Benedict himself was the author both of RM and RSB: the first in his youth at Subiaco, the second in riper years at Monte Cassino.

A word about editions of RM. The handiest Latin text—though not a good one—is still the text in Migne, *Patrologia Latina*, Vol. 88, coll. 943–1052. The year 1953 saw the production of a diplomatic edition, based upon the oldest manuscript evidence (of around A.D. 600), and edited by Dom Hubert Vanderhoven and M. François Masai. This is a finely printed volume and the editors have taken immense pains over their work. Yet the book does not provide the critical text which scholars have so long desired.

There is no English translation of RM, apart from the pieces translated by the present writer and printed in the *Downside Review* (1939, 1940) or in his edition of St. Benedict's Rule (1952).

Concluding this Note about the Master's Rule, I would express my feeling that the controversy is showing signs of exhaustion. For all the work that has been put into it, it is difficult to point to any positive results. Unless some new evidence is discovered, I should not be surprised if it died a natural death.

It is possible, however, that this twenty-year controversy over the relation between the Rules of St. Benedict and the Master is now approaching its end. We are promised for the year 1958 an elaborate edition of Saint Benedict's Rule in the 'Vienna Corpus' (i.e., *Corpus Scriptorum Ecclesiasticorum Latinorum*). The editor (Professor Rudolf Hanslik) has made a very extensive study of the manuscripts of the Rule, collating as many as three hundred, and promises to supply his text with an exceptionally full *apparatus criticus*. He has described his edition and outlined his purpose in *Studia Anselmiana* (1957); and it would seem probable that his edition will supersede all existing editions of the Rule. But, neglecting general considerations, we would wish to report here what Professor Hanslik has to say in passing about the relations between the Rules of St. Benedict and the Master. He does not say much, but what he says is of a decisive character and, if established, will sweep away most of the ingenuities and extravagances of the above-mentioned controversy. Here is a translation of Professor Hanslik's brief allusion to the matter:

'On the basis of the manuscript situation I have no doubt whatever that, in the chapters where the two Rules are in verbal agreement, the Master—whose Rule I would date around A.D. 580—has used St. Benedict's Rule.'

INDEX

Aachen, 97, 179

abbot, St. Benedict's conception of, 79–80, 82, 84, 86, 104–105

election of, 105–106, 106 n.

Abundantia, mother of St. Benedict, 31

Acacian schism, 41 ff.

Acacius, Patriarch of Constantinople, 41–42

active life, the, 128 ff.

Adalbert, St., 178
of Fleury, 167, 168

admittance to the community, 109 ff.

Ado the martyrologist, St., 213

Adrevald of Fleury, 167, 169

Adrian of Canterbury, 152

Africa, 18, 19, 20, 25

Agapetus, Pope, 148, 148 n.

Agapitus, subdeacon, 145

Agatho, Pope, 177 n.

Aigulf, St. of Fleury and Lerins, 168

Alans, 20

Alaric, King of the Visigoths, 18, 20, 37

Albers, Dom Bruno, 98

Albi, bishop of and diocese, 111, 175, 176 n.

Alboin, King of the Lombards, 25, 37, 38

Alcuin of York, 213

Alexandria, Patriarchate of, 42

Anastasius II, Pope, 42

anchorites, see hermits

Andrew, St., monastery of, 148 n., 171–172, 199

Angelo della Noce, Abbot, 217

Anician gens, 31, 39, 40

Anio river, 48–49, 54, 58

Anschar, St., 184

Anselm, St., 77, 189

Antonius the noble, 197

Antony, Mark, 30
of Egypt, St., 47, 50, 57, 109

Apollo, altar of, at Monte Cassino, 67–68, 70, 161, 201

aqueducts, 38

Arianism, 24

Arles, 175

asceticism, Christian, 47

Ataulf, King of the Visigoths, 20

Athanasius, St., 43, 171

Attila, King of the Huns, 20, 37

Augustine of Canterbury, St., 101, 172–173, 175, 177, 189
of Hippo, St., 18, 102, 102 n., 127 n., 153

Augustus Caesar, 17, 30

austerity of the Rule, 109, 135–136, 137

Autun, Council of, 176

Avienus, 201

Baronius, 149, 163

Basil, St., 102, 127 n., 139

Bede the Venerable, St., 77, 101, 152, 177–178, 177 n., 188–189

Beech, Dom Anselm, 183–184

Belisarius, 25, 158

Benedict of Aniane, St., 97, 179, 181
of Nursia, St., sources for his life, 7–12, 194–208; his historical setting, 17–26; birth and early years, 29–36; in Rome, 37–46; at Subiaco, 47–65; at Monte Cassino, 67–78; character, 79–88, 136–137, 139–140; later life, 143–148; relation to Cassiodorus, 148–153; last years and death, 155–161; translation to France, 163–170; sketch of his institute, 171–189. See also Rule and passim

Benedictine polity, 179–182

Benedictinism, 171–189

Benet Biscop, St., 174, 177–178, 178 n.

Berlière, Dom Ursmer, 184 n., 187 n., 222

Image Books

OUR LADY OF FATIMA
By William Thomas Walsh
D1—75¢

THE SPIRIT OF CATHOLICISM
By Karl Adam   D2—75¢

DAMIEN THE LEPER
By John Farrow   D3—85¢

A POPULAR HISTORY OF THE CATHOLIC CHURCH
By Philip Hughes   D4—95¢

MR. BLUE
By Myles Connolly   D5—50¢

THE DIARY OF A COUNTRY PRIEST
By Georges Bernanos D6—65¢

THE CHURCH SPEAKS TO THE MODERN WORLD:
The Social Teachings of Leo XIII. Edited by Etienne Gilson
D7—95¢

PEACE OF SOUL
By Fulton J. Sheen D8—75¢

LIFT UP YOUR HEART
By Fulton J. Sheen D9—75¢

STORM OF GLORY
The Story of St. Thérèse of Lisieux. By John Beevers
D10—65¢

THE PERFECT JOY OF ST. FRANCIS
By Felix Timmermans
D11—75¢

SAINTS FOR OUR TIMES
By Theodore Maynard
D12—85¢

INTRODUCTION TO THE DEVOUT LIFE
By St. Francis de Sales. Newly translated and edited by John K. Ryan   D13—85¢

THE ROAD TO DAMASCUS
Edited by John A. O'Brien
D14—75¢

JOYCE KILMER'S ANTHOLOGY OF CATHOLIC POETS With a new supplement by James Edward Tobin   D15—$1.25

BERNADETTE AND LOURDES
By Michel de Saint-Pierre
D16—75¢

THE IMITATION OF CHRIST
By Thomas à Kempis. A Modern Version edited with an Introduction by Harold C. Gardiner, S.J.   D17—75¢

THE EVERLASTING MAN
By G. K. Chesterton D18—85¢

A GRAMMAR OF ASSENT
By John Henry Cardinal Newman with an Introduction by Etienne Gilson   D19—95¢

A WATCH IN THE NIGHT
By Helen C. White D20—95¢

BROTHER PETROC'S RETURN
By S. M. C.   D21—65¢

ST. FRANCIS OF ASSISI
By Johannes Jörgensen
D22—95¢

STORIES OF OUR CENTURY BY CATHOLIC AUTHORS
Edited by John Gilland Brunini and Francis X. Connolly
D23—85¢

AUTOBIOGRAPHY OF A HUNTED PRIEST
By John Gerard. Introduction by Graham Greene D24—85¢

FATHER MALACHY'S MIRACLE
By Bruce Marshall D25—65¢

ON THE TRUTH OF THE CATHOLIC FAITH   Summa Contra Gentiles Book I: God. Newly translated, with Introduction and notes by Anton C. Pegis
D26—95¢

Image Books

. . . making the world's finest Catholic literature available to all

THE WORLD'S FIRST LOVE
by Fulton J. Sheen
The whole story of Mary, Mother of God, lovingly and reverently portrayed in the inimitable style of the great Bishop. **D30—75¢**

THE SIGN OF JONAS
by Thomas Merton
The absorbing day-by-day account of life in a Trappist monastery by one of the great spiritual writers of our times. **D31—95¢**

PARENTS, CHILDREN AND THE FACTS OF LIFE
by Henry V. Sattler, C.Ss.R.
An invaluable guide for parents and teachers for sex instruction of children, based on tested and approved Catholic methods and principles. **D32—75¢**

LIGHT ON THE MOUNTAIN
The Story of LaSalette
by John S. Kennedy
The miraculous appearance of the Blessed Virgin Mary at LaSalette in 1846 dramatically and inspiringly portrayed. **D33—65¢**

EDMUND CAMPION
by Evelyn Waugh
The heroic life of the great English Jesuit and martyr told in the matchless prose of one of England's greatest authors. **D34—65¢**

HUMBLE POWERS
by Paul Horgan
Three beautifully told novelettes which magnificently emphasize the eternal power of faith, love and sacrifice. **D35—75¢**

SAINT THOMAS AQUINAS
by G. K. Chesterton
A superb introduction to the work and personality of the Angelic Doctor by the scintillating and irresistible G.K.C. **D36—75¢**

ON THE TRUTH OF THE CATHOLIC FAITH (SUMMA CONTRA GENTILES) BOOK TWO: CREATION
by St. Thomas Aquinas, newly translated, with an Introduction and notes, by James F. Anderson.
The second volume of the new translation of St. Thomas Aquinas' great classic *Summa Contra Gentiles*. **D27—95¢**

If your bookseller is unable to supply certain titles, write to Image Books, Department MIB, Garden City, New York, stating the titles you desire and enclosing the price of each book (plus 5¢ per book to cover cost of postage and handling). Prices are subject to change without notice.

Image Books

. . . making the world's finest
Catholic literature available to all

APOLOGIA PRO VITA SUA
by John Henry Newman
Introduction by Philip Hughes
Definitive edition of the great
English cardinal's superb spiritual autobiography.   D37—95¢

A HANDBOOK OF THE CATHOLIC FAITH
by Dr. N. G. M. Van Doornik,
Rev. S. Jelsma, Rev. A. Van De
Lisdonk. Edited by Rev. John
Greenwood.
A complete summary of every
aspect of Catholic doctrine and
practice. 520 pp.   D38—$1.35

THE NEW TESTAMENT
Official Catholic edition
Newly translated into English
by members of the Catholic
Biblical Association of America
under the supervision of the
Episcopal Committee of the
Archconfraternity of Christian
Doctrine.   D39—95¢

ON THE TRUTH OF THE CATHOLIC FAITH (SUMMA CONTRA GENTILES) Book Three: Providence, Part 1
by St. Thomas Aquinas, newly
translated, with an Introduction
and notes, by Vernon J. Bourke
The third book of the new
translation of St. Thomas' magnificent classic *Summa Contra
Gentiles*. Part 1 contains chapters 1 to 83.   D28A—85¢

MARIA CHAPDELAINE
by Louis Hémon
A novel of French-Canadian
life which has justly been called
an idyllic epic.   D40—65¢

SAINT AMONG THE HURONS
by Francis X. Talbot, S.J.
The stirring and inspiring story
of Jean de Brébeuf, one of the
American martyrs, who was
tortured and put to death by
the Indians.   D41—95¢

THE PATH TO ROME
by Hilaire Belloc
The delightful account of a
most unusual pilgrimage on foot
to Rome. Illustrated by the
author.   D42—85¢

SORROW BUILT A BRIDGE
by Katherine Burton
The biography of Nathaniel
Hawthorne's daughter—her conversion to Catholicism and her
work as Mother Alphonsa,
founder of a religious order.
   D43—75¢

ON THE TRUTH OF THE CATHOLIC FAITH (SUMMA CONTRA GENTILES) Book Three: Providence, Part 2
by St. Thomas Aquinas, newly
translated, with an Introduction
and notes, by Vernon J. Bourke
Part 2 contains chapters 84 to
163.   D28B—85¢

If your bookseller is unable to supply certain titles, write to Image
Books, Department MIB, Garden City, New York, stating the titles
you desire and enclosing the price of each book (plus 5¢ per book
to cover cost of postage and handling). Prices are subject to change
without notice.

Image Books

*. . . making the world's finest
Catholic literature available to all*

THE WISE MAN FROM THE WEST
by Vincent Cronin
Vivid, fascinating account of a remarkable priest who brought Christianity to the strange world of sixteenth century China.
D44—85¢

EXISTENCE AND THE EXISTENT
by Jacques Maritain
Existentialism, the most discussed trend in modern philosophy, examined in the light of Thomist thought by a world-famed Catholic philosopher.
D45—75¢

THE STORY OF THE TRAPP FAMILY SINGERS
by Maria Augusta Trapp
The delightful story of a remarkable family. "Engrossing, humorous, poignant," says Boston Traveler.
D46—85¢

THE WORLD, THE FLESH AND FATHER SMITH
by Bruce Marshall
The heartwarming story of a lovable priest. "Delightfully written," said the New York Times of this wise and witty book.
D47—65¢

THE CHRIST OF CATHOLICISM
by Dom Aelred Graham
A full, well-rounded study of Christ, His personality and teaching, by the distinguished Benedictine writer.
D48—95¢

ST. FRANCIS XAVIER
by James Brodrick, S.J.
A new condensed version for modern readers of the biography of St. Francis that the New York Times calls: "the best book on Francis Xavier in any language."
D49—95¢

ST. FRANCIS OF ASSISI
by G. K. Chesterton
A fresh, fascinating study of one of the best-loved saints—by one of the outstanding writers of our time.
D50—65¢

ON THE TRUTH OF THE CATHOLIC FAITH (SUMMA CONTRA GENTILES) BOOK FOUR: SALVATION
by St. Thomas Aquinas. Translated, with an Introduction and notes, by Charles J. O'Neil
The final volume of the superb new English translation of this great Christian classic.
D29—95¢

If your bookseller is unable to supply certain titles, write to Image Books, Department MIB, Garden City, New York, stating the titles you desire and enclosing the price of each book (plus 5¢ per book to cover cost of postage and handling). Prices are subject to change without notice.

Image Books

VIPERS' TANGLE
by François Mauriac

A penetrating novel of evil and redemption by one of the world's greatest writers, and winner of the Nobel Prize.   **D51—75¢**

THE MANNER IS ORDINARY
by John LaFarge, S.J.

Delightful autobiography of a famous Jesuit priest and his full, rich life of service for God and his fellow man.   **D52—95¢**

MY LIFE FOR MY SHEEP
by Alfred Duggan

A fictionalized biography of St. Thomas à Becket, twelfth century Archbishop of Canterbury who was martyred by Henry II for opposing the King's efforts to bring the Church in England under royal domination.

D53—90¢

THE CHURCH AND THE RECONSTRUCTION OF THE MODERN WORLD
The Social Encyclicals of Pius XI, Edited by T. P. McLaughlin, C.S.B.

The definitive English edition of the major encyclicals of Pope Pius XI. These works are among the most important body of authoritative teaching on the attitude of the Catholic Church toward modern problems.

D54—$1.25

A GILSON READER:
Selections from the Writings of Etienne Gilson
Edited by Anton C. Pegis

This book distills all the writings of Etienne Gilson, one of the greatest living philosophers, into a single volume that captures the essence of his thought and presents it as an integrated system.   **D55—95¢**

THE AUTOBIOGRAPHY OF ST. THÉRÈSE OF LISIEUX:
The Story of a Soul
A new translation by John Beevers

A new and distinguished translation of the outstanding spiritual book of our century—a book that is ranked among the foremost spiritual classics of all time.   **D56—65¢**

HELENA
by Evelyn Waugh

Brilliant historical novel about St. Helena, mother of Constantine the Great and founder of Christ's Cross, by one of the foremost novelists in the English-speaking world.   **D57—65¢**

THE GREATEST BIBLE STORIES:
A Catholic Anthology from World Literature
Edited by Anne Fremantle

Imaginative re-creations of fifteen Bible stories by many of the foremost authors in world literature.   **D58—75¢**

Image Books

. . . making the world's finest
Catholic literature available to all . . .

THE CITY OF GOD
by St. Augustine; edited with Introduction by Vernon J. Bourke; Foreword by Etienne Gilson

A great Christian classic, specially abridged for modern readers.
D59—$1.45

SUPERSTITION CORNER
by Sheila Kaye-Smith

Fast-moving historical novel of a girl's lonely struggle for her Faith in Elizabethan England.
D60—65¢

SAINTS AND OURSELVES
Edited by Philip Caraman, S.J.

24 outstanding Catholic writers portray their favorite saints in vivid profiles written especially for today's Catholic. **D61—95¢**

CANA IS FOREVER
by Rev. Charles Hugo Doyle

The complete Catholic guide to dating, courtship, and marriage —a unique blend of the ideal and the practical. **D62—75¢**

ASCENT OF MOUNT CARMEL
by St. John of the Cross; translated and edited by E. Allison Peers.

A classic guide to the spiritual life by the saint who is widely regarded as the greatest of all mystical theologians.
D63—$1.25

RELIGION AND THE RISE OF WESTERN CULTURE
by Christopher Dawson

Brilliant interpretation, in terms of culture, of Europe from the late Roman Empire to the end of the Middle Ages. **D64—85¢**

PRINCE OF DARKNESS AND OTHER STORIES
by J. F. Powers

Eleven superb stories by one of America's finest writers.
D65—85¢

ST. THOMAS MORE
by E. E. Reynolds

Vivid biography of England's best-loved saint, portraying his court, family, social, and intellectual activity as well as his spiritual life. **D66—95¢**

If your bookseller is unable to supply certain titles, write to Image Books, Department MIB, Garden City, New York, stating the titles you desire and enclosing the price of each book (plus 5¢ per book to cover cost of postage and handling). Prices are subject to change without notice.

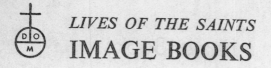

LIVES OF THE SAINTS
IMAGE BOOKS

SAINTS FOR OUR TIMES
by Theodore Maynard
Brief biographies of 18 saints whose lives have special meaning for modern Catholics.

D12—85¢

AUTOBIOGRAPHY OF ST. THÉRÈSE OF LISIEUX: The Story of a Soul
Newly translated by John Beevers
The outstanding spiritual book of our century, already a classic of the first rank.

D56—65¢

STORM OF GLORY:
The Story of St. Thérèse of Lisieux
by John Beevers
Best-selling and very readable biography of the Little Flower.

D10—65¢

ST. FRANCIS XAVIER
by James Brodrick, S.J.
Condensed version of the biography the New York *Times* calls "the best book on Francis Xavier in any language."

D49—95¢

MY LIFE FOR MY SHEEP
by Alfred Duggan
Fictionalized life of St. Thomas Becket, martyred by Henry II for opposing that King's efforts to control the Church in England.

D53—90¢

SAINTS AND OURSELVES
Edited by Philip Caraman, S.J.
24 outstanding writers portray their favorite saints in profiles written especially for today's Catholic.

D61—95¢

EDMUND CAMPION
by Evelyn Waugh
Gripping, adventure-filled life of the great Jesuit martyr, a Hawthornden Prize book.

D34—65¢

ST. FRANCIS OF ASSISI
by Johannes Jorgensen
Definitive biography of the best-loved of all saints.

D22—95¢

ST. FRANCIS OF ASSISI
by G. K. Chesterton
Fresh, fascinating interpretation by one of the outstanding writers of our century.

D50—65¢

SAINT AMONG THE HURONS
by Francis X. Talbot, S.J.
Exciting story of Jean de Brébeuf, missionary martyred by the Indians.

D43—75¢

BERNADETTE AND LOURDES
by Michel de Saint-Pierre
The whole inspiring story of Our Lady's appearances at Lourdes and the subsequent happenings in Bernadette's life which led to her canonization.

D16—75¢

If your bookseller is unable to supply certain titles, write to Image Books, Department MIB, Garden City, New York, stating the titles you desire and enclosing the price of each book (plus 5¢ per book to cover cost of postage and handling). Prices are subject to change without notice.